Secrets of Good French Cooking

Prestige des Grands Chefs

Secrets of Good French Cooking

by

Pierre Paillon

under the direction of
Pierre Michalet
Translated by Anne Sterling

A copublication of

and

L'Academie Culinaire de France
National Organization to
Promote Culinary Excellence

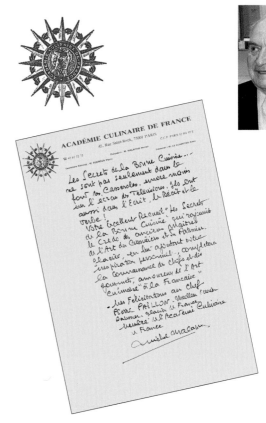

Like the other fine arts; Music, Painting, Architecture and Poetry, the Culinary Arts are highly regarded in France and high standards are maintained through the hard work and dedication of the professionals in the field.

In the late 1880's, well known chef Joseph Favre wrote the "Dictionnaire Universal de la Cuisine Practique et de l'Hygiène Alimentaire" a comprehensive culinary work in four volumes.

The complete reperatoire of French cooking at the time, from regional dishes to haute cuisine, was recorded for posterity. Based on his work, he founded the "Académie de la Cuisine" in 1885 which became the "Académie Culinaire de la France" in 1887.

Each month, under the leadership of the present president Michel Malapris, the distinguished members of the Academy unite in Paris to discuss and analyze recipes and trends in French cuisine. Their goal is to assure the continuation of the great traditions established over the centuries by the chefs of great restaurants and those before who worked for royalty.

There are 50 elected officials and several hundred members from the ranks of top chefs in France. There are a few honorary members who are not professional chefs but who have contributed in a significant way to "la cuisine française".

The Academy has also established international branches of the organization is the United States, Great Britain, Canada, Autralia, Japon, and Belgium-Netherlands-Luxemburg (Bénélux).

A culinary competition is organized each year and the prestigious "Trophée National de Cuisine" is awarded.

Also of interest is the annual dinner during the hunting season which features the very best dishes served with top wines. Such events honor the chefs of today who are perpetuating the grand traditions of French cooking.

The "Académie Culinaire de la France" protects these traditions and insures the future of the great cuisine of France.

Pierre Paillon is shown demonstrating his craft in Japan, accompanied by Jean Millet, President of the «Confédération Nationale de la Pâtisserie».

The secrets of good French cooking are not found only in the kitchens of the great chefs. They can be shared with the public through the written word.
"Secrets of Good French Cooking" is an excellent collection of recipes from renowned "Maîtres de l'Art du Cuisinier et du Pâtissier-Glacier" ("Masters of Cooking and Pastry"), selected by Chef Paillon. The knowledge in this book will inspire restaurant chefs and all good cooks who love French food.
Congratulations to Chef Pierre Paillon, "Meilleur Ouvrier Patissier-Glacier de France" and member of the "Academie Culinaire de France.

Michel MALAPRIS
President, l'Academie Culinaire de France

La Chaîne des Rôtisseurs (1248-1950)
"Defenders of Haute Cuisine in 116 countries"

In 1248, under Saint Louis, King of France, the "Corporation des Rôtisseurs" was founded and included only the official goose roasters or "Ayeurs". This organization was officially recognized by the throne in 1610 and remained strong until the French Revolution in 1789 when all such groups were disbanded.

On Easter in 1950, professional chefs and great "gastronomes" came to Paris to reestablish the organization. The great Curnonsky, "Prince élu des Gastronomes" became the first honorary president, the "Confrérie de la Chaîne des Rôtisseurs" became official and the coat of arms were created.

The goal of this group is to bring together food enthusiasts the world over to enjoy the bounty of the table. Roasted meats, in the tradition of the original "Corporation" are always a highlight of the meals shared by the members.

To join, one must accept the high standards set forth by the organization, learn the oath and be approved for membership by an official chapter.

Members must wear the special insignia of the "Chaîne" at all official functions. When a "Rôtisseur" meets another in a restaurant they show their insignias.

This organization is a legion of honor and members deserve the highest respect.

Oath of the "Rôtisseurs" (translated from the French)

" I swear to never speak badly of and to always properly cook roasted and grilled meat. I swear to uphold our goals and to respect all members of the Chaîne des Rotisseurs."

I am honored to introduce this collection of recipes from chefs working in a variety of restaurants from humble to the most famous.
They are continuing in the footsteps of the chefs who came before them with ideas that are solidly based in traditional cuisine.
Now it is their turn to contribute their ideas and innovations and pass them on to future generations as in the spirit of the "Chaîne des Rôtisseurs".

Robert BATY
Grand Chancelier
President, Chaîne des Rôtisseurs

A cook book not like the others....

Frozen foods, powdered sauces and vacuum-packed, ready-to-serve dishes are beginning to creep into restaurant kitchens, replacing fresh natural foods that «taste like what they are», an idea promoted by the great gastronome Curnonsky. Luckily there are chefs all over France who are perpetuating the great culinary traditions of the past while giving a personal touch to their cuisine. But much too often these worthy cooks are not well known. The dining guides lavish praise on the star chefs of the moment but overlook the fine cooking being produced in more humble restaurants.
«The Secrets of Good French Cooking» includes the recipes of great chefs from the four corners of France who, through their work, show their respect for the canons of «real cooking» and are proud to share their secrets. The recipes reflect the individual style of each author. The dishes were photographed in the kitchens where they were created and the regional products used to make the dishes are often pictured as well.
The recipes include a complete list of ingredients, instructions and the chef's secrets for successfully recreating the dish. Here the reader will find inspiration for original and traditional cold and hot first courses, main dishes made with seafood, meat, poultry and game and a stunning selection of desserts to end the meal on a happy note.
The best of good French cuisine, made with top-quality, natural ingredients is represented in this book.
«The Secrets of Good French Cooking» is an indispensible tool for restaurant and catering chefs as well as amateur cooks the world over who would like to serve the best dishes of France to their clients and friends.

Pierre Paillon

Pierre PAILLON
Meilleur Ouvrier de France *(Section : Glaces & Sorbets)*

Cuisinier Breveté d'Etat - Médaille d'Or 1951 - Diplôme de Mérites Exceptionnels 1953 - Lauréat de Preis Der Kochkunt Eugen Lacroix à Francfort sur Main 1953 - Membre du Jury aux Expositions - Hors Concours Saint-Etienne 1965 - Membre de l'Académie Culinaire de France - Membre du Conseil d'Administration de la Chaîne des Rotisseurs

Table of Contents

Chapter 1 - Cold First Courses

In the intoduction to each chapter, Pierre Paillon offers a historic and informative view on the subject covered in that chapter. This pertinent information, tracing the evolution of "good French cooking", gives background which will help the reader to appreciate the recipes. The cooking methods, for example, are explained in detail. A deep understanding and mastery of these techniques will often make the difference between a good dish and a great one. The reader will be able to apply the lessons learned in the introduction to the preparation of the recipes offered by these great chefs.

On the subject of first courses...

In the 18th century, the host went to any expense to honor his guests. On arriving at the table, diners were greeted with a virtual avalanche of dishes. With great pageantry and zeal, the food was brought to the table in a spirit of good will. The master of the household would personally choose the menu which never included fewer than 6 courses. In addition, were served a copious selection of desserts. Of course, the beverages flowed freely throughout the evening, served from pewter pitchers.

The numerous first courses ("entrées» in French) were actually the fourth course to be served after the soup, hors d'oeuvres and "relevés" (dishes following the soup). It's no wonder that these copious feasts lasted for 10 hours. In his book, "History of French Cuisine", Christian Guy describes a dinner offered by the Duc de Richelieu, a man as renowned for his gourmandise as for his political power. In hommage to the members of royalty being held prisoner by his troops, he served them a six course banquet comprised only of beef dishes.

A soup of beef consommé began the meal, followed by four hors d'oeuvres then a potage "relevé".

The "entrées" or "first courses" courses that were served next included:
Oxtail with chestnut purée
Beef tongue civet à la Bourguignon
Paupiettes of beef with candied nastursiams
Braised beef with celery
Fried beef with hazelnut purée

Beef marrow on toast
These gargantuan feasts provided a real challenge to the guest to pace himself with just a taste of each dish so that his appetite would last to the end of the meal.

When one examines the menus of the era, it is impressive to note not only the great number of "entrées" but the level of sophistication as well. The elaborate dishes were carefully chosen to compliment each other. The techniques and ingredients used can be seen today in the dishes of top restaurants...toasted bread topped with meat has become a torte or pâté "en croûte", and simple fried foods have been made light and crispy with batter and improved frying equipment.

"Entrées" are no longer the fourth offering in a menu of six courses (plus dessert). Now the "entrée" or first course is served immediately following the hors d'oeuvres and is a single dish that is a main part of the meal.

With our busy schedules, time at the table is limited and the average budget no longer permits such extravagance. There is no time in our modern lifestyle for lengthy, copious dinners. A good meal now consists of an hors d'oeuvre, an "entrée" or fish dish, a poultry or meat dish followed by cheese and/or dessert. (For a fancy meal, both a first course and fish course may be offered, but for more casual dining, the diner usually chooses one or the other.)

Whether hot or cold, the first course must compliment the main course which follows.

Terrines and Pâtés

Explanation of terms

The word terrine refers to the earthenware mold the dish is cooked in ("terre" means earth). Terrines are glazed clay molds and can be round, oval or rectangular. The top of the terrine can be plain and flat or adorned with the sculpture of an animal (rabbit or duck or fish, for example). The meat used to make the dish usually is chosen to "match" the decoration on the mold.

A variety of ingredients can be used to make a terrine; chicken, duck, rabbit, hare, fish, shellfish, pork, foie gras orvegetables. Vegetables can be used alone (often layered to make the most of the various colors) or cut in shapes to add color and texture to meat or seafood terrines.
Terrines, therefore, consist of a forcemeat (ground or chopped ingredients bound with eggs or other ingredient) molded in an earthenware container. To maintain moisture during cooking, the terrine often is lined with strips of bacon or larding fat. The mixture is cooked at a moderate temperature with the mold set in a waterbath.

Pâté, on the other hand, means "cooked in pastry" and in its truest sense, refers to a mixture of ground meat or seafood that is wrapped in dough and baked. A pâté can be free-standing, formed and cooked directly on the baking sheet or molded by lining an embossed metal mold with sheets of dough, filling with forcemeat, covering with pastry and baking without a cover. Although the title "pâté en croûte" is actually redundant, forcemeats in a pastry crust are often called this to distinguish them from "terrines".

Often the terms "pâté" and "terrine" are confused and even used together to describe a single preparation such as "pâté en terrine du chef" or "terrine de pâté de foie gras".

Monkfish and Tomato Terrine

« Relais Ste-Victoire »
(Beaurecueil)
Chef : René Bergés

Ingredients
(3-4 servings)
500 g (1 lb) monkfish
500 g (1 lb) tomatoes
4 large eggs
3 shallots, peeled, chopped
1 branch fresh basil,
leaves chopped
1 tbl tomato concentrate
100 ml (3.5 fl oz) olive oil

Plate Presentation

At the restaurant this cold first course is sliced and arranged on the plate with a garnish of green pepper mousse.

Procedure

To peel the tomatoes, make a slit in the bottom, plunge into boiling water a few seconds, transfer to cold water then pull off the loosened skins. Cut in half, remove the seeds, chop coarsely and cook over medium heat in half of the olive oil. Add the shallots and basil, season with salt and pepper and cook over low heat to thicken. Stir in the tomato paste and set aside.
Trim the monkfish. Heat the remaining olive oil and sear the fish. Season with salt and pepper then cut into large dice.

Beat the eggs and stir them into the tomato mixture. Gently stir in the pieces of fish.
Butter a porcelain mold, fill with the mixture.
Bake in a water bath in a moderate oven (350-375 F) 20-25 minutes or until the tomato mixture is set. Cool at room temperature then cover and refrigerate.

Garlic Terrine with Parsley and Pink Peppercorns

« Le Mas du Soleil »
(Salon-de-Provence)

Chef : Francis Robin

Ingredients
(4 servings)

1.5 kg (about 3 lbs) garlic, peeled
100 g (3 1/2 oz) parsley leaves, chopped
125 ml (4 fl oz) chicken broth
Salt, pepper
1 tbl powdered gelatin, softened
100 ml (3.5 fl oz) olive oil
Pink peppercorns

Procedure

Cut the peeled garlic cloves in half and remove the green sprout from the center. Cover with cold water, bring to a boil, rinse under cold water. Steam the blanched garlic for 6-8 minutes.
Bring the chicken broth to a simmer, add the softened gelatin. Stir the olive oil into the broth and season with salt and pepper. Place a sheet of plastic wrap in the bottom of a rectangular loaf pan and spread an even layer of the cooked garlic cloves on the bottom. Cover with coarsely chopped parsley and pink peppercorns then repeat the layers, using all the garlic.
Pour the chicken broth with olive oil over the ingredients, knock the mold on the work surface to distribute the liquid, cover and refrigerate, with a weight on top, 24 hours.

Plate Presentation

Serve slices of this terrine as a side dish with chicken, rabbit or a green salad with herbs.

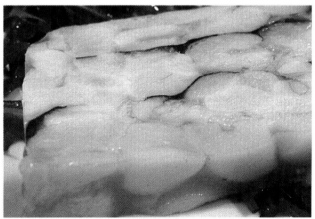

11

Terrine of Duck Foie Gras

« La Toque Blanche » *(Pujols)*
Chef : Bernard Lebrun

Ingredients (10 servings)

Barding fat
1.6 kg (about 3 1/4 lbs) fresh foie gras
20 ml (2 tbl) Armagnac
24 g (5 tsp) Kosher salt
10 g (scant 2 tsp) freshly ground pepper
Chilled aspic (chopped), field greens

Procedure

Carefully slice down the length of the lobes of foie gras. Trim away the dark vein that branches out in the center of the lobes.
Season evenly with the salt, pepper and Armagnac.
Cover and refrigerate 2 hours.
Line a terrine mold with the barding fat. Place the largest piece of foie gras on the bottom, smooth side down. Fill the terrine with foie gras, placing the pieces together like a puzzle and pressing down as you go to eliminate air pockets. Cover the top with barding fat.
Place the filled terrine in a water bath and cook in a preheated 130 C (270 F) degree oven for 40 minutes.
Remove the cooked terrine from the water bath, place a board on top of the terrine and a 3 lb weight (this can be done with a rectangle of cardboard wrapped in foil and three soup cans).
Refrigerate 24 hours so the pieces of liver will chill and mold together.

Plate Presentation

Remove the barding fat from the top, cut thin slices of the terrine and remove the barding fat from the slices.
Place a slice on each plate and decorate with chopped aspic and a few pretty lettuce leaves. Serve with toasted French bread.
Foie gras terrine is also delicious with onion compote and prunes cooked in red wine.
The richness of the liver is complimented by late harvest wines with a honey-like sweetness and flavor.

Duck Foie Gras Marinated with Four Peppercorns

«Les Délices du Château» *(Saumur)*
Chef : Pierre Millon

Ingredients
(8 servings)

1 duck foie gras (500-600 g (about 1 1/4 lbs))
20 g (2/3 oz) black peppercorns
20 g (2/3 oz) dried green peppercorns
20 g (2/3 oz) white and pink peppercorns
4 large onions
2 tbls red currant jelly
2 branches rhubarb
20 g (2/3 oz) sugar
1 tsp grenadine syrup
1/2 bottle dry red wine
Salt (not iodized)

Note: Make sure that the foie gras is very fresh and of the best quality as it is "cooked" by only the marinade.

Procedure
Remove the veins from the interior of the liver and degorge the liver in cold water for 2 hours. Drain on a towel and season with salt (20 g (4 tsp) per kilo (2.2 lbs)). Press the pieces of liver together to form a cylinder and roll in the four peppercorns (crushed coarsely and mixed together).

Wrap the cylinder tightly in a sheet of plastic wrap. Refrigerate 48 hours.

Onion compote: Cut the onions into small dice and brown in a little oil or butter, add the grenadine, currant jelly and red wine. Cook over very low heat about 1 1/2 hours. Cool.

Rhubarb: Peel the rhubarb and cut into strips about the size of a thin green bean. Add a few drops of grenadine and the sugar, and macerate about 1/2 hour.

Plate Presentation
Cut the cylinder of foie gras into 8 medallions.
Place a medallion on each plate and spoon some of the onion compote and macerated rhubarb next to the liver.
Decorate with chopped chicken aspic and serve with slices of toasted French bread.

13

Sweetbreads and Foie Gras Terrine with Jerusalem Artichokes

« La Cognette »
(Issoudun)

Chef : Alain Nonnet

Ingredients
(12 servings)

Sauce:
1 cup heavy cream
15 g (1/2 oz) chopped truffles
Truffle juice (from canned truffles)
Juice of 1 small lemon
Salt and cayenne pepper

500 g (1 lb) sweetbreads
200 ml (7 fl oz) Madeira
100 g (3 1/2 oz) carrots, sliced
100 g (3 1/2 oz) onions, sliced
1 bouquet garni
500 ml (2 cups) beef broth
300 g (10 oz) foie gras, cooked
1 1/2 tsps powdered gelatin, softened
1 cup duck fat
1 kg (about 2 lbs) Jerusalem artichokes - 100 g (3 1/2 oz) smoked bacon strips

Procedure

Degorge the sweetbreads in cold water then blanch in lightly salted water. Pull off the thin membrane that covers the sweetbreads. Brown the carrots and onions in a little butter, place the blanched sweetbreads on top and add the beef broth and Madeira, cover and braise the sweetbreads over low heat for 40 minutes.
Peel the Jerusalem artichokes and rinse well under cold water. Bring the duck fat to a simmer, add the artichokes, season lightly with salt and cook about 15 minutes or until tender. Remove with a slotted spoon and drain.
Remove the sweetbreads with a slotted spoon, and cut into 1 cm (3/8 in) slices. Pour the braising juices through a sieve, bring to a simmer and stir in the softened gelatin.
Cut the foie gras into 1 cm (3/8 in) slices.
Assemble the terrine. Line the rectangular mold with the bacon strips. Place the slices of sweetbreads in the bottom, moisten with broth, add a layer of sliced artichokes then cover with foie gras. Pour the remaining broth over the top and knock the mold on the counter to settle the liquid. Cover with plastic wrap, cut a board to fit the top and place a few cans on top to gently press the ingredients together. Refrigerate overnight. Make the sauce. Mix the cream, truffles with their liquid and lemon juice, season to taste with salt and pepper. Refrigerate until service.

Asparagus with Marinated Salmon

«Le Prieuré»
(Villeneuve-Lès-Avignon)

Chef : Serge Chenet

Ingredients(4 servings)

800 g (1 lb 10 oz) fresh salmon fillet
28 asparagus spears
150 ml (5 fl oz) virgin olive oil
1 hard boiled egg
1 lemon
20 g (2/3 oz) salmon caviar
1 bunch chives
1 lime
20 g (2/3 oz) sturgeon caviar

To marinate the salmon:
8 star anise
10 g (2/3 oz) fennel seed
10 g (2/3 oz) coriander seeds
3 g (scant tsp) freshly ground pepper
10 g (2 tsp) sugar
10 g (2 tsp) sea salt

Procedure

Marinate the salmon 48 hours in advance. Grind the spices to a powder and rub them into the flesh of the salmon. Sprinkle the juice of 1/2 lime over the salmon, cover with plastic wrap and refrigerate.
Rinse the marinated salmon under cold running water and dry with a clean kitchen towel. Cut four thin slices of salmon, lay them flat on a plate and cover with plastic wrap.
Make a classic vinaigrette (see recipe for "Monkfish with Caviar").

Chop the whites and yolks of the eggs separately and chop the chives. Stir these ingredients into the vinaigrette just before serving.
Peel the asparagus, keeping as much of the green color as possible. Rinse the asparagus and tie in two bundles for easier cooking. Cook the asparagus in salted boiling water about 8 minutes or until the point of a knife can pierce the stem.

Plate Presentation

Place 7 hot asparagus on each plate. Cover the asparagus with a slice of salmon. Stir the chopped eggs and chives into the vinaigrette and spoon over the ends of the asparagus.
Brush olive oil over the salmon to make it shine and grind a little pepper over the top.

15

Oyster Remoulade

"Hostellerie de La Fuste" *(Valensole)*
Chef: M. Bucaille

Ingredients (4 servings)

24 oysters (about 2 kg (4 1/2 lbs))
1 celery root
1 egg yolk
1 tbl mustard
1 tsp heavy cream
Olive oil
2 tomatoes
Parsley, chives
Caviar*
Salt, freshly ground pepper

Procedure

Stir the mustard and egg yolk together. Whisk in about 1 cup olive oil to make a thick mayonnaise, season with salt and pepper. Peel the celery root, grate to cut into very fine julienne and season with salt and freshly ground pepper. Toss the celery root in the mayonnaise to coat evenly.

*Chef Bucaille uses "poutarque", or mullet eggs, a specialty product of his region.

Presentation

Mound the celery remoulade on the plates and arrange the oysters with the small end in the middle of the plate and the large end toward the rim to give a petaled effect. Place tomato wedges between the oysters.
Place a little caviar on each oyster and sprinkle freshly chopped herbs over the dish.

Vegetable Pyramid with Balsamic Vinaigrette

«L'Etape Lani» (Bouc-Bel-Air)
Chefs : Lucien and Joël Lani

Ingredients (4 servings)

Mixed salad greens
4 tomatoes, sliced
200 g (7 oz) thin green beans, cooked
2 Belgian endives, sliced
4 slices smoked salmon
4 artichokes
4 slices foie gras terrine
1 carrot, peeled
1 turnip, peeled
1 beet, peeled
Balsamic vinaigrette

Procedure

Trim the leaves from the artichoke, leaving only the heart. Cook in simmering salted water until tender. Trim the tips from the green beans and cook in boiling, salted water until «al dente». Slice the carrot, turnip and beet very thinly, then cut into matchsticks («julienne) and soak briefly in ice water to crispen.
Season each vegetable with salt and pepper.
Layer the salad, beans, endives, tomatoes and salmon separately in 4 high-sided 10 cm (4 in) rings (tuna fish cans with top and bottom removed can be used). Press on the layers, then unmold onto four plates.

Plate Presentation

Sprinkle vinaigrette over the molded vegetables and salmon. Top the «pyramids» with slices of foie gras, artichoke hearts and julienned vegetables.

Sweetbreads and Crayfish Salad

"Hostellerie Lenoir" *(Auvillers-Les-Forges)*
Chef : Jean Lenoir

Ingredients (4 servings)

12-16 crayfish
280 g (9 oz) sweetbreads
Flour, curry powder
Salt, pepper
Mixed salad greens, cleaned
Carrot, julienned
Red cabbage, julienned
Avocado, sliced
Vinaigrette made with walnut oil

Procedure

Cut the sweetbreads into 1/2 cm (1/4 in) slices. Blanch, drain and pull off the membrane that covers the slices.
Mix equal parts flour and curry powder and lightly coat the slices.
Heat oil and butter over medium high heat and pan fry the slices, season with salt and pepper.
Remove the shells from the crayfish, boil the heads (for garnish) and pan fry the tail meat. Keep warm until service.

Plate Presentation

Arrange the fresh greens on the plate in an attractive pattern.
Mix the carrot and cabbage julienne together and mound in the center and place the slices of avocado around.
Make a vinaigrette with walnut oil and wine vinegar, seasoned with curry and drizzle over the salad.
Place the just-cooked crayfish tails and heads on the greens.
Arrange the slices of sweetbreads in the center.
Serve immediately.

Note that the crayfish can be replaced with shrimp or slices of lobster and the sweetbreads can be replaced with slices of chicken breast.

Lobster
with Two Vinaigrettes

"Auberge du Père Bise" *(Talloires)*
Chef : Sophie Bise

Ingredients
(4 servings)

2 fresh lobsters
  (600 g (1 1/4 lbs) each))
3 large leeks
Salt and pepper
2 cooked beets
Olive oil
Wine vinegar
1 garlic clove, finely chopped
Dijon mustard
1 tsp capers
1/2 onion, finely chopped
4 cornichons
(small tarragon pickles)
Chives, chopped
1 hard-boiled egg, chopped
Dill, chervil

Procedure

Cook the lobsters over low heat in a court bouillon for 20 minutes, remove the flesh. Cut the meat from the tails into 16 medaillons and cut the claw meat in half.
Cut the whites of the leeks into 2.5 cm (1 in) pieces and cook in boiling salted water.
Wash and trim the green portion of the leeks, cut into julienne and deep fry in peanut oil, being careful not to brown the leeks.
Beet vinaigrette: Puree the beets and whisk in vinegar and olive oil, season with salt and pepper.
Vinaigrette "ravigotte": Make a classic vinaigrette with mustard. Stir in finely chopped onion, a minced garlic clove, capers, chopped cornichons, chopped chives and chopped hard boiled egg.

Plate Presentation

Spoon the beet vinaigrette around the edge of the plate.
Spoon the "ravigotte" in the center.
Arrange the slices of leeks in the center and overlap the lobster medaillons on top of the leeks.
Place the claw meat on the side and decorate with chervil and dill sprigs and the fried leek julienne.

Lobster Salad

"La Renaissance" (Magny-Cours)
Chef : Jean-Claude Dray

Ingredients
(4 servings)

2 lobsters 800 g each
  (1 lb 12 oz))
2 heads Boston lettuce, washed
2 egg yolks
1 tbl paprika
Pinch nutmeg
1 tsp Cognac
1 tsp tomato paste
125 ml (1/2 cup) olive oil
1/4 cup crème fraîche or heavy
  cream
Chervil and tarragon, chopped
1 truffle (20 g (2/3 oz)), chopped

Plate Presentation

Choose the greenest leaves of lettuce and arrange them around the rim of the plates.
Place the white, central leaves in the center of the plates.
Divide the lobster medallions among the four plates and arrange on the lettuce leaves.
Sprinkle the top with chopped truffle, chervil and tarragon.

Procedure

Cook the lobsters in a full-flavored court bouillon. Cool, remove the shells and cut the tail meat into 1/2 cm (1/4 in) slices. Blend together the 2 egg yolks with the paparika, a pinch of freshly grated nutmeg, a few drops of Cognac and the tomato paste. Whisk in the olive oil in a steady stream to emulsify the sauce. Stir in the cream. Season to taste. Marinate the slices of lobster in this sauce about 30 minutes.

Salad with Foie Gras, Prawns, and Duck Gizzards

"La Toque Blanche" *(Pujols)*
Chef: Bernard Lebrun

Ingredients (4 servings)

120 g (scant 4 oz) foie gras terrine
20 Dublin Bay Prawns
4 preserved ("confit") duck gizzards*
16 cherry tomatoes
1 shallot, finely chopped
1 garlic clove, finely chopped
Field salad ("mesclun")
60 ml (2 fl oz) vinaigrette
(red wine vinegar, olive oil, mustard)
1 small bunch chives, chopped
1 small buch flat parsley, chopped
3 large basil leaves, chopped
Salt and pepper
Chervil leaves

Note: Gizzards "confit" are prepared by slow, low cooking in duck fat. They are available in jars from specialty shops. See "Cooking of Southwestern France" by Paula Wolfert for more information.

Procedure

Remove the shells from the prawns. Heat a little oil in a heavy pan and sauté the tail meat for 3 minutes. Season with salt and pepper, add chopped shallot, garlic and parsley, cook another minute and keep warm until service.

Meanwhile warm the gizzards in the oven, slice thinly and keep warm.

Whisk together Dijon mustard and red wine vinegar then slowly add the olive oil. Add chopped chives, basil and parsley to the vinaigrette.

Plate Presentation

Toss the greens in the vinaigrette and mound in the center of the plate. Place the slices of gizzards and foie gras on top. Place the prawns and cherry tomatoes around the edge. Decorate with chervil leaves.

When in season add other vegetables to this salad such as asparagus tips, artichoke hearts, peeled tomato quarters or thin green beans.

21

Marinated Scallops with Truffles and Cabbage Salad

« El Chiquito » (Rueil-Malmaison)
Chef : M. Pichois

Ingredients (4 servings)

12 large sea scallops
(sliced thinly)

Cabbage Salad

Slice a small green cabbage very thinly. Toss with raisins, chopped walnuts, diced tomatoes, chopped chives, salt and pepper.

Marinade (for scallops):

Stir together the juice of one lemon, salt, pepper and a pinch of curry powder, whisk in olive oil.

Plate Presentation

Overlap the thin slices of scallops around the plate, leaving a place in the center for the salad. Add 1 tbl chopped truffles to the marinade and brush over the scallops several times. Toss the cabbage salad in the remaining marinade and mound in the center.
Decorate with a few chervil sprigs.

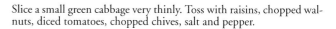

Scallop Salad with Endive and Clementines

« Hôtel du Dauphin » *(L'Aigle)*
Chefs : Michel Bernard and
Jean-Pierre Fulep

Ingredients
(4 servings)

480 g (scant 1 lb) sea scallops
Juice of 1 lemon
200 ml (7 fl oz) vinaigrette
  (olive oil and lemon juice)
200 g (7 oz) lamb's lettuce
  («mâche»)
400 g (14 oz) Belgian endives
80 g (2 2/3 oz) sugar
600 g (1 1/4 lbs) clementines
80 ml (1/3 cup) vinegar
200 g (7 oz) unsalted butter
1 bunch chives
chopped tomatoes

Procedure
To prepare the butter sauce: Cook the sugar and vinegar over low heat for 5 minutes. Peel and section the clementines and add them to the reduction and simmer until the fruit is lightly candied. Remove with a slotted spoon and set aside. Whisk in a little heavy cream then, off the heat, whisk in the butter a little at a time to obtain a smooth, shiny sauce. Keep warm in a water bath.
Clean and julienne the endives and steam with a little lemon juice. Season with salt and pepper and keep warm.
Cut each scallop into 4 «medallions», spread in a single layer on a buttered baking sheet and cook at about 190 C (375) 1-2 minutes.
Just before serving, toss the lettuce in the vinaigrette.

Plate Presentation
Spread the julienned endive in the center of each plate and arrange the scallop slices on top.
Spoon the sauce over the scallops.
Mound three spoonfuls of salad around the edge.
Decorate with warm clementine sections, chopped tomatoes and pieces of chives.

Snails in a Crispy Crust with Garlic Cream and Field Greens

"Restaurant Vidal" *(St-Julien-Chapteuil)*
Chef : Jean-Pierre Vidal

Ingredients (4 servings)

100 g (3 1/2 oz) leeks (white portion) - 500 g (1 lb) potatoes
100 g (3 1/2 oz) unsalted butter
Cream puff dough made with:
100 ml (3.5 fl oz) water, 100 ml (3.5 fl oz) milk, 5 g (1 tsp) sugar, 5 g (1 tsp) salt, 80 g (2 2/3 oz) unsalted butter, 120 g (scant 1 cup) flour, 4 large eggs, nutmeg, salt, pepper 32 snails - 300 g (10 oz)

garlic, peeled, germ removed
500 ml (2 cups) heavy cream
500 ml (2 cups) veal or chicken stock
Field greens for 4 servings
Dill, chives and chervil sprigs
Vinaigrette: hazelnut oil, wine vinegar, mustard
1 large beet, cooked - 500 ml (2 cups) peanut oil for frying

Procedure

Rinse the snails and sauté briefly in butter, set aside.
Peel and cook the potatoes in salted water, mash while warm (use a ricer or food mill so there are no lumps).
Cut the leeks into a fine julienne and cook in butter over low heat.
Make the cream puff dough. Combine the water, milk, salt, sugar and butter in a large saucepan and bring to a boil. When the butter is melted, remove from the heat, add the flour and stir. Dry out the mixture a little over low heat until smooth. Off the heat, beat in the eggs one at a time and season with salt, pepper and ground nutmeg. Mix together the mashed potatoes, cream puff dough and leeks.
Mold a little of this dough around each snail (snail with the coating should be about 3 cm (1 1/4 inch) in diameter). Place on a tray in the freezer.
Make the garlic cream. Cover the garlic cloves with cold water, bring to a simmer, rinse. Blanch three times in all. Cook the blanched garlic in the cream and stock then purée in the blender and season with salt and pepper.

Plate Presentation

Heat the oil to 170 C (350 F), deep fry the snails and drain on paper towels. Add the herbs to the salad greens and toss with hazelnut vinaigrette.
Place a mound of dressed salad in the center of each plate with a colorful decoration of julienned beet.
Spoon the hot garlic cream around the edge of each plate and place 8 hot snails on top of the sauce. Serve immediately.
This original first course is a successful marriage of creamy garlic and crispy fritter coating on the snails which goes well with the mild acidity of the hazelnut vinaigrette.

Lobster "Blanquette" with Basil

"Le Jardin Gourmand" *(Sartrouville)*
Chefs : Régis Ligot and Christian Gipteau

Ingredients (4 servings)

4 lobsters (400 g (14 oz each))
2 L (2 qts) court bouillon
200 g (6 1/2 oz) buttom
  mushrooms
4-5 small turnips, peeled
4-5 small carrots, peeled
4-5 small zucchini
20 basil leaves
400 g (14 oz) unsalted butter
400 ml (14 fl oz) dry white wine
60 g (2 oz) chopped shallots
1 L (1 qt) heavy cream
Salt, pepper
2 large baked potatoes

Procedure

Poach the lobsters in the court bouillon, remove the meat from the tails and claws and reserve the shells.
Cut the vegetables into small, even pieces and cover with water, add a little salt and butter and cook until tender and lightly glazed.
Cut the mushrooms into large dice and sauté in butter.
Press the warm baked potatoes through a sieve and stir in 300 g (10 oz) butter.

Sauce:

Crush the lobster shells, add the white wine, shallots and basil. Simmer until all the liquid is evaporated. Add the cream and simmer until the cream thickens enough to coat a spoon. Pour the sauce through a fine sieve. Whisk in the potato mixture to bind the sauce and whisk in 50 g butter to enrich the sauce and make it shine.

Plate Presentation

Combine the lobster meat and sauce and divide the "blanquette" between four plates. Arrange the vegetables around and garnish with julienned basil leaves. Serve with fresh pasta (linguini).

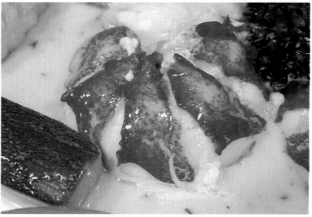

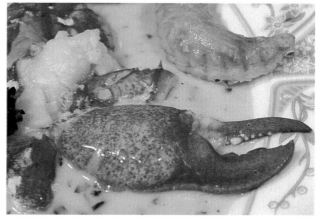

Salad with Scrambled Eggs and Fricassée of Snails

"Château-Hôtel de Nieul" *(Nieul)*
Chef : Luce Bodinaud

Ingredients
(4 servings)

1 small head Boston lettuce
1 small head red oak leaf lettuce
1 bunch lamb's lettuce
 or watercress
100 g (3 1/2 oz) button
 mushrooms
1/2 raw beet
Chives and parsley, chopped
Vinaigrette
6 large eggs
1 tbl heavy cream
Salt, pepper, chives
Butter

For the fricassée of snails:
200-250 g (7-8oz) snails
(cooked in broth)

100 g (3/12 oz) bacon
2 garlic cloves
Parsley, chopped
Butter

Procedure

Drain the snails, sauté briefly in butter with a little salt and pepper. Cut thick-sliced bacon into short strips, add to the snails and cook over medium heat about five minutes. Towards the end of cooking, add chopped garlic and parsley.
Meanwhile clean the greens, dry and mix with finely julienned beet and thinly sliced mushrooms. Make a vinaigrette with walnut oil, wine vinegar, chopped chives and parsley and salt and pepper.
Just before service, beat the eggs with a little salt and pepper. Cook them in a little butter over very low heat, stirring constantly to make very creamy, moist scrambled eggs. Sprinkle with chopped chives.

Plate Presentation

Toss the greens in the vinaigrette and mound on the plates. Arrange the scrambled eggs and fricasée of snails around the plate in an attractive pattern.

Vegetable Tart with Anchovy Vinaigrette

"Le Lingusto" *(Cuers)*
Chef : Alain Rion

Ingredients
(4 servings)
3 tomatoes
3 zucchini
200 g (6 1/2 oz) pumpkin
  flesh
2 eggplant
2 g (pinch) saffron
20 g (2/3 oz) garlic cloves
400 g (14 oz) prepared puff
  pastry
125 ml (1 cup) olive oil
100 g (3 1/2 oz) anchovies

Procedure
Cut the prepared puff pastry into 4 circles (12 cm (4 1/2 in)).
Prick with a fork and bake at 200 C (400 F) about 10 minutes.
When browned a little, place another baking sheet on top to com-
press the layers and continue cooking about 10-15 minutes or
until golden brown and crispy. Trim the edges if necessary.
Peel the tomatoes, cut in half then into thin slices.
Cut the zucchini and eggplant lengthwise and cut into 3 mm (1/8
in) slices. Cut the pumpkin into slices about the same size as the
other vegetables. Blanch the slices of pumpkin and zucchini
separately (until "al dente") and cool in cold water, drain.
Sauté the eggplant slices briefly in olive oil.
Alternate the slices of vegetables, standing on end, and arrange
them tightly in the mold (individual non-stick 10 cm (4 in)) so
they stay in place during cooking. Cook at 120 C (250 F) for 1
hour or until the pumpkin is very tender.

Plate Presentation
Place the rounds of puff pastry over the cooked vegetables and
invert the vegetables over onto the pastry.
Pour a little olive oil on the plates and arrange anchovies around
the edge, sprinkle with saffron.
Place the warm tart in the center and serve immediately.

Chapter 2 - Hot First Courses

Rediscover Vegetables

France is an immense garden. Vegetables grow in abundance and are freshly picked and rushed to market. In the hands of great chefs and talented home cooks, their wonderful flavors are released. By definition, "vegetables" refers to garden plants destined for human consumption.

Depending on the plant, various parts are eaten:
- Leaves: spinach, chard, endives, cabbage, lettuce...
- Stems: asparagus, chard, leeks...
- Roots, bulbs and tubers: carrots, onions, potatoes, radishes, salsify...

The very best produce available comes from the small farms that sell directly to the market. Very fresh, often picked the same day or at most the day before, the leaves are bright green and stems and tubers have no soft spots. Very fresh vegetables are firm to the touch and have a beautiful appearance. Having reached full maturity "on the vine" and not subjected to lengthy transport, the flavor of these farm-raised foods are perfect.

To prepare, trim the leaves and peel as necessary and rinse in a basin of cold water with a little vinegar.

For most vegetables, the best cooking method to preserve flavor and color is to cook in rapidly boiling water. Bring a large pot of water to a boil, just before adding the vegetables, salt the water (never add salt until this point).

It is important not to overcook vegetables. If they become too soft, the texture, which plays an important role in overall taste, is lost. It is recommended to cook them "al dente", with just a little crunch when bitten. When the vegetables are perfectly cooked, drain and refresh under cold running water to stop the cooking.

Leafy vegetables (and some roots like carrots) are cooked with butter and salt in a covered pan where moisture is released from the vegetables and they cook in their own juices.

For vegetables that have a tendency to turn brown during cooking, a "blanc" (meaning "white") can be used. This is done by adding 1 large spoonful of flour to 2-3 liters (2-3 quarts) of water, bringing the water to a boil, adding salt and lemon juice (or clear vinegar) then proceeding to cook the vegetables as described above. Vegetables prepared for a gratin dish are often cooked with a "blanc" as a matter of course.

Another trick is to add a slice of bread to the water in which cauliflower is cooked to absorb some of the strong odor.

The amount of time each vegetable cooks is a function of freshness and size. Tender spring vegetables will need less cooking than hardy winter ones.

Check the doneness with a skewer to check that they are just soft enough to penetrate without falling apart.

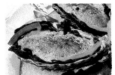

The History of Souffléed Potatoes

Thanks to our friend and colleague Roger Lallemand, former cooking instructor and well-known author, who wrote «The History of Souffléed Potatoes», the fascinating story and recipe for this delicious sidedish has been recorded for posterity.

On August 26, 1837, the new railroad line connecting Paris and Saint-Germain-en-Laye was inaugurated. Of course the day's celebration would end with a banquet. On the menu, among the many dishes was Filet of Beef with Deep Fried Potatoes. The chef had ordered just the right amount of food for the number of guests and was preparing the meal according to schedule. He started frying the potatoes one hour before the guests were to arrive, but catastrophe struck! The train was delayed and the poor chef, fearing a great embarrassment and the end of his career, quickly removed the potatoes from the hot oil, set them aside and waited impatiently. The train finally arrived, puffing into the station and the guests made their way to the banquet hall

led by King Lois Philippe and Queen Amélie.

The chef proceeded with the preparation of the potatoes and plunged them into very hot oil to crispen them. To his surprise each one blew up like a golden balloon, light as air and crispy. He had created a most delicious potato dish that is still served today.

According to the chemist Chevreul who has studied the phenomenon of the souffléed potato, here is how it happens: the starch in the potato transforms into dextrine in the first «bath» of oil. The albumine partially coagulates and forms an envelope which holds the steam created by the second frying which causes the potato inflate like a balloon.

In principle, the method should work with all potatoes, but for best results use a yellow «fleshed» elongated variety. Peel them well and square off the sides. Cut long slices that are 3-5 mm (1/8 in) thick (this is an important step). For perfectly even slices,

it is recommended to use a «mandoline» or other vegetable slicer. Pat them dry with a clean dish towel.

Use two deep frying vessels, filled with peanut oil. Heat the first to 110 C and the second to 210 C. Plunge the potatoes into the cooler oil and cook about 6 minutes, stirring constantly to keep the slices from sticking to each other. They should not brown at this point. Remove the potatoes with a large wire skimmer and plunge them immediately into the hot oil for about one minute to puff and become golden brown. Sprinkle with fine, plain (not iodized) salt and serve hot. Chef Dumont-Lespine advises:

1. Don't fry too many potatoes at once as this would lower the temperature of the oil.

2. As soon as the frying is completed, remove the oil from the heat and lower the temperature rapidly (to keep it from burning) by placing an onion or slice of bread in the oil.

Hot Oysters
with Hazelnut Butter

"La Châtaigneraie"
(Sucé-sur-Erdre)
Chef : J. Delphin

Ingredients
(4 servings)

6 oysters
75 g (2 1/2 oz) hazelnuts, toasted
200 g (6 1/2 oz) unsalted butter,
 softened
Coarse salt for presentation

Plate Presentation

Place the oysters under the broiler to brown the tops, heat them through and release the delicious hazelnut aroma of the butter. Serve immediately.

Procedure

Open the oysters.
Detach the muscle and leave the oysters in their shell to keep all the flavorful liquid in the shell. Cover the surface of heatproof plates with coarse salt and place the oysters on top.

Finely chop the toasted hazelnuts and blend them into the softened butter.

Just before service, place a spoonful of hazelnut butter on each oyster.

30

Warm Oysters with Paprika

"La Tour du Roy" *(Vervins-en-Thièrache)*
Chef : Annie Desvignes

Ingredients (4 servings)

24 oysters
2 heads Bibb lettuce
6 eeg yolks
100 ml (3.5 fl oz) heavy cream
180 g (6 oz) unsalted butter
1/2 tsp curry powder
1/4 tsp paprika

Procedure

Open the oysters and remove them from the shells.
Pour the oyster liquor into a saucepan and gently poach the oysters to warm them though without overcooking.
Wash the deep half of the shells in boiling water with vinegar, wipe them clean and dry.
Trim and wash the lettuce and reform the leaves into the original shape. Heat 40 g (1 1/3 oz) butter in a saucepan, add the lettuce, season with salt and pepper, cover and cook over low heat until tender.
To make the hollandaise, whisk together the egg yolks with 100 ml (3.5 fl oz) water over low heat until the mixture is warm, thick and foamy. Whisk in the curry powder, softened butter and crème fraîche.
Fill the bottom of each oyster with chopped, braised lettuce, place an oyster on top. Spoon hollandaise over each oyster and sprinkle the entire surface of sauce with paprika.

Plate Presentation

Cover 6 plates with seaweed (or coarse salt).
Just before serving, warm the oysters under the broiler. The hollandaise will brown slightly.
Arrange 6 oysters on each plate and serve immediately.

Crayfish Gratin

"Auberge du Père Bise" *(Talloires)*
Chef : Sophie Bise

Ingredients (4 servings)

3 kg (6 1/2 lbs) crayfish
2 carrots, 1 onions,
3 shallots, peeled, diced
1 celery stalk
1 branch of thyme, 1 bay leaf,
1/2 head of garlic
500 ml (2 cups) dry white wine
Cayenne pepper
Coarsely ground black pepper
100 ml (3 1/2 fl oz) peanut oil
500 ml (2 cups) crème fraîche
30 ml (1 fl oz) Cognac

Procedure

If using live, wild crayfish, pull out the intestine from the tail.
Sauté the crayfish in a large pot with a little oil.
When the crayfish have turned red, add the vegetables (cut in small dice) to the pot and cook for about 2 minutes.
Add the Cognac, wine, pepper and enough water to cover the crayfish, bring to a simmer and cook 1 minute.
Remove the crayfish with a slotted spoon, cool for 10 minutes, remove the meat and put the shells back into the liquid.
Reduce the liquid by 3/4, then strain through a conical sieve, pressing on the shells and vegetables to extract flavor.
Reduce the strained liquid by half, add the crème fraîche (or heavy cream) and reduce to thicken.
Put the crayfish meat in the sauce, stir to coat evenly.
Spoon the mixture into 4 gratin dishes and set aside about 1/2 hour for the sauce to form a "skin" on the surface (which browns evenly).

Plate Presentation

Just before serving, warm in the oven then brown the top under the broiler.

Mussel Gratin with Saffron Sauce

"Le Cyrano" *(Bergerac)*
Chef : Jean-Paul Turon

Ingredients (4 servings)

500 g (1 lb) mussels
300 g (10 oz) tomatoes
1 large onion
3-4 cloves garlic
1 hot pepper
Bouquet garni

Salmon mousseline:
500 g (1 lb) salmon
4 large eggs
120 g (4 oz) unsalted butter
150 ml (5 fl oz) heavy cream
Salt, pepper, cayenne, saffron

Procedure

Make a rich, zesty sauce with the tomatoes, onions, pepper, garlic and the bouquet garni.
Make a salmon mousseline by puréeing the salmon then adding the the eggs, cream, butter and seasonings and blending until smooth.

Clean the mussels, pull off any barnacles and seaweed that are attached and open the mussels with a paring knife. Pull off the top shell without detaching the mussel.
Pipe a little salmon mousseline on each mussel.
Steam for about 10 minutes.

Plate Presentation
Place the cooked mussels on a heatproof plate.
Cover with tomato sauce and sprinkle with grated Swiss cheese, brown under the broiler and serve immediely.

Scallops Sautéed in Olive oil with Eggplant Roulades

« Le Vieux Castillon » (Castillon-du-Gard)
Chef : Gilles Dauteuil

Ingredients (10 servings)

60 large sea scallops
2 kg (2 lbs) eggplant
5 kg (11 lbs) tomatoes
2 red peppers
1 yellow pepper
100 g (3 1/2 oz) black olives, pitted, chopped
500 ml (1 cup) olive oil
Chervil, chives, basil, salt, pepper

Procedure

Cut each eggplant lengthwise into thin slices. Pan-fry in olive oil, reserve.

Peel and seed the tomatoes. Chop and cook with olive oil, thyme and salt. Spread the purée on a baking sheet lined with parchment and dry in a very low oven (80 C (150 F)) for 4 hours.

Lay the slices of eggplant on the work surface. Cut strips of the dried tomato the same size as the slices and roll together.

Cut them in half and group 6 together and wrap another slice of eggplant around the roulades.

Grill the pepper or bake in a very hot oven. Peel, seed and cut into very small dice. Make a vinaigrette with olive oil, wine vinegar and mustard. Stir in the diced peppers, chopped olives and herbs.

Pan-fry the scallops in olive oil and season lightly.

Plate Presentation

Place an eggplant roulade in the center and arrange the scallops around. Spoon the vinaigrette over the dish and decorate with sprigs of fresh herbs.

Prawn Brochettes with Pesto Noodles

"Auberge du Père Bise" *(Talloires)*
Chef : Sophie Bise

Ingredients (4 servings)

24 fresh Dublin Bay prawns	1 L (1 qt) dry white wine
180 g (6 oz) fresh pasta	200 ml (scant cup) crème fraîche
24 cherry tomatoes	2 egg yolks
24 pieces of celery	Parmesan
2 small onions	Basil, chopped
1 head of garlic	Chives, chopped
2 medium carrots	50 g (1 2/3 oz) unsalted butter
1 small, dried chili pepper	Olive oil
Thyme and bay leaf	Salt and pepper

Procedure

Twist the prawns to separate the tail from the head.
Remove the shell from the tails. Cook the shells with olive oil, diced vegetables, pepper and herbs.
Add the white wine and 2 L (2 qts) water, bring to a simmer, skim the surface and continue to simmer 1 hour. Pass through a conical sieve and continue reducing.
Peel and cut celery into 24 pieces and cook until tender in the reducing liquid, remove with a slotted spoon and set aside.
When the strained liquid is reduced by half, whisk in the crème fraîche and set the sauce aside.
Meanwhile, sauté the prawn tails in butter, season with salt and pepper, set aside.

Peel the cherry tomatoes.
Alternate the cooked tail meat, cherry tomatoes and cooked celery chunks on 8 bamboo skewers.
Cook the pasta "al dente" in boiling salted water, drain.
To make the pesto sauce, mix together finely chopped garlic with the egg yolks, parmesan and chopped basil. Whisk in olive oil to make a smooth, emulsified sauce.

Plate Presentation

Reheat the pasta with the pesto sauce, stir in the butter and mound the pasta in the center of four heated plates. Place 2 brochettes on top of the pasta and sprinkle with chopped chives.

Shrimp in Red Wine

"Hôtel d'Espagne" *(Valençay)*
Chef : Maurice Fourré

Ingredients
(4 servings)

20 large shrimp, shells removed
50 ml (4 tbls) olive oil
Sauce:
100 g (3 1/2 oz) flour
100 g (3 1/2 oz) unsalted butter
1 L (1 qt) red wine
500 ml (2 cups) chicken stock
Salt, pepper, thyme, bay leaf
2 carrots, 3 onions, sliced
Garnish:
200 g (7 oz) spring or pearl
    onions, peeled
200 g (7 oz) button mushrooms
100 g (3 1/2 oz) thick-sliced bacon
1 bunch chives

Procedure

Sauté the sliced carrots and onions in the butter until lightly browned, season with a little salt and pepper. Stir in the flour and cook for a minute. Add the thyme, bay leaf, red wine and chicken stock. Bring to a boil, skim, lower the heat and simmer about 40 minutes.
Cut the bacon into short strips ("lardons") and blanch in boiling water. Cook the onions separately in lightly salted boiling water until tender.
Pass the sauce through a sieve and add the lardons and onions. Pan fry the shrimp in olive oil, turning them over to cook on both sides.
Cut the mushrooms into match sticks ("julienne") and chop the chives.

Plate Presentation

Ladle the red wine sauce onto plates and add the shrimp. Garnish the top with raw mushroom julienne and chopped chives.

"Gambas" and Wild Mushrooms in Red Wine

"Le Bourbon" *(Yssingeaux)*
Chef : André Perrier

Ingredients (5 servings)

5 "gambas" (jumbo shrimp), shells removed
5 large pleurottes or portabellos (tops only)
Garlic, shallots, chives, chopped

Lentil flan:
750 ml (3 cups) heavy cream
9 large eggs, salt, pepper
100 g (3 1/2 oz) cooked lentils

For the wine sauce:
300 ml (10 fl oz) fish stock
300 ml (10 fl oz) red wine
100 ml (3.5 fl oz) brown sauce
2-3 tbls. unsalted butter

Procedure

Lentil flans: Butter 5 individual soufflé dishes and place a few cooked lentils in the bottom. In the blender or food processor, mix together the cream, eggs and remaining lentils and season with salt and pepper. Pour the custard into the molds and cook in a water bath at 100 C (200 F) about 1 hour or until set.

Wine sauce: Reduce the full-flavored fish stock by 1/2, add the wine and reduce by 3/4. Add the brown sauce and reduce until the sauce coats a spoon. Just before serving, whisk in a little butter to enrich the sauce and make it shine.

Gambas: Place one shrimp and one mushroom cap each on 5 skewers. Pan-fry the brochettes with butter and chopped garlic and shallots. Sprinkle the cooked brochettes with chopped chives.

Plate Presentation

Ladle the sauce on the bottom of the plates.
Place a brochette and a flan on each plate.
Garnish with cooked "pearls" of vegetables (cut with a tiny melon baller).

37

Warm Bouquet of Seafood with Field Greens

« Aux Armes de Champagne » (L'Epine)
Chef : Patrick Michelon

Ingredients (2 servings)

1 red mullet (250 g (8 oz))
1 lobster (500 g (1 lb))
4 large sea scallops
150 g (5 oz) thin green beans
1 shallot
Assorted seasonal greens:
2 leaves Boston lettuce
2 leaves raddichio
4 leaves Belgian endive
Bunch lamb's lettuce or arugula
Salt, pepper

Procedure

Cook the seafood and beans at the last minute so they are still warm when ready to assemble the dish. Roast the lobster in a hot oven for 7 minutes, remove the shell and cut the tail into medallions. Pan-fry the mullet fillets and scallops. Blanch the green beans in boiling salted water.

Plate Presentation

Arrange the greens on the plates. Place one lobster claw on each plate. Arrange the warm lobster medallions, scallops, beans and slices of mullet in an attractive pattern. Combine the chicken broth, vinegar and oil and drizzle over the dish. Decorate with fresh herbs and a few grains of coarse sea salt.

Snails in Filo

« Le Vieux Castillon » (Castillon-du-Gard)
Chef : Gilles Dauteuil

Ingredients (10 servings)

10 dozen snails
2 kg (2 lbs) root vegetables:
carrots, Chinese and Jerusalem
artichokes, beets, cerlery root
10 zucchini flowers
10 sheets filo dough
4 tbls chopped herbs:
  parsley, tarragon, chervil
2 bunches watercress, trimmed
1 bunch flat parsley, chopped
1 head garlic
250 g (8 oz) unsalted butter
Salt, pepper

Procedure

Wash and peel the root vegetables and cut into small dice («brunoise»). Cook each separately in boiling water. Reserve 2 cups of liquid. Toss with the chopped herbs and season with salt and pepper.

Sauté the snails in a little butter with 4 chopped garlic cloves and 2 tbls chopped parsley.

Brush the filo sheets with melted butter and fold in half. Place 12 snails in the center with 1 tbl vegetable dice, fold like a package and brush with butter. Bake at 180 C (365 F) for 10 minutes. The pastry should be brown and crispy.

In a heavy pot, melt 1 tbl butter and add the watercress (stems trimmed). Add the 2 cups of vegetable broth, 3 garlic cloves and the remaining parsley. Simmer and reduce by 2/3. Purée in a food processor and whisk in 200 g (7 oz) butter.

Deep fry the zucchini blossoms.

Plate Presentation

Place a snail package on each plate. Spoon watercress sauce around and garnish with the remaining vegetable dice and a zucchini blossom.

Snail Raviolis
with Morels

"Château de Vauchoux" *(Port-sur-Saône)*
Chef : Jean-Michel Turin

ngredients
(4 servings)

30 snails, cooked
100 g (3 1/2 oz) carrots, peeled
50 g (1 2/3 oz) shallots, chopped
20 g (2/3 oz) unsalted butter
100 g (3 1/2 oz) dried morels
300 ml (10 fl oz) crème fraîche
   or heavy cream
500 ml (2 cups) white wine
300 ml (10 fl oz) reduced chicken
   stock
1 bunch chervil
Salt, pepper
Fresh pasta dough:
500 g (1 lb) flour, 5 whole eggs,
2 egg yolks, 2 tbls peanut or olive
oil, pinch of salt

CHATEAU DE VAUCHOUX

Plate Presentation

Ladle the morels and cooking liquid on the plates. Place the raviolis on top and garnish with a warmed snail and chervil leaves. Serve very hot.

Procedure

To make the pasta dough, mix the eggs and oil into the flour and salt and knead until smooth. Cover and refrigerate 2 hours.
Cut the carrots into small dice ("brunoise") and cook them in butter with the chopped shallots and a pinch of salt until tender. Set aside.
Soak the dried morels in water, cut in half and rinse thoroughly to remove all dirt and sand.
Combine the mushrooms with the wine, cream and stock in a large saucepan and simmer about 20 minutes. Season with salt and pepper.

Drain the snails.
Roll out the pasta dough and cut into 48 small squares.
Place a snail and a spoonful of cooked carrots and shallots on half of the squares. Brush water around the edge of the dough, place another square of pasta on top and press to seal.
Cook the raviolis 4 minutes in boiling, salted water.

40

Snails and Smoked Trout with Honey Sauce

"Le Bourbon" *(Yssingeaux)*
Chef : André Perrier

Ingredients
(2 servings)

24 snails
160 g (5 1/3 oz) smoked trout
Chopped shallots
30 g (1 oz) honey
300 ml (10 fl oz) reduced fish stock
100 ml (3 1/2 fl oz) heavy cream
Salt, cayenne pepper, curry powder
Leeks, julienned
Tomatoe "compote" with thyme

Note that tomato "compote" a simple mixture of stewed, chopped tomatoes is a standby garnish and flavoring component in many French kitchens. See recipe for "Tomato Omelette".

Procedure

Cut the smoked trout fillets into strips and roll into spirals. Alternate three smoked trout spirals and 2 snails on wooden skewers. Make 6 brochettes per serving.
Honey sauce: Cook the honey to a caramel. Add the full-flavored fish stock and reduce. Add the cream, reduce to thicken enough so that the sauce coats a spoon. Season to taste with salt, Cayenne pepper and curry powder.
Sauté the snail brochettes in butter with chopped shallots. Add the sauce, bring to a simmer and remove from the heat.
Steam the julienned leeks.

Plate Presentation

Place the warm julienned leeks on the bottom of the plate.
Arrange the brochettes in a star around the plate.
Ladle the sauce over the brochettes and garnish with tiny spoonfuls of tomato compote.

Lentil Soup with Truffles

"La Cognette" *(Issoudun)*
Chef : Alain Nonnet

Ingredients
(8 servings)

250 g (8 oz) green lentils
100 g (3 1/2 oz) carrots, peeled
100 g (3 1/2 oz) onions, peeled
50 g (1 2/3 oz) smoked bacon
500 ml (2 cups) light cream
1 bouquet garni
100 g (3 1/2 oz) unsalted butter
1 small canned truffle with juice
Croutons

Procedure

Cut the aromatic ingredients (carrots, onions) into dice. Cook the bacon a little to melt the fat, add the vegetables and cook together until the vegetables are soft and lightly browned.
Add the lentils and water (according to package directions). Add the bouquet garni and simmer 25 minutes.
Remove the bacon and bouquet garni from the cooked lentils. Purée the lentils in the food processor and add cream. Pour the mixture through a sieve.
Just before serving, stir in the truffle juice and whisk in the butter.

Plate Presentation

Garnish the soup with truffle slices and fresh croutons made from "pain de mie" or "pullman loaf", cut in small cubes and sautéed in butter until crisp.

Pumpkin Soup with Polenta and Truffles

«Hostellerie de la Fuste» (Valensole)
Chef : M. Bucaille

Ingredients
(8 servings)

1 kg (2.2 lbs) pumpkin
250 g (8 oz) unsalted butter
250 ml (1 cup) heavy ceam
200 g (7 oz) polenta
1 bouquet garni
200 g (7 oz) truffles
Nutmeg, salt, pepper

Procedure

Peel the pumpkin and cut into chunks. Place in a heavy pot with the butter, season with salt, pepper and freshly grated nutmeg. Cover and cook over low heat until the pumpkin is soft.

Add cream to cover the pumpkin, add the bouquet garni and simmer until the cream thickens enough to coat a spoon.

Remove the bouquet garni and purée the pumpkin and cream together in the food processor until smooth.

Return to the heat, bring to a simmer then pour through a sieve. Meanwhile, cook the polenta according to package directions and pour into a shallow dish. Set aside to cool.

Plate Presentation

Serve the soup in heated soup dishes.

Scoop the polenta to make small oval-shaped «quenelles» to garnish the soup.

Further embellish the soup with slices of truffle.

Place a serving dome over the soup to keep it piping hot and serve immediately.

Zucchini Blossoms with Prawns

"Les Délices du Château" *(Saumur)*
Chef : Pierre Millon

Ingredients
(4 servings)

8 tiny zucchini with blossoms attached
2 kg (4.4 lbs) large Dublin Bay Prawns
(shrimp can be substituted for prawns)
300 ml (10 fl oz) heavy cream
5 shallots, chopped
1 bottle dry white wine
5 large tomatoes, cut in large dice
1 garlic clove, chopped
1 egg white
Cayenne pepper
Olive oil
Chervil

Plate Presentation

Slice and fan out the cooked zucchini and arrange them on plates with the cooked blossoms. Ladle sauce around and decorate with the steamed prawn tails and sprigs of fresh chervil. Serve very hot.

Procedure
Prepare the zucchini.
Separate the blossoms from the zucchini. Carefully wash the blossoms and cut away the pistols. Cook the zucchini in boiling, salted water for about 5 minutes, refresh in cold water, then drain.
Prepare the sauce.
Remove the shells from the prawns and set aside the tail meat. Chop the shells and sauté in olive oil with the shallots. Add the garlic and tomatoes. When the vegetables have softened, crush the ingredients with a potato masher.
Add the white wine and season with salt and cayenne pepper, simmer for 45 minutes.

Pour the ingredients through a sieve and press on the shells and vegetables to extract flavor. Stir in 100 ml (3.5 fl oz) cream, reduce to thicken, and keep warm until service.
Prepare the filling.
Set aside the 4 best looking pieces of tail meat for garnish. Purée the remaining prawns until smooth and add the egg white. Whip the remaining cream to very soft peaks and gently stir into the puréed prawns and season with salt.
Pipe this smooth mixture into the zucchini blossoms.
Just before service, steam the stuffed blossoms for 10 minutes and the prawn tails for 3 minutes. Warm the zucchini.

Blood Sausage Lasagna with Prawns

"Restaurant Vidal" *(St-Julien-Chapteuil)*
Chef : Jean-Pierre Vidal

Ingredients (8 servings)

48 medium Dublin Bay prawns
300 g (10 oz) fresh lasagna noodles
100 g (3 1/2 oz) carrots
100 g (3 1/2 oz) onions
100 g (3 1/2 g) shallots
2 garlic cloves
500 ml (2 cups) dry white wine
1 L (1 qt) crème fraîche or heavy
  cream

1 L (1 qt) fish stock
200 g (6 1/2 oz) unsalted butter
800 g (1 lb 12 oz) blood sausage
Olive oil
Salt, cayenne pepper, star anise
200 g (6 1/2 oz) spice bread,
  crumbled
8 cherry tomatoes, 1 bunch fresh
  dill

Procedure

Cook the lasagna in salted water, set aside in cold water.
Remove the shells from the prawns. Refrigerate the tail meat.
Make a sauce from the shells. Heat the olive oil, cook the shells briefly then add the vegetables and spices and cook until soft. Add the wine, fish stock and cream. Simmer until reduced by about half. Strain, whisk in pieces of butter and keep warm in a water bath
Remove the casing from the blood sausage and stir until smooth with a little butter and cream. Keep warm until service.
Press the spice bread crumbs onto the prawns and sauté in olive oil until just firm, don't overcook. (Note that French "spice bread" is similar to gingerbread.)

Plate Presentation

Warm the cooked lasagna and layer with hot blood sausage purée and place in the center of heated bowls (low and wide).
Arrange 6 prawns around the lasagna.
Spoon sauce over on the dish without coating the prawns.
Decorate with a cherry tomato and dill sprig.
Place the bowl on a plate with a doilie and serve hot.

Truffle Soufflé with Foie Gras Mousse

"La Tour du Roy" *(Vervins-en-Thiérache)*
Chef : Annie Desvignes

Ingredients
(4 servings)

150 g (5 oz) foie gras mousse (duck)
150 g (5 oz) poached chicken breast
30 g (1 oz) chopped truffle peelings
250 ml (8 fl oz) crème fraîche
4 egg whites
1/2 cup Port
Salt and freshly ground pepper

Plate Presentation

Unmold the soufflés onto 4 heated plates and ladle sauce around each souffle. Serve at once.

Procedure

Cut the cooked chicken breast into dice. In a food processor, purée the chicken and foie gras until smooth. Transfer to a cold bowl and stir in 100 ml (3 .5 fl oz) crème fraîche a little at a time. Season with salt and pepper. Stir in 1/3 of the truffles.
Beat the egg whites to stiff peaks and gently fold them into the foie gras and truffle mixture.
Spoon the mixture into 4 buttered ramekins, place in a water bath with boiling water and cook cook until puffed in a 200 C (400F) oven.

To make the sauce, simmer the Port with the remaining truffles until reduced by 3/4. Whisk in the remaining crème fraîche, bring to a simmer to reduce the cream a little. Season with salt and pepper.

46

Cabbage Stuffed with Salmon Mousseline

"Restaurant Vidal" *(St-Julien-Chapteuil)*
Chef : Jean-Pierre Vidal

Ingredients (4 servings)

1 kg (2.2 lbs) salmon fillet
6 egg whites
500 ml (2 cups) heavy cream
2 small curly-leafed cabbages
1 L (1 qt) fish stock
80 g (2 2/3 oz) shallots
80 ml (1/3 cup) dry white wine
250 ml (1 cup) heavy cream

100 g (3 1/2 oz) unsalted
butter
100 g (3 1/2 oz) lemon zest,
blanched
1.5 kg (3 lbs) carrots
1.5 kg (3 lbs) zucchini
200 g (6 1/2 oz) flour

Procedure

Make the salmon mousseline. Cut the salmon in chunks and purée in the food processor. Add the egg whites and cream and process until smooth without heating the mixture. Refrigerate. Pull off the leaves of the cabbage, trim the thick center vein and blanch in boiling salted water, drain on paper towels.
Place a tablespoon of mousseline on each leaf and wrap like a parcel. Steam the stuffed cabbage leaves for 20 minutes.

To make the sauce, first combine the fish stock, white wine and chopped shallots in a heavy saucepan. Reduce by half, add the cream and reduce by half. Just before service, whisk in the cold butter pieces and the blanched julienned lemon zest.

Cut the carrots and zucchini in julienne, toss in flour and deep fry. Drain on paper towels.

Plate Presentation

Spoon the sauce onto the plates, place the stuffed cabbage leaves in the center and the fried vegetable julienne around the sides.

Cabbage "Beggars Purses" with Scallops and Orange Sauce

"Le Bourbon"
(Yssingeaux)
Chef : André Perrier

Ingredients
(4 servings)

8 large scallops
8 cabbage leaves
Basil, chopped
Salt, pepper
Onions, sliced

Orange sauce:
300 ml (10 fl oz) fish stock
100 ml (3.5 fl oz) orange juice
100 ml (3.5 fl oz) heavy cream

Garnish:
Tomato compote with basil
Zest of 1 orange
Orange slices
Zucchini

Plate Presentation

Ladle sauce on the bottom of the plate and place two "purses" in the center. Arrange the garnishes around the edge. Serve immediately.

Procedure

Separate the leaves of the cabbage, cut away the central rib and blanch in salted boiling water, refresh in cold water and drain. Place a scallop in each leaf and season with chopped basil, salt and pepper. Tie with blanched strips of orange zest or leek. Just before serving, place the "purses" on a bed of sliced onions cooked in fish stock and add fish stock to cover the bottom of the dish. Cook a few minutes in a hot oven.

To make the orange sauce, reduce the full-flavored fish stock by half, add the orange juice and reduce by half. Whisk in the cream and reduce until the sauce coats a spoon.
To make the garnishes, cut strips of orange zest and blanch, cut the zucchini into small even-sized pieces and cook in boiling salted water and cook fresh, chopped tomatoes with basil until thick.

48

Stuffed Cabbage "Grand-Mère"

"Château-Hôtel de Nieuil" *(Nieuil)*
Chef : Luce Bodinaud

Ingredients (6 to 8 servings)

1 large or 2 small cabbage	6 large eggs
6 leaves swiss chard	Salt and pepper
(or 500 g (8 oz) fresh spinach)	4-5 L (about 10 qts) broth
6 sorrel leaves	
1 bunch chives, chopped	Make the stuffed cabbage a day
1 bunch parsley, stems removed	in advance for better slicing. It
5-6 garlic cloves, peeled	can even be made up to 1 week in
750 g (1 1/2 lbs) pork belly,	advance and stored in its cooking
ground	liquid in the refrigerator. The reci-
500 g (1 lb) stale bread	pe can be doubled for a larger
1/2 L (2 cups) whole milk	group.

Procedure

Prepare the cabbage.
Separate the cabbage leaves. Wash then blanch the large, who-le, green leaves in salted boiling water, stop the cooking in cold water then drain on paper towels. Cut the compact center of the cabbage into quarters.

Prepare the vegetables and herbs.
Cut the pieces of cabbage into strips, eliminating the hard core.
Cut away the tough center vein of the swiss chard, cut in strips.
Remove the stems from the sorrel and cut in strips.
Chop the chives finely (1/4 cup).
Chop the garlic cloves and parsley leaves in a food processor.

Prepare the bread.
Trim the crust from the bread, break up the "crumb" of the bread and combine with the milk.

Prepare the stuffing.
In a large bowl combine the strips of cabbage, swiss chard and sorrel and the chopped chives, garlic and parsley.
Squeeze the excess milk from the bread and add to the bowl along with the ground pork.
Crack the eggs, and beat with salt and pepper.

Mix all these ingredients together with your hands to make a homogenous mixture. Cook a small spoonful to check seasoning.

Stuff the cabbage.
Use cheesecloth in a bowl or round strainer to mold the cabba-ge. Cut the tough center vein of the cabbage leaves.
Line the mold with the leaves, smoothest side out. Overlap the leaves to the top of the mold with the top of the leaves hanging over the edge to fold over the top of the stuffing.
Fill the shell of cabbage leaves with the stuffing, pressing on the mixture to eliminate air pockets. Fold the ends of the leaves over the top of the stuffing and cover completely with leaves of cab-bage.
Gather the ends of the cheesecloth and twist to give the prepa-ration the shape of a cabbage. Tie kitchen string securely around the ends.

Cook the stuffed cabbage.
Bring the chicken or veal broth to a simmer.
Place the stuffed cabbage in the liquid and poach for 2 1/2 hours.

Transfer the cooked stuffed cabbage to a strainer. Place a board or plate with a weight on top and leave the cabbage to cool and drain for several hours.

Plate Presentation

When the cabbage has cooled, remove the cheesecloth, slice thinly and arrange the slices on a platter (ideal for a cold buffet).
The slices can also be reheated in a pan with butter, about 2 minutes on each side to brown and warm through.
Serve warm slices of the stuffed cabbage with a simple accom-paniment like baked tomatoes.

 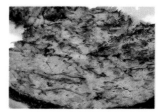

Open Faced Grilled Blue Cheese

"Restaurant Vidal" *(St-Julien-Chapteuil)*
Chef : Jean-Pierre Vidal

Ingredients (6 servings)

1 baguette (large diameter)
2 apples, peeled, cored
400 g (14 oz) blue cheese
2 heads Boston lettuce, cleaned
Vinaigrette
Bunch of red currants or grapes
Walnut halves

Note : Chef Vidal uses a local cheese "fourme bleue d'Yssingeaux" to make this dish. Choose a top quality blue that is creamy, not too salty, and slices well.

Procedure

Cut thin slices of bread (depending on the diameter, prepare one or two per person). Cut the apples into thin slices and place one or two slices on each slice of bread. Remove the outer crust of the cheese if necessary and place a slice on top of each sandwich.
Place the sandwiches on a baking sheet and toast in a 200 C (400 F) oven about 5 minutes or until the cheese begins to melt and the top browns a little.
Meanwhile, toss the cleaned lettuce leaves in the vinaigrette and arrange on 6 plates. Place the toasted sandwiches on top of the salad.

Plate Presentation

For a fancy touch, garnish each plate with a small bunch of red currants (or grapes) and a few walnuts.

Cured Ham Galettes with Fresh Goat Cheese Sauce

Restaurant Vidal *(St-Julien-Chapteuil)*
Chef : Jean-Pierre Vidal

Ingredients (4 servings)

50 g (1 2/3 oz) flour
50 g (1 2/3 oz) semolina
2 large eggs
30 g (1 oz) unsalted butter, melted
100 ml (3.5 fl oz) dry white wine
250 g (8 oz) fresh goat cheese
Salt, pepper, paprika
125 ml (1/2 cup) heavy cream
3-4 shallots, sliced, cooked in butter
4 slices cured ham
Tomato (diced), olive oil
Chervil sprigs

Procedure

Whisk together the flour, semolina, eggs, melted butter and wine.
Pan fry small "galettes" (pancakes) in a non-stick pan, set aside.
Whisk enough crème fraîche (or heavy cream) into the goat cheese to make a sauce, stir in a little mustard and season with salt, pepper and chopped chives.
Whip the remaining cream until thickened. Layer the cream with the cooled galettes, slices of ham and cooked shallots.

Plate Presentation

Spread the goat cheese sauce on four plates.
Place the layered galettes in the center and decorate with diced tomato marinated in olive oil and sprigs of chervil.
Serve chilled.

Foie Gras Ravioli with Spring Vegetables

"Le Prieuré" *(Villeneuve-Lès-Avignon)*
Chef : Serge Chenet

Ingredients (4 servings)

4 baby artichokes
4 spring onions
4 broccoli flowerettes
4 asparagus spears, peeled
1 branch celery, cut into 4 pieces
Green beans, snow peas, broad beans
4 baby carrots, peeled
4 cauliflower flowerettes
4 baby turnips, peeled
1 small fennel bulb, sliced
4 button mushrooms

150 g (5 oz) chicken forcemeat (see "Panaché of Lamb")
4 zucchini blossoms
8 wonton wrappers
1 egg (for glaze)
100 g (3 1/2 oz) fresh foie gras
1 leek, white portion
250 g (8 oz) fresh peas
250 ml (1 cup) chicken broth
100 ml (3.5 fl oz) light cream
50 g (1 2/3 oz) unsalted butter

Choose a variety of small, tender spring vegetables in a wide range of colors for a stunning presentation. Use what is best at the market (at least 8-9 different vegetables). The following recipe, therefore, is an example of a combination that works well.

Preparing the fresh pea sauce:
Heat 50 g (1 2/3 oz) unsalted butter in a heavy saucepan. Add the white portion of the leek (washed and sliced) and cook on low heat about 2 minutes. Add the chicken broth and bring to a simmer. Add the fresh peas, season with salt, pepper and a little sugar and cook about 20 minutes. Transfer the cooked peas and broth to a food processor and purée. Add the cream to make a smooth mixture. Pour the sauce through a conical strainer and check the seasoning. Bring back to simmer and whisk in 40 g (1 1/3 oz) unsalted butter, cut in small pieces.
Keep the sauce warm in a water bath.

Plate Presentation
Reheat the vegetables in a little butter mixed with olive oil.
Steam the stuffed zucchini blossoms.
Cook the raviolis in salted boiling water.
Spoon the fresh pea sauce onto four plates.
Mound the vegetables in the center and place the zucchini blossom on the side and the ravioli on top.

Procedure
Preparing the vegetables:
Artichokes: Cut off the tough, top portion of the leaves. Scoop out the choke with a melon baller. Add salt, juice of 1/2 lemon and 2 tsp olive oil to boiling water and cook until artichokes are tender.
Carrots, turnips, asparagus, celery, fennel snowpeas: Cook separately in boiling chicken broth, refresh in cold water to keep the bright color. Keep the broth for the sauce and set aside the vegetables separately.
Mushrooms: Cook over high heat in a covered saucepan with a little salt, water, lemon juice and butter
Onions: Cook over medium heat in a covered saucepan with a little salt, sugar, water and butter.
Zucchini blossoms: Stuff with the chicken forcemeat and slice through the zucchini for more even cooking.
Preparing the raviolis:
Cut the slice of foie gras into four pieces, season with salt and pepper and place in the center of 4 wonton wrappers. Brush the edges with beaten egg. Place another wonton wrapper on top and press to seal the edges. Cut into circles with a scalloped-edged cutter.

Lentil Tarts
with Cured Ham

"Restaurant Vidal" *(St-Julien-Chapteuil)*
Chef : Jean-Pierre Vidal

Ingredients (4 servings)

500 g (1 lb) flour
300 g (10 oz) unsalted butter
10 g (2 tsp) salt
1 large egg plus 1 egg yolk
300 g (10 oz) green lentils

80 g (2 2/3 oz) carrots
80 g (2 2/3 oz) onions
40 g (1 1/3 oz) butter
200 g (6 1/2 oz) cured ham, sliced

Procedure

Make a well in the flour and place the butter, eggs and salt in the center. Mix the wet ingredients with fingertips to soften the butter and little by little incorporate the flour to form a smooth dough. Don't overmix. Wrap and refrigerate.

Roll out the dough about 2 mm (1/8 in), cut neat circles. Lightly butter the molds and press the dough firmly into the molds. Bake the unfilled pastry at 210 C (415 F) oven for about 20 minutes.

Peel the carrots and onions, cut into small dice, season with salt and cook in butter until soft. Add the lentils and 1 1/2 times their volume in water, bring to a simmer, cover and cook 18 minutes. Set aside to cool.

Plate Presentation

Spoon the cooled lentils into the pastry shells and top with a thin slice of cured ham.

53

Pumpkin Galette

Hôtel d'Espagne *(Valençay)*
Chef : Maurice Fourré

Ingredients (4 servings)

1 kg (2.2 lbs) pumpkin
200 g (6 1/2 oz) onions, chopped
1 bunch chervil, chopped
45 g (1 1/2 oz) parsley, chopped
20 ml (2/3 fl oz) olive oil

Salt, pepper
1 kg (2 lbs) puff pastry
(made with 500 g (1 lb) flour,
500 g (1 lb) unsalted butter,
125 ml (1 cup) water, 12 g (2 tsp) salt
Egg glaze

Roll out the pastry into two rectangles. Brush one with egg glaze and spoon the pumpkin mixture in the center, leaving a 1 inch border. Place the second rectangle of dough on top, press to seal the edges. Brush egg glaze over the top, pierce a small hole for steam to escape and bake at 200 C (400 F) one hour or until puffed and golden brown. Serve warm.

Procedure

Puff pastry: Mix the flour, (cold) water, 125 g (4 oz) butter and salt to make a smooth dough. Cover and refrigerate 1 hour. Roll out the dough into a circle, place the remaining butter in the center and pull the edges of dough over to cover completely, seal the edges. Roll the square of dough into a long rectangle, fold into thirds. Turn the dough 180 dgrees so that an open end is towards you. Repeat this process a total of 6 times, resting the dough in the refrigerator 1/2 hour every two "turns".

Peel the pumpkin and cut the flesh into 1/2 cm (1/4 in) cubes. Season with salt and pepper, place in a large sieve and leave to degorge about 4 hours.
Cook the chopped onions in a little oil until translucent and toss with the diced pumpkin and chopped herbs.

54

Tomato Omelette

"La Régalido" *(Fontvieille)*
Chef : Jean-Pierre Michel

Ingredients
(4 servings)

12 large eggs
125 ml (1 cup) olive oil
8 black olives, pitted, quartered
1 kg (2 lbs) ripe tomatoes
1 medium onion, finely chopped
1 garlic clove, finely chopped
1 bouquet garni with basil

Procedure

Make a thick tomato "compote". Cut out the stem end of the tomatoes and plunge into boiling water a few seconds to loosen

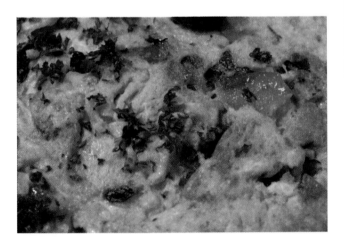

the skins then refresh in ice cold water. Peel, cut in half and squeeze out all the seeds. Coarsely chop the tomatoes.

Brown the chopped onion with half the olive oil, add the garlic, bouquet garni and the tomatoes. Season with a little salt and pepper and cook over medium high heat until the mixture thickens.

For each omelette, whisk three eggs in a bowl and stir in one heaping tablespoon of tomato mixture, 2 sliced olives, 1 tsp. olive oil and season to taste with salt and pepper.

Use a 18 cm (about 8 in) heavy skillet (cast iron works well) to cook each omelette. Heat 1 tsp of olive oil in the pan, pour in the egg mixture. Cook until the eggs are set on the bottom, fold over one edge of the omelette.

Plate Presentation

Serve the omelette on a warm plate and sprinkle the top with chopped parsley and basil.

Foie Gras with Pineapple Compote

"La Renaissance" *(Magny-Cours)*
Chef : Jean-Claude Dray

Ingredients (4 servings)

800 g (1 lb 10 oz) fresh duck foie gras
1 ripe pineapple
100 ml (3.5 fl oz) distilled vinegar
50 ml (4 tbls) red wine vinegar
80 g (6 tbls) sugar
10 g (1/3 oz) black peppercorns
2 inches fresh gingerroot, grated
200 ml (7 fl oz) reduced veal or chicken stock
Juice of 2 small limes
100 g (3 1/2 oz) unsalted butter

Procedure

Remove the veins and nerves that run through the center of the foie gras without breaking it apart too much.

Cut into 12 even slices (about 60 g (2 oz) each), cover and refrigerate.

Peel the pineapple, remove the «eyes» and cut away the tough core. Reserve the nicest looking leaves for decoration.

Cut the pineapple into chunks. Recuperate any juice that exudes.

Combine the two vinegars, sugar and peppercorns and simmer until mixture thickens to a syrup.

Add the pineapple and juice. Cook over low heat about 20 minutes or until the pineapple is very soft. Keep warm.

Lightly season the slices of foie gras with salt and freshly ground pepper. Pan fry in a non-stick skillet 45 seconds on each side. Transfer with a slotted spatula and keep warm.

Deglaze the pan with stock and lime juice. Add the ginger and simmer to infuse the flavor and thicken the liquid a little.

Whisk in pieces of cold butter to thicken the sauce and make it shine.

Plate Presentation

Place the pineapple compote in the center of four preheated plates.

Spoon the sauce over the pineapple and arrange the slices of foie gras on top. Decorate the plate with a few pretty pineapple leaves.

56

Duck Foie Gras with Watermelon Preserves and Sweet Sour Sauce

«L'Etape Lani» (Bouc-Bel-Air)
Chef : Lucien Lani

Ingredients (4 servings)

1 lobe duck foie gras (about 3/4 -1 lb)
200 g (7 oz) watermelon preserves (see below)
Sweet and sour sauce (see below)
Chervil (for garnish)

Procedure

To make the watermelon preserves:
Choose a small, firm, underripe watermelon. Remove the skin and seeds. Cut the watermelon into small cubes, weigh and add 2/3 of its weight in sugar. Put in a heavy, non-reactive pot cook over very low heat for about 4 hours.

To make the sweet and sour sauce:
Reduce 100 ml (3.5 fl oz) vinegar and 1 tbl apricot jam with 1 small chopped shallot. Add 200 ml (7 fl oz) veal stock and reduce to concentrate the flavor and thicken. Season to taste with salt and pepper.

To prepare the foie gras:
Cut the lobe of foie gras into medium slices. Coat lightly with flour. Heat a heavy skillet and cook the foie gras over high heat until browned on each side. Transfer to paper towels to absorb excess fat.

Plate Presentation

Place a heaping tablespoon of warm watermelon preserves in the center of each plate.
Arrange slices of foie gras around and coat with a little sauce. Decorate with fresh chervil.

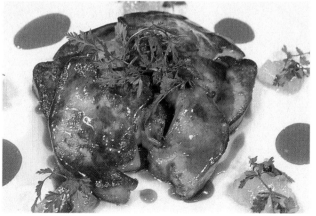

Foie Gras with Sausage and Ham Brochettes

"Le Bourbon" *(Yssingeaux)*
Chef : André Perrier

Ingredients

(1 serving)
90 g (3 oz) foie gras per eperson
25 g (scant 1 oz) cooked ham
25 g (scant 1 oz) cooked sausage
50 ml (4 tbls) Madiera
Brown sauce (made with duck)
Heavy cream

(Note that chef Perrier has used high quality homemade sausage and ham from his region, choose the best products available.)

Procedure

Cut the foie gras into slices, cover and refrigerate.
Cut the sauasage and ham into small cubes and alternate them on wooden skewers.
Just before serving, season the foie gras and pan fry in a hot non-stick skillet. Drain on a towel. Heat the brochettes in the same pan.
Pour the fat from the pan, add the Madiera and reduce. Add a little brown sauce and cream and reduce until thickened.

Plate Presentation

Ladle sauce onto hot plates. Arrange the slices of foie gras and mini brochettes on the plate.
A delicious garnish would be sautéed wild mushrooms (when in season).
This dish is quick to make and should be assembled just before serving.

58

Veal Kidneys with Mustard Butter

« Hôtel du Dauphin » *(L'Aigle)*
Chefs : Michel Bernard and Jean-Pierre Fulep

Ingredients (4 servings)

3 veal kidneys
(700-800 g (about 1 1/2 lbs))
300 g (10 oz) unsalted butter
70 g (2 1/2 oz) Dijon mustard
1 tbl chopped shallots
1 tbl heavy cream
Salt, pepper
60 ml (1/4 cup) Calvados

Procedure

Heat a little butter in a skillet and brown the kidneys on all sides. Lower the heat and continue cooking to the doneness desired. Set aside and keep warm.
While the kidneys are cooking, make the sauce. Cook the shallots in a little butter over low heat to soften without browning. Deglaze with Calvados, season very lightly and reduce by half. Stir in the cream.
Blend together the butter and mustard. Off the heat, whisk in the butter to obtain a smooth, rich sauce. Season to taste and keep warm in a water bath.

Plate Presentation

Slice the kidneys 1/2 cm (1/4 in) and arrange on the plates. Coat with sauce and serve with sautéed mushrooms.

Sweetbreads with Morels

"Auberge du Vieux Moulin"
Chef : Élisabeth Mirbey

Ingredients (4 servings)

4 sweetbreads (about 180 g (6 oz each))
2 carrots, peeled
1 leek, cleaned
6 shallots, chopped
2 L (2 qts) veal stock
150 g (5 oz) fresh morels
250 ml (1 cup) heavy cream
1 tbl each unsalted butter, olive oil
Salt, pepper, nutmeg

Procedure

Gently poach the sweetbreads in the veal stock about 15 minutes.
Trim all fat and the thin membrane from the poached sweetbreads.
Soak the morels in cold water and rinse several times to eliminate
all sand and dirt in the mushrooms.
Cut the carrots into 4 cm (1 1/2 in) sticks and cut the leek into
julienne.
In a heavy saucepan, melt the butter and cook the shallots until
soft then add the washed morels. Add the cream, season with salt,
pepper and a little nutmeg and simmer until the cream thickens.
In another heavy saucepan, (large enough to hold the
sweetbreads), melt a little butter with olive oil and cook the
carrots and leeks a few minutes over low heat. Place the
sweetbreads on the bed of carrots and leeks and braise over low
heat about 15 minutes.

Plate Presentation

Place each portion of sweetbreads in the center of the plate.
Arrange morels and carrots with leeks on the plate.
Pour morel sauce around the meat and finish with freshly ground
pepper on the top.

Veal Kidneys and Sweetbreads with Sauternes

« Le Jardin Gourmand » *(Sartrouville)*
Chefs : Régis Ligot

Ingredients (3-4 servings)

350 g (12 oz) veal kidneys
350 g (12 oz) veal sweetbreads
Unsalted butter
200 ml (7 fl oz) Sauternes
200 ml (7 fl oz) veal stock
300 ml (10 fl oz) heavy cream
Salt, pepper
Pasta (large, flat noodles), cooked

Procedure

Choose firm kidneys with a shiny appearance. Cut in half to remove the fat in the center. Season the kidneys and pan fry in butter to desired doneness. Place between two large plates and set aside in a warm place.
Blanch the sweetbreads in lightly salted water. Remove the thin outer skin and cut into 8 mm (1/3 in) slices. Pan fry the slices in butter until golden brown. Season with salt and pepper.
Place between two large plates and set aside in a warm place.
Pour the fat off the pan and deglaze with Sauternes. Reduce by half, add the veal stock and reduce by half. Add the cream and continue to simmer the sauce until it thickens enough to coat a spoon. Taste and add seasonings if necessary.
Place the cooked sweetbreads in the sauce and simmer over very low heat a few minutes.

Plate Presentation

Mound noodles in the center of the plates and arrange the slices of sweetbreads on the pasta.
Slice the kidneys and arrange around the noodles.
Ladle sauce over the meats and noodles and serve immediately.

Lamb Brains with Avocado and Walnut Oil

"La Belle Époque" *(Bellegarde-sur-Valserine)*
Chef : Michel Sevin

Ingredients
(4 servings)

4 lamb brains
3 avocados
2 tomatoes
1 onion, diced
1 carrot, diced
Bay leaf, parsley, chervil, thyme
1/4 cup wine vinegar
1/2 cup French walnut oil
1 lemon
Salt and pepper to taste

Procedure

Degorge the lamb brains under cold running water for 1 hour. Remove the thin outer skin and bloody veins.
Prepare a "court bouillon". Combine 1 liter (1 qt) water with the carrot, onion, and herbs and simmer 1/2 hour. Add the vinegar. Bring to a boil, skim the surface, add the lamb brains to the boiling court bouillon then lower the heat immediately to a simmer.
Gently poach the brains for 3 minutes. Remove with a slotted spoon, trim and set aside.
Peel the tomatoes, chop coarsely, and season with salt and pepper.
Peel the avocados, remove the pits and slice lengthwise.

Plate Presentation

Just before service, separate the lobes of the brains, pat dry, dust with flour and brown in butter. Heat the plates.
Spoon the walnut oil onto the hot plates and add a squeeze of lemon.
Arrange the two lobes of each brain on the back side of the plate, and fan out several avocado slices in front.
Sprinkle lemon juice over the avocado and brains and place a small spoonful of the chopped tomatoes on the ends of the avocado slices.

Foie Gras
Cooked in Salmon

« Hôtel du Dauphin » *(L'Aigle)*
Chefs : Michel Bernard and
Jean-Pierre Fulep

ngredients
(4 servings)

4 thin slices salmon
120 g (1/4 lb) foie gras
150 g (5 oz) lentils
300 ml (10 fl oz) red wine
300 ml (10 fl oz) fish stock
150 ml (5 fl oz) veal stock
50 g (1 2/3 oz) unsalted butter
50 ml (4 tbls) crème fraîche
1 bunch chives

Procedure

Cook the lentils according to package directions with an addition of diced onions and carrots.
Butterfly and flatten the slices of salmon so that they are no thicker than 1 cm (3/8 in). Season with salt and pepper.
Cut the foie gras into four pieces and enclose them like a package in the slices of salmon. Cook them about 3-4 minutes.
Meanwhile make the sauce. Reduce the wine by 2/3, add the fish stock and reduce by 1/3. Add the veal stock and simmer 15 minutes.
Off the heat, whisk in the butter a little at a time to obtain a smooth, shiny sauce.
(Note: Chef Fulep uses «Banyuls», a slightly sweet red wine from his region.)

Plate Presentation

Place a mound of lentils at the top of the plate.
Ladle sauce on the bottom of the plate and place the foie gras/salmon «package» on top.
Pipe crème fraîche with a paper cone in a decorative design and decorate with the tips of the chives.

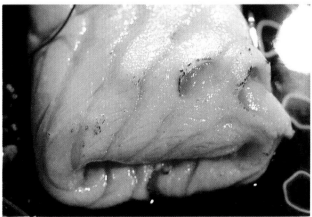

French Andouillette with White Wine

"Auberge du Vieux Moulin"
Chef : Elisabeth Mirbey

Ingredients (4 servings)

4 French andouillette sausages	2 garlic cloves, chopped
300 g (10 oz) dried white beans	50 ml (4 tbls) white wine
2 carrots, peeled	Bouquet garni
2 onions, peeled	Salt and pepper
100 g (3 1/2 oz) salt pork	Unsalted butter
2 shallots, chopped	

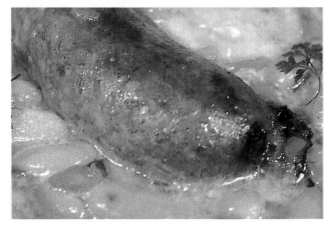

Procedure

Soak the beans overnight so that they will cook more quickly.
Cut the fat into dice and melt in a large heavy pot over low heat.
Cut the carrots and onions into small dice ("mirepoix"), add to the pot and cook a few minutes. Add the beans, add cold water to one inch above the beans and cook over low heat 2-3 hours. Make sure the beans are always covered with liquid as the cook. When they are cooked, there should be a thickened "juice" with the beans.
Melt a little butter in a pan. Cook the chopped shallots and garlic a little then add the cooked beans and heat through, stirring occasionally.

Pan fry the sausage over low heat without bursting the casing.

Plate Presentation

Spoon the beans into shallow, heat-proof dishes, place the hot andouillette on top and keep warm. Pour off the fat from the pan and deglaze with wine. Simmer a few minutes then pour a little liquid over each sausage just before serving.
Place the dish on a serving plate and serve very hot.

Note that French "andouillette" is a sausage made with intestines. Chef Mirbey uses "vin jaune" ("yellow wine") a rich golden wine made in Franche Comté

64

Tripe in Riesling

«Hostellerie Les Bas Rupts» (Gérardmer)
Chef : Michel Phillippe

Ingredients
(4 servings)

1 kg (2.2 lbs) cooked tripe
1 large onion, finely chopped
80 g (2 2/3 oz) unsalted butter
100 ml (3.5 fl oz) heavy cream
1 tbl tomato paste
3 tbls Dijon mustard
Salt, freshly ground pepper
1 bottle Riesling

Procedure

In a large heavy pot, sauté the onions in the butter until soft.
Cut the tripe into 1 inch squares and place on top of the onions.
Add the remaining ingredients, season lightly, cover and simmer gently about 1 hour.
Taste and add more salt and freshly ground pepper if necessary.

Plate Presentation

Traditionally, tripe is served piping hot in small earthenware dishes.
Garnish with croutons and serve with boiled potatoes.

Chapter 3 - Fish Dishes

The Art of Cooking Fish

Fish is a food product that must be transported, cleaned and prepared with great care. Once scaled, gutted, rinsed and dried, fish can then be prepared in six principle ways:

1. Poached in a court bouillon

- Court bouillon made with water: spring water, sea salt, peppercorns, bouquet garni, one onion with a clove, one carrot, and one garlic clove.
- White wine court bouillon: Half water, half dry white wine, same aromatics as above. Simmer 1/2 hour then cool before using.
- Vinegar court bouillon: Used primarily for "truite au bleu", a preparation of trout that is plunged alive into the simmering cooking liquid. Half water and half vinegar with the same aromatics.
- Court bouillon "Nantais": Half water, half milk, bouquet garni, salt and peppercorns.
- Bouillabaise: Each region in the south of France uses a slightly different combination of aromatics. In Marseille, for example, there is always saffron, olive oil and tomato (and potatoes are added to the soup with the fish).

Note: Chopped or ground raw fish can be mixed with cream or choux pastry to make quenelles which are then poached in court bouillon.

2. Cooked in white wine or red wine

- "Matelote": Authentic "matelote" is always prepared with red wine and eel. Start with spring or pearl onions and a few crushed garlic cloves. Add eel cut in pieces, a bouquet garni and red wine to cover. Bring to a boil, flame with Cognac, cover and simmer gently 20-25 minutes.

Remove the eel with a slotted spoon and place in buttered shallow dishes. Add sautéed mushrooms and the cooked onions. Pour the cooking liquid through a sieve, reduce by 2/3 and thicken with "beurre manié". Ladle the sauce over the eel and vegetables and decorate with a few cooked crayfish.

- "Meurette": This is a "matelote" enjoyed in Burgundy and made with an assortment of fresh water fish. Red Burgundy wine is always used and the dish is flamed with "Marc de Bourgogne". "Meurette" is garnished with square croutons that are baked until crispy and rubbed with garlic.
- "Pochouse": Similar to "matelote", made with dry white wine. Cooking liquid is reduced and thickened with cream and the dish is garnished with bacon "lardons" (small strips, fried), glazed onions, small sautéed button mushrooms, and garlic croutons. "Pochouse" is prepared with eel, pike, carp, brill, and/or monkfish.

3. Deep fried fish

- Fillets or pieces of fish can be cleaned, dried and deep fried "au naturel" in hot oil. When the fish comes to the surface, drain excess oil and serve very hot with slices of lemon and a mayonnaise sauce.
- For a thin crust on the fried fish, soak the raw fillets in milk or beer for 15-20 minutes. Pat dry and coat lightly with flour. Deep fry as above. Cut large fillets into "gougonettes" (thin strips cut at an angle acrosss the grain).
- Batter-dipped fish: Sprinkle the fish with salt and pepper then dip into the batter then plunge into hot oil. Drain excess oil and serve the fish on a folded napkin with a sprinkling of fine salt. "Accra" is a fried fritter made with salt cod.

4. Baked fish

- Whole fish: A whole fish can be cleaned, brushed with buttered and baked with or without a stuffing. (Depending on the fish the stuffing can be made with pork, seafood or vegetables.)
- With a sauce, "gratin": Many sauces marry well with fish; Bordelaise, Bechamel, Mornay.
- Braised fish: Prepare a "bed" of sautéed chopped onions, shallots, parsley, a little garlic, one clove. Cover with dry white wine and water and place the fish on top. Cook in a moderate oven, basting often. Mushrooms and mussels can be added for flavor as well.

Bream, cod, mackerel, and hake are good when braised.

- En croûte": This is a wonderful method for cooking a whole fish. For example, a whole salmon, stuffed with cooked spinach and lentils, wrapped in puff pastry. With large fish, it is necessary to poach partially, cool then wrap in pastry. Wrap the dough around the fish to give the form of the fish. Make "scales" by scoring overlapping semicircles in the pastry with the wide end of a pastry tip. "Coulibiac" is a fine example of how elegant this cooking method is.

5. "Meunière": Trout and other fish with small fillets that make a single serving can be cooked using this method.

Soak the fillets in milk, pat dry and coat lightly in flour. Pan fry in butter, a few minutes on each side. Prepare just before serving so that the skin is very crisp.

Traditionally, "truite meunière" is served with browned butter, chopped parsley and a lemon wedge.

"Truite à l'Auvergnate" is a variation served with cooked strips of thick-sliced bacon. The pan is deglazed with cream and poured around the fish.

6. Grilled or broiled fish

Grilled or broiled fish is always a favorite. It works well with flat fish like sole and flounder and fatty fish such as salmon.

Keep the skin on the fish and heat the grill very hot before placing the fish on it. Large and/or round fish can be cut into steaks to facilitate even cooking.

Grilled fish are usually served with melted butter, hollandaise, or chopped parsley.

Grilled sardines are delicious but give off a strong odor. It is best to grill them outdoors.

A new method that has become very popular is to grill or broil one side only with very high heat to achieve a crispy skin or top with the flesh just barely cooked inside. Fish cooked this way is served with the browned side up and accompanied by browned butter spooned around the fish.

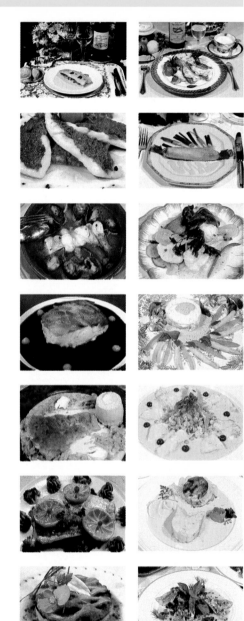

Braised Trout

"Auberge du Vieux Moulin"
Chef : Élisabeth Mirbey

Ingredients (4 servings)

1 large trout (2 kg (about 4 lbs))
3 shallots, chopped
1 medium onion, sliced
100 ml (3.5 fl oz) dry white wine
50 g (1 2/3 oz) unsalted butter
1/2 lemon
Fresh fennel
200 ml (7 fl oz) heavy cream
500 g (1 lb) potatoes
100 g (3 1/2 oz) Comté cheese
500 ml (2 cups) milk
2 garlic cloves
Salt, pepper, nutmeg

Procedure

To make the potato gratin, cut the onions and potatoes into 1/4 inch slices. Rub the bottom and sides of a gratin dish with the garlic cloves then brush with softened butter. Layer the potatoes and onions in the dish, sprinkling with salt and pepper between each layer. Heat the milk, whisk in the nutmeg and pour over the potatoes. Bake at 375 F for 1 hour. After 45 minutes, sprinkle the top with grated cheese (Comté or a Swiss type) then finish cooking.

Gut the trout and cut four even steaks across the body beginning behind the gills. Combine the white wine, chopped shallots, the butter and juice of 1/2 lemon in a heavy pan and bring to a simmer. Add the trout steaks to the pan, season with salt and pepper, cover and cook over low heat 10 minutes. Remove the trout with a spatula, keep warm. Add the cream and reduce, check the seasoning.

Plate Presentation

Serve this dish on a large, hot plate.
Pour the sauce through a sieve and ladle some on each plate.
Place a portion of potatoes and a trout steak on each plate.
Garnish with slices of lemon and pieces of fresh fennel.

Trout Stuffed with Lentils Served with Mussels in Verveine

"Restaurant Vidal"
(St-Julien-Chapteuil)

Chef:
Jean-Pierre Vidal

Ingredients (4 servings)

4 small trout
1 sea trout fillet
200 g (about 3/4 cup) heavy cream
100 g (3 1/2 oz) cooked green lentils
100 g (3 1/2 oz) unsalted butter
1 L (1 qt) mussels

100 g (3 1/2 oz) shallots, chopped
1 onion, chopped
Parsley, chopped
250 ml (1 cup) dry white wine
2 lemons, sliced
Juice of 1 lemon
Salt, pepper, clove
Verveine (verbena) leaves

Procedure

Bone the small trout and season with salt and pepper. Purée the sea trout fillet in the food processor and add cold cream and seasonings to make a mousse. Stuff the trout with the mousse and cooked lentils.

To make the mussels "marinière", combine the parsley, onion, shallots and lemon juice in a large pot, add the mussels, cover and cook over high heat until the mussels open. Remove with a slotted spoon. Add the trout bones and clove to the mussel juice, add water to cover and simmer a few minutes. Strain the liquid over the stuffed trout and poach the fish.

Remove the trout and infuse the verveine into the liquid, reduce. Season, if necessary, with salt and pepper.

Plate Presentation

Warm the mussels in the reduced liquid. Arrange the stuffed trout and mussels in deep dishes, ladle the full-flavored cooking liquid over the seafood and decorate with lemon slices.

Salmon Trout Stuffed with Cèpes

"Le Moulin du Roc" *(Champagnac-de-Belair)*
Chef: Solange Gardillou

Ingredients
(4 servings)

4 salmon trout (220 g (7 oz) each)
200 g (6 1/2 oz) cèpes
40 g (1 1/3 oz) goose rillettes
Small garlic clove (optional)
1 bunch flat parsley, chopped
1 bunch chives, chopped
1 tbl unsalted butter
Salt and pepper

to make a "papillotte" and cook in a hot oven 8-10 minutes. Meanwhile, make a wine and butter sauce ("beurre blanc") or simply mix fresh lemon juice with clarified butter.

Plate Presentation
Gently open the foil packages and lift the fish onto heated plates and serve with "beurre blanc" or melted butter.

Procedure
Remove the filets of salmon trout, remove the skin and check for any small bones that may remain. Season with salt and pepper, cover and refrigerate.

Trim, wash and slice the mushrooms. (If cèpes are not available substitiute another wild mushroom.) Sauté in butter over high heat until they are golden brown. Mix the cooked mushrooms with the goose rillettes, crushed garlic, and chopped herbs. Place in a food processor and pulse the machine to achieve a finely chopped, homogenous mixture. Season with salt and pepper. Brush butter on four squares of aluminum foil, place one fish fillet in the center of each and spread with the mushroom mixture. Place a second fillet on top and press to eliminate air pockets and seal the fish and filling together. Close the foil around the fish

Salmon with Sherry Vinegar

«La Renaissance» (Magny-Cours)
Chef : Jean-Claude Fray

Ingredients
(6 servings)

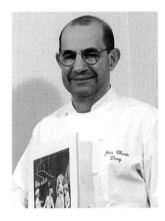

3 salmon steaks, cut in half
100 ml (3.5 fl oz) sherry vinegar
(«Xeres»)
100 ml (3.5 fl oz) sweet sherry
2 tbls. chopped shallots
100 g (3 1/2 oz) unsalted butter
6 tomatoes
Fresh herbs, chopped

Procedure

Cut thick steaks of salmon and cut in half through the bone.

Combine the shallots, vinegar and sherry in a non-reative saucepan and simmer until most the liquid is evaporated. Set aside.
Bake the tomatoes in a hot oven until soft; keep warm.
Lightly season the salmon and sear on a hot grill, skin side down. Place the fish, skin side up in a buttered baking dish and heat through in a hot oven about 1 minute. The salmon should remain a little rare in the center.
Just before serving, whisk the butter into the shallot/sherry reduction.

Plate Presentation

Ladle the sauce onto 6 preheated plates.
Pull the skin off the salmon and place in the center.
Garnish each plate with a baked tomato and chopped herbs.

Salmon
with Chinese Artichokes

"Le Bourbon" *(Yssingeaux)*
Chef : André Perrier

Ingredients (4 servings)

600 g (1 b 3 1/2 oz) salmon fillets
50 g (1 2/3 oz) semi-soft or Swiss cheese
50 ml (4 tbls) dry white wine
300 ml 10 fl oz) fish stock
100 ml (3.5 fl oz) heavy cream
Shallots, chopped
1 small green cabbage
200 g (6 1/2 oz) Chinese artichokes

50 g 1 2/3 oz) fresh bread crumbs
Unsalted butter, salt, pepper
Note: If Chinese artichokes ("crosnes") are not available, use another vegetable, cut into small even shapes.
Chef Perrier uses a local cheese, "Tome d'Araules"

Procedure
Garnishes:
Separate the cabbage leaves and cut into thin strips. Cook the cabbage strips with a little water, salt and butter until tender. Set aside. Clean the Chinese artichokes, cook with a little water, salt and butter until "al dente".

Salmon:
Cut the salmon fillet into 4 thin slices and season with salt and pepper. Mix the cheese, breadcrumbs, and butter in the food processor and grind without making a purée, season with salt and pepper, refrigerate. Cut the chilled mixture into "petals" and overlap them on the salmon.

Sauce:
Combine the chopped shallots, fish stock and white wine and reduce by half. Add the cream and reduce until thickened slightly. Season with salt and pepper and stir in a few cabbage strips.

Plate Presentation
Warm the remaining cabbage strips in a little butter and place in the bottom of the plates. Warm the "crosnes" in butter, season and place on top of the cabbage.
Broil the salmon fillets a few minutes to brown the top then finish cooking at 200 C (400 F).
Place the salmon on the cabbage and spoon the sauce around the salmon.

"Tagle" with Sesame Seeds, Sweet Peppers and Pumpkin Sabayon

"Auberge de l"Ill *(Illhaeusern)*
Chef : Marc Haeberlin

Ingredients (6 serving)

1 tagle (2 kg (about 4 1/2 lbs))(see note)
4 tbls sesame seed
4 tbls olive oil
1 medium onion, chopped
300 g (10 oz) pumpkin flesh, diced
25 g (scant 1 oz) short grain rice
1 small red pepper
1 large egg
125 g (4 oz) unsalted butter
125 ml (1/2 cup) heavy cream
2 egg yolks
Cayenne pepper
Salt, pepper

Note that "tagle" is a fish found in the fresh water streams of Alsace. Pike perch would be a good substitute

Procedure

Remove the skin from the fish and bone the fillets.

Cut each fillet in half. Season with salt and pepper and brush the top with beaten egg.

Finely chop the pepper, mix with the sesame seeds and spread on top of the fish.

Sauce
Cook the chopped onion in a little butter. Add the diced pumpkin and rice, season with salt and a pinch of cayenne pepper. Add water to cover and simmer 1/2 hour.

When the rice is cooked, puree the mixture in a food processor until very smooth. Add the egg yolks to the hot mixture then the cream and butter.

Meanwhile pan fry the fish fillets in olive oil, about 3-4 minutes on each side. drain on paper towels to absorb excess oil.

Plate Presentation

Ladle the pumpkin sabayon in the center of each plate and place a portion of fish on top.

Garnish with fresh chervil sprigs and julienned vegetables cooked in butter.

Whiting in Filo Papillotte with Puréed Garlic

"La Fenière" *(Loumarin)*
Chef : Reine Sammut

Ingredients (6 servings)

12 whiting fillets
8 garlic cloves, peeled
6 sheets filo dough, olive oil
500 ml (2 cups) fish stock
Sea salt and freshly ground pepper

12 baby carrots
12 small fennel bulbs
12 small leeks

Sauce:
250 ml (1 cup) olive oil
3 garlic cloves, peeled
5 egg yolks

Procedure

Preheat the oven to 200 C (400 F).
Cover the 8 cloves of garlic with cold water, bring to a simmer and rinse under cold water. Repeat 4-5 times until the garlic is soft.
Mash the garlic into a smooth purée.
Brush the sheets of filo dough with a little oil, fold in half and place one fillet of fish in the center, season with salt and pepper. Spread garlic purée over the fish and cover with a second fillet. Fold the sides of filo dough over the fish and tie the ends with a string. Brush with olive oil and bake for about 10 minutes.

To make the sauce bourride, purée the 3 garlic cloves, stir in the egg yolks and whisk in the olive oil to make an emulsified sauce.
Whisk in hot fish stock, place over a water bath and stir as it warms and thickens. Steam the vegetables.

Plate Presentation

Remove the strings from the papillottes and place them on the plates. Pour sauce around the fish and arrange the vegetables on the plate.

Turbot with Red Wine

« La Toque Blanche » *(Pujols)*
Chef : Bernard Lebrun

Ingredients (4 servings)

700 g (1 lb 7 oz) turbot fillets
   (plus bones for sauce)
1 leek,
4 carrots
1 onion
1 garlic clove
1 bay leaf
1 branch fresh thyme
1 bottle red wine
200 ml (7 fl oz) veal stock
1 tsp sugar
50 g (1 2/3 oz) unsalted butter
3 potatoes
3 turnips
8 pitted prunes
Sea salt and freshly ground
   pepper
Fresh chervil

Procedure

Combine in a small stockpot, the fish bones, leek, 1 carrot and onion (cut in pieces), chopped garlic, thyme and bay leaf. Add the wine, sugar and a pinch of salt and pepper. Simmer about 15 minutes, skimming all impurities that rise to the surface in the form of a froth.
Strain and reduce by half. Add the veal stock and reduce by half.
Pour the sauce through a fine-meshed conical sieve and taste for seasoning. Whisk in the butter, add the prunes and keep warm in a water bath.
Cut 3 carrots, the turnips and potatoes into even sized, attractive shapes. Cook the carrots and turnips, separately, in a little water with unsalted butter, salt, pepper and sugar until softened and glazed. Steam, boil or sauté the potatoes.
Cut the fillets into 4 servings and season with salt and pepper. Steam the fish about 5 minutes or until the flesh flakes apart.

Plate Presentation

Pour sauce on the plates and place the fish fillets in the center. Arrange the carrots, turnips and potatoes around the fish.
Decorate with fresh chervil sprigs.
At "La Toque Blanche", chef Lebrun makes this dish with the local red wine "Côtes de Buzet", a full-flavored wine typical of the region.

Use a good quality red wine to make the sauce and plan to serve the same wine with the dish.

Turbot with Caviar

«Château de Vauchoux» (Port-sur-Saône)
Chef : Jean-Michel Turin

Ingredients (6 servings)

6 turbot fillets, skinned (150 g (5 oz) each)	2 shallots, chopped
1 L (1 qt) reduced fish stock	30 g (1 oz) caviar
300 ml (10 fl oz) heavy cream	1 cucumber
50 g (1 2/3 oz) unsalted butter	Chervil
100 ml (3.5 fl oz) Champagne or Chablis	Salt, pepper

Procedure

Rinse the fillets under cold water, set aside.

Peel the cucumber and remove the seeds. Cut into four sections then slice thinly. Cut the slices into thin strips («julienne») and set aside.

Combine the stock and cream in a large pan and bring to a boil. Off the heat, add the turbot fillets return to very low heat and simmer gently 8-10 minutes. Remove with a slotted spatula and keep warm.

Divide the poaching liquid between two saucepans. To one add the shallots and wine and reduce by half.

To the other, add the cucumber julienne, bring to a simmer then remove the cucumber with a slotted spoon and set aside. Combine the two sauces then pour through a sieve. Bring to a simmer, whisk in cold butter.

Plate Presentation

Place the warm turbot fillets in the center of preheated plates. Ladle the sauce over the fish and mound a little cucumber julienne on each side.

Garnish the top of the fish with grains of caviar. Snip the chervil with scissors and sprinkle over the dish.

Turbot
with Green Olive Purée

«L'Etape Lani» (Bouc-Bel-Air)
Chefs : Lucien and Joël Lani

Ingredients (4 servings)

4 turbot fillets (200 g (7 oz) each)	3 shallots
200 g (7 oz) green olive purée	Extra virgin olive oil
12 ripe tomatoes, peeled, seeded,	Thyme, bay leaf, salt, pepper
3 garlic cloves,	Juice of 1 lemon

Procedure

To make the «concassé» of tomatoes: Coarsely chop the tomatoes and finely chop the garlic (reserve 1/3 of garlic for sauce) and shallots. Heat olive oil in a large, heavy pot. Add the tomatoes, garlic, shallots, thyme and bay leaf. Season lightly with salt and pepper and cook over medium heat until thick.

To make the sauce: Combine 200 ml (7 fl oz) olive oil, lemon juice, the remaining garlic and 4 teaspoons of olive purée. Set aside.

To prepare the turbot: Spread the remaining olive purée on the four turbot fillets and sprinkle with olive oil.
Cook at 220 C (425 F) for about 8 minutes.

Plate Presentation

Place the turbot fillets in the center of the plates.

Use two large spoons to form three «football-shaped» scoops of tomato concassé around the fish. Ladle sauce onto the plate.

John Dory
with Wild Mushrooms

"La Châtaigneraie" *(Sucé-sur-Erdre)*
Chef : J. Delphin

Ingredients (4 servings)

1.8 kg (about 4 lbs) John Dory
Olive oil
200 ml (scant cup) grapefruit juice
50 g (1 2/3 oz) sugar
100 g (3 1/2 oz) unsalted butter
500 g (1 lb) fresh wild mushrooms
1 bunch chives, chopped

Procedure

Bone the fish fillets, cut in portions and marinate in olive oil.
Cook the sugar with a little grapefruit juice to a light caramel.
Add 100 ml (3.5 fl oz) of juice to the caramel, stir to dissolve and reduce by half. Reserve the remaining juice.
Clean and trim the mushrooms. Cook in half the butter with a little salt, season the cooked mushrooms with some chopped chives.
Cook the fish fillets in a non-stick pan.
Heat the sweet and sour sauce and whisk in the remaining butter and juice.

Plate Presentation

Mound the mushrooms in the center of the plates.
Arrange the fish fillets around the mushrooms and spoon the sweet and sour sauce over the fish.
Sprinkle chopped chives over the dish.

Turbot
Cooked in Muscadet

"La Châtaigneraie"
(Sucé-sur-Erdre)
Chef : J. Delphin

Ingredients
(4 servings)

1 turbot (2 kg (about 2 lbs))
2 shallots, chopped
2 leeks, white portion
4 carrots, cut in small dice
500 ml (2 cups) Muscadet
250 ml (1 cup) crème
  fraîche
1 bunch grapes
100 g (3 1/2 oz) unsalted
  butter
Salt and pepper

Procedure

In a large heavy saucepan, cook the chopped shallots in half the butter until soft. Slice the leeks and add them to the shallots. Blanch the diced carrots and add those to the pot.

Bone the turbot and cut the fillets into 1/2 inch cubes and place them on top of the vegetables.

Add the Muscadet, cover and bring to a simmer then remove from the heat. The fish will finish cooking with the heat held in the pot.

Transfer the fish and vegetables with a slotted spoon to a plate, cover and keep warm.

Reduce the liquid in the pot to a syrupy consistency, add the cream and reduce again until the sauce coats a spoon. Season with salt and pepper. Off the heat, whisk in the remaining butter.

Peel the grapes and remove the seeds.

Plate Presentation

Spoon the vegetables and fish onto the center of the plates.

Arrange grapes around the mixture.

Ladle the sauce over the fish.

Decorate the dish with coarsely chopped chervil.

John Dory with Potatoes

« Aux Armes de Champagne » (L'Epine)
Chef : Patrick Michelon

Ingredients (2 servings)

1 small John Dory (700-800 g (1 1/2 lbs))
400 g (14 oz) cockles
1 shallot, chopped
1 branch celery, chopped
6 strands saffron
50 ml (4 tbls) dry white wine
Chives, chopped
Dill
1 salsify
Fresh dill
Coarse sea salt, white pepper

Procedure

Rinse the shellfish well several times to eliminate sand.
Sauté the shallot in a little butter. Add a branch of celery, the safran, white wine and cockles. Bring to a boil to open the shells. Transfer the cockles to a bowl with a slotted spoon, remove the shells and reserve the «meat». Pour the liquid through a cheese-cloth or coffee filter.
Peel and slice the potatoes. Arrange in a baking dish and cover with the shellfish liquid. Bake at 375 F. When the potatoes are almost done, stir in the cockles and chopped chives and continue cooking until the potatoes are just tender.
Clean and trim the fish and cut off the head. Brown it on both sides.
Season with salt and pepper, place it on the «bed» of cooked potatoes and finish cooking at 180 C (360 F) about 7 minutes. Peel and cut the salsify into thin strips and deep fry.

Plate Presentation

Serve the dish as soon as the fish is cooked. Garnish with fried salsify, sprigs of fresh dill and grains of coarse sea salt.

Monkfish Simmered with Seasonal Vegetables

«Hostellerie de la Fuste» (Valensole)
Chef : M. Bucaille

Ingredients (4 servings)

800 g (1 lb 10 oz) cleaned monkfish
1 clove garlic, chopped
100 g (3 1/2 oz) tomatoes
100 g (3 1/2 oz) zucchini
100 g (3 1/2 oz) onions
100 g (3 1/2 oz) swiss chard
Seasonal vegetables
1 bunch tarragon, chopped
1 bunch flat parsley, celery leaves
Olive oil
Coarse sea salt

Procedure

Wash the vegetables and cut into even shapes.
Blanch the green leaves of the swiss chard and set aside for garnish.
In a large heavy pot, combine the vegetables, a little olive oil, the garlic and tarragon and season lightly with salt.
Cover and cook at 175 C (350 F) 1 hour. Baste the fish often with the juices exuded from the vegetables.
Pluck the leaves off the parsley and celery. Wash and completely dry. Deep fry (medium heat to maintain the green color). Drain excess oil and set aside.

Plate Presentation

Once the fish is very tender, serve the dish with the garnish of fried parsley and celery. (The crunchy, fried parsley provides a pleasant contrast to the succulent fish and vegetables.)
Sprinkle with a little coarse sea salt to heighten the flavors and serve immediately.

Red Mullet with Artichoke «Barigoule»

« L'Etape Lani » (Bouc-Bel-Air)
Chefs : Lucien and Joël Lani

Ingredients (4 servings)

Fish:
8 red mullets (200 g (7 oz) each)

« Barigoule »:
4 artichokes
1/2 red pepper
1 potato
100 g (3 1/2 oz) thick-sliced bacon
200 ml (7 fl oz) olive oil
1 shallot, choped
1 garlic clove, chopped
100 ml (3.5 fl oz) dry white wine
Fish fumet (see recipe)
1 bunch chives, chopped

Fumet:
1 tbl unsalted butter
1 onion, sliced
1 leek, white portion, sliced
100 g (3 1/2 oz) mushrooms, sliced
Parsley stems
1 tsp peppercorns
Juice of 1 lemon

Plate Presentation

Mound a little «Barigoule» in the center of the plates.
Lean the fillets on the vegetables and spoon more «Barigoule» around the fish.

Procedure

To prepare the fish:

Use a thin, flexible knife to remove the fillets. Keep the bones and trimmings to make the fumet.
With tweezers, pull out the bones that remain.
Drizzle olive oil over the fillets, season with salt and pepper.
Cover and refrigerate.

Fish fumet:

Cook the onions and fish bones in butter without browning. Add the leek, mushrooms, parsley stems, peppercorns and lemon juice. Add water and white wine to cover. Simmer for 20 minutes, skimming impurities that rise to the surface, then strain.

Artichoke «Barigoule»:

Trim the artichokes to obtain the hearts, cut into small dice. Cut the potato and pepper into small dice. Sauté in a little olive oil (vegetables should remain crunchy at this point).
Cut the bacon into thin strips («lardons») and blanch.
Add the chopped garlic and shallot and lardons to the diced vegetables. Deglaze with the fumet and white wine.
Season lightly and cook over low heat about 15 minutes.

When the vegetables are cooked but still firm, add the chopped chives.
Just before serving, cook the fillets in a very hot oven (500 F) for 3-4 minutes.

Red Mullet with Sherry Vinegar

« El Chiquito » *(Rueil-Malmaison)*
Chef : M. Pichois

Ingredients
(4 servings)

2 red mullets 400 g (14 oz) each
50 ml (4 tbls) olive oil

Butter Sauce:
3 shallots, chopped
2 tbls Sherry vinegar («Xeres»)
4 tbls dry white wine
300 g (10 oz) unsalted butter,
    room temperature
1 small lemon, sectioned, diced
1 small firm tomato, peeld, diced
1 tbls cooked cranberries
1 bunch each chives, chopped
Salt, white pepper, thyme, bay leaf

Garnish:
Ratatouille
Broccoli flowerettes
Chervil

*From left to right: Laurent Pichois, Sylvain Oudoyer
and Jean-Pierre Pichois*

Procedure

Remove the scales from the mullet and rinse under cold water. Use a thin, flexible knife to remove the fillets and check for bones.
Lightly season both sides of the fillets.
Heat olive oil in a skillet, place the fish skin side down and cook about 1 minute. Turn over the fillets and finish cooking in the oven.

To make the butter sauce:

Combine the chopped shallots, thyme, bay, vinegar and wine in a non-reactive saucepan. Simmer until the liquid is «syrupy».

Whisk in the butter a little at a time to make a smooth sauce. Season to taste with salt and pepper.
Just before serving, add the diced lemon, tomato, chopped chives and cooked cranberries.

Plate Presentation

Ladle sauce on the plates and arrange the fish on top.
Garnish with a spoonful of ratatouille and cooked broccoli.
Decorate with a few sprigs of fresh chervil.

85

Fresh Cod «Fougasse» with «Brandade»

« Le Vieux Castillon » *(Castillon-du-Gard)*
Chef : Gilles Dauteuil

Ingredients (10 servings)

1 kg (2 lbs) tomatoes	***Brandade (salt cod purée):***
1 kg (2 lbs) eggplant	600 g (1 lb 3 1/2 oz) salt cod
2 onions, chopped	750 ml (3 cups) olive oil
3 garlic cloves	750 ml (3 cups) whole milk
Olive oil	Parsely, thyme, bay leaf, garlic,
Salt, pepper	lemon juice, nutmeg
1 bunch basil, chopped	
1 kg (2 lbs) fresh cod	
300 g (10 oz) bread dough with thyme	
300 g (10 oz) «brandade» (see recipe)	

Plate Presentation

Transfer the circles of fresh cod to the center of the plates. Pose the baked bread with vegetables on top. Add a scoop of brandade on the fougasse.
Whisk a little olive oil and chopped basil into the reserved vegetable juices and ladle around the dish.

Procedure

To make the brandade:
Soak the salt cod for 48 hours in cold water, changing the water several times. Cut into pieces and poach for 8-10 minutes in water infused with thyme, bay leaf, parsley and a squeeze of lemon juice. Drain and cool.
Remove all the bones and any dry bits of fish that remain. Break into little pieces and put into a large casserole.
Warm the oil and the milk in two separate pots. Alternate, adding a little of each, stirring well with a wooden spatula.
The brandade will be very creamy, like smooth mashed potatoes. Season with a few drops of lemon juice and a pinch of nutmeg.

To make the «Fougasse» (flat bread):
Cut up the eggplant, sprinkle with salt, cover and leave to degorge overnight in the refrigerator. Rinse with cold water and drain.
Peel the tomatoes, cut in half and squeeze out the seeds.
Heat olive oil in a large, heavy pot. Add the chopped onions, tomatoes, eggplant, crushed garlic cloves and basil. Cover and cook in a medium-hot oven about 1 hour. (This combination of vegetables is called «Bohemian» in French cooking.)
Drain the juices and reserve. Mold the cooked vegetables in 8 cm (about 3 in) rings. Form the thyme-flavored bread dough into circles 8 cm (3 in) and place on top of the vegetables. Bake at 180 C (375 F) for 15 minutes.
Meanwhile, cook the fresh cod in olive oil and form into circles with the same rings.

Sea Bass Soufflé with Aspargus and Sorrel Sabayon

« Hostellerie Lenoir » *(Auvillers-Les-Forges)*
Chef : Jean Lenoir

Ingredients (4 servings)

Sea bass (600-700 g)
  (1 1/4-1 1/2 lbs)
16 asparagus tips, blanched
300 ml (10 fl oz) heavy cream
2 large eggs
Sea salt, freshly ground pepper
Cayenne pepper

Sabayon
125 ml (1 cup) heavy cream
1 shallot
5-6 sorrel leaves
4 egg yolks
Salt, pepper

Procedure

Remove the fillets from the bass. Remove the skin and pull out any bones that remain. Rinse under cold water and cut each fillet in half.

Cut half of the fish in small pieces and reserve.

Purée half of the fish in the food processor and press the purée through a drum sieve to eliminate nerves and make a smooth purée.

Place the purée in a bowl over ice and season with 1 tsp salt and beat in the eggs. Add the cream a little at a time, beating the mixture well to make it very smooth and homogenous.

Add a pinch of cayenne pepper and freshly ground white pepper then poach a spoonful of mixture to check the seasoning.

Butter the soufflé dishes (8 cm (3 in)) and fill halfway with fish mousse. Place two asparagus tips and 2-3 pieces of fish on top of the purée. Fill the molds with soufflé mixture and smooth the top.

Place the molds on a baking sheet, place a sheet of oiled parchment paper on top and bake at 220 C (425 F) about 30 minutes or until the soufflés are puffed and set in the center.

Meanwhile make the sorrel sabayon. Bring the heavy cream to a boil and add the chopped shallot and the puréed sorrel leaves and boil a few minutes. Place the egg yolks in the top of a double boiler and gradually pour the hot cream into the egg yolks, whisking constantly.

Continue whisking over the hot water until the sauce thickens like a hollandaise sauce. Season with salt and pepper.

Plate Presentation

Unmold the soufflés as soon as they are cooked and place in the center of the plates.

Ladle sorrel sabayon over the the soufflés and serve immediately before they deflate.

Bream with Lemon

« El Chiquito » *(Rueil-Malmaison)*
Chef : M. Pichois

Ingredients (4 servings)

2 bream (700 g (1 lb 7 oz))
50 ml (4 tbls) olive oil
500 ml (2 cups) fish stock
   (made with bream bones)

Sauce:
200 ml (7 fl oz) reduced fish stock
Juice of 1/2 lemon
100 ml (3.5 fl oz) olive oil
Salt, freshly ground pepper

Garnish:
Seasonal vegetables, stewed leek,
steamed green beans

Decoration:
Chopped tomatoes, broccoli flowerettes,
chervil, slices of candied lemon

Procedure

To make the candied lemon slices: Wash two lemons and cut in medium slices. Combine clarified butter and sugar in a pan and cook over low heat to soften without browning. Transfer to a rack to drain.
Scale, clean and rinse the fish under running cold water. Bone the fillets and with tweezers, remove any bones that remain. Make a stock with the bones.
Season the fish on both sides. heat a little oil in a heavy skillet and sear the fish fillets, skin side down. Add fish stock to the pan and finish cooking the fish by poaching.
Separately, reduce some fish stock, add lemon juice and off the heat, whisk in olive oil. Season to taste.

Plate Presentation

Arrange the garnish of choice in the center of the plate. Ladle sauce in a ribbon around the plate.
Warm the slices of candied lemon and place on the garnish, then place the fish fillets on top.
Around the edge, add chopped tomato and broccoli for color.
Add a few sprigs of chervil just before serving.

Bouillabaise "Régalido"

"La Regalido" *(Fontvielle)*
Chef: Jean-Pierre Michel

Ingredients (3 servings)
2 onions, sliced
3 garlic cloves, peeled and crushed
Peel of one orange
Bouquet garni made with parsley
stems, fennel, celeri and bay leaf
3 potatoes, peeled
2 ripe tomatoes, coarsely chopped
Olive oil
French bread, sliced, toasted,
  rubbed with garlic
1 L (1 qt) Provençale fish soup
450 g (about 1 lb) prepared fish
  fillet (sole, monkfish, pike perch,
  sea bass)
500 g (1 lb) mussels, 500 g (1 lb)
  squid
Rouille (optional) (see note)

Note: The "fish soup" in the recipe, available prepared in France, is a flavorful fish stock, thickened with puréed cooked fish and flavored with tomatoes. The "rouille" is a garlic mayonnaise with tomato paste that is a traditional accompaniment to Provençale fish soups.

Procedure
Clean and steam the mussels with white wine, chopped shallots and parsley. Reserve the mussels and the cooking liquid.
Clean the squid and cut into 5 mm (1/4 in) rings.
Cut the fish fillets and potatoes into 2 cm (3/4 in) slices.
In a large, heavy pot, heat the olive oil and cook the onions, garlic, tomatoes, with the bouquet garni and orange peel. Add the mussel liquid, fish soup and the sliced squid. Bring to a boil, then simmer for 10 minutes.
Add the sliced potatoes and cook until the potatoes are tender.
Add the sliced fish and cook about 5 minutes. Just before serving, add the mussels (with or without the shells).

Plate Presentation
Ladle the bouillabaise into wide, shallow soup bowls and pass the toasted bread slices and rouille separately.

Bass "Frère Joseph"

Auberge des Cimes *(St-Bonnet-Le-Froid)*
Chef : Régis Marcon

Ingredients (6/8 servings)

2 bass each 1-1.2 kg (2 1/4 lbs)
1 lobster, cooked
12 Dublin Bay prawns, cooked
6 sea scallops
6 medium potatoes, cut into cylinders
500 ml (2 cups) crème fraîche
1 bottle "St Joseph" or other red wine
1 bottle dry white wine
250 ml (1 cup) verjus*
250 g (8 oz) unsalted butter
125 g (4 oz) wild mushrooms
1 onion, 1 shallot
30 g (1 oz) dried cepes
250 g (8 oz) small leeks
250 g (8 oz) pie pastry with garlic
Fresh fennel, fennel seed, thyme, bay leaf
1 small green cabbage
4 egg whites
Fresh chervil - Salt, pepper
*Verjus is the tart juice from unripe grapes. Add a little lemon or lime juice instead.

Procedure

Cut open one bass along the backbone, remove the bones and spread out the fillets (that are still attached to the belly side of the fish).
Trim about 1/3 of the flesh and make a mousseline with salt, pepper, egg white and cream. Dice the lobster tail and stir the dice into the mousseline. Fill the cavity of the boned fish. Cook small leeks (and other colorful vegetables cut the same size) in consommé and decorate the top of the bass. Steam the fish over low heat.
Remove the fillets of the second fish. Leave the skin on and cut into thick strips across the grain. Cook them on a grill, turning them to mark the skin.
Make a sauce with the lobster carcass, red wine, verjus, herbs, seasonings and aromatics. Simmer 30 minutes, strain, reduce and thicken with butter.
Make a second sauce with the white wine, fennel and fennel seeds. Simmer 30 minutes, strain, reduce to a glaze, and whisk in cream and butter.

Blanch the cabbage leaves then braise. Sauté the scallops with the eggs from the lobster and make miniature stuffed cabbages filled with scallops.

Make individual round tart shells with the pie pastry and fill with prawns and julienned leeks.

Cut the potato cylinders into pieces, hollow them out and cook in boiling salted waer. Fill with a duxelle of the two wild mushrooms and garnish with chervil.

Presentation

On a large, oval platter, place the whole bass. Arrange the grilled slices around the edge, alternating with the other garnishes.
Pour the wine sauces on the platter in a pretty pattern and serve the remaining sauce separately.
Alternatively, the fish can be served cold with aspic.

Pike Perch with Spinach and Pitty Pan Squash

"Le grand Ecuyer"
(Cordes)
Chef : Yves Thuriès

Ingredients
(4 servings)

600 g (about 1 1/4 lb) pike perch
  fillets
2 medium pitty pan squash
Mint leaves, cut in strips
1 kg (about 2 lbs) fresh spinach
Garlic
Shallots, chopped
Fish stock, dry white wine, vinegar
Pimento cut in strips, fresh chervil
Salt, pepper butter

Procedure

Peel the squash, cut in half in a zigzag pattern, remove the seeds and cut away a layer of the flesh from the inside to leave a thin shell.
Steam or braise the peeled squash until just tender. Cut the squash flesh into large dice and cook, covered, in a heavy pot with a little butter, salt and strips of mint leaves.

Wash the spinach and cook over high heat in a large pan. Cook a few minutes in the liquid exuded from the spinach, drain if necessary then add a little butter and chopped garlic and cook a few minutes.

Cut the pike perch into 12 thin slices, season with salt and pepper and pan-fry in butter, about 2 minutes on each side.
To make the sauce, combine the chopped shallots, coarsely ground pepper, vinegar and dry white wine in a sauce pan and reduce to a glaze. Add a tablespoon of water or fish stock, reduce then whisk in 4-6 tablespoons cold butter in pieces. Pass the sauce through a conical strainer, season to taste.

Plate Presentation

Mound the diced squash and cooked spinach in the center of the plates and invert the pitty pan shell on top. Pour sauce around the edges and arrange the slices of fish on top of the sauce.

Decorate with long strips of cooked red pepper and fresh chervil leaves.

Pike Perch with Crispy Skin

"Le Bourbon"
(Yssingeaux)
Chef André Perrier

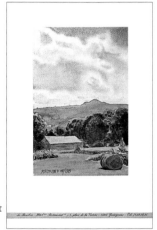

Ingredients
(4-6 servings)

600 g (1 1/4 lb) pike perch fillets
50 ml (4 tbls) almond or walnut
   oil
500 ml (2 cups) fish stock
150 ml (5 fl oz) dry white wine
100 ml (3.5 fl oz) heavy cream
60 g (2 oz) unsalted butter
1/2 lb fresh spinach, blanched
100 g (3 1/2 oz) raviolis (or walnut
   flan)

Walnut Flan:
750 ml (3 cups) heavy cream
9 large eggs
50 g (1 2/3 oz) walnuts (ground)

Whisk together ingredients and season with salt. Pour into individual molds and cook in a water bath at 175 C (350 F) about 1 hour or until set.

Procedure

Use very fresh fish fillets with the skin attached. Divide into even portions and keep refrigerated until ready to use.
Reduce the fish stock and wine to a glaze, whisk in the cream and reduce a little to thicken then enrich with butter.

Meanwhile, place the fish, skin side up on a baking sheet. Season with salt, brush with almond oil and place under the broiler to cook the skin and make it crisp.

Transfer the fish to a 240 C (475 F) oven to finish cooking.

Plate Presentation

Ladle sauce on the plates and mound a few cooked spinach leaves in the center. Place the fish fillets on top.

each plate with a walnut flan, a few raviolis or mushrooms sautéed with garlic.

Pike Perch with Potato "Scales"

"Les Délices du Château" *(Saumur)*
Chef: Pierre Millon

Ingredients
(6 servings)

1 pike perch (2.5-2.8 kg
(5-5 1/2 lbs)
1 bottle red wine
3 large potatoes
4 shallots, sliced
1 bouquet garni
1 tsp seedless raspberry jam
300 g (10 oz) unsalted butter
1 tbl potato starch

Procedure

Bone the fish, remove the skin and rinse the fillets under cold water.
Cut each fillet into three even portions. Reserve the bones.
Peel the potatoes and trim them into cylinders using a round cutter and slice thinly. Cook the slices in simmering water a minute or two until "al dente". Transfer to paper towels to dry.

Melt 100 g (3 1/2 oz) butter and stir in the potato starch. Carefully coat the potato slices in the starch then overlap them on the fish fillets to resemble scales. Cover and refrigerate.

In a heavy pot, combine the bones and sliced shallots and cook in a little oil or butter until lightly browned. Add the jam and 1/2 bottle of wine and reduce by half. Add the remaining wine and the bouquet garni and reduce by half. Pour the sauce through a fine-meshed conical sieve then whisk in 200 g (6 1/2 oz) cold unsalted butter a little at a time. Season to taste. Keep warm in a water bath.

Meanwhile, heat a few drops of olive oil in a non-stick skillet and invert the fish filets into the pan to brown the "scales". Turn the fillets over and place on a baking sheet to finish cooking in a hot oven for about 15 minutes.

Plate Presentation

Ladle sauce on the plates and place the fish on top.

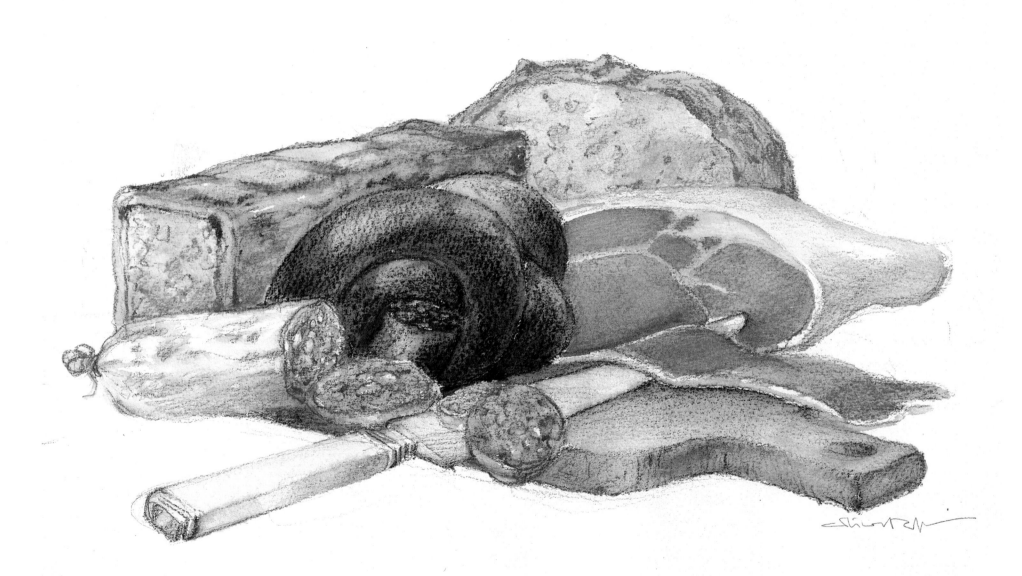

Chapter 4 - Meat Dishes

Meat has been a main source of nutrition for man since the dawn of time. Although at the beginning meat was eaten raw, man soon discovered the gustatory pleasure of eating cooked meat. Aside from a few specialties like «steak tartar» and «carpaccio» meat is now served cooked. There are five main ways to cook meat:

1. Boiled meat

The making of the classic "pot au feu" and other boiled meat preparations can be approached two ways:

In the past, the meat was placed in cold cooking liquid, seasoned then brought to a boil. With this method, the meat loses much of its texture and soluble nutrients. The flavorful juices are transferred to the cooking liquid which becomes a rich broth and delicious ingredient for soups. (The broth needs to be chilled to eliminate the fat.)

After coming to a boil, the impurities that rise to the surface in the form of a froth are carefully skimmed and discarded. The heat is then lowered so that the liquid is barely simmering and the vegetables are added according to how long they need to cook.

The meat cooks over low heat for 2-21/2 hours (depending on the size of course) until very tender. The surface should be skimmed of impurities from time to time.

For the alternative method, bring the liquid to a boil first then add the meat. Blade roast or beef ribs are used and some chefs add a marrow bone for flavor. When the meat comes in contact with the hot liquid it is immediately seared and the connective tissues are kept intact. The juices are held in the meat through quick coagulatoin of the albumine.

There is less shrinkage of the meat with this method and the meat is more flavorful and nutritious. However, the trade off is that the broth is not as flavorful and nutritious as when the meat is started in cold water.

As with the first method, the heat is lowered to a simmer and the meat cooks about 2-2 1/2 hours and the vegetables are added during cooking.

The meat retains more texture and flavor and the broth, although good, is simply used to moisten the meat and is not the main feature of the dish.

2. Roasted meats

In France there are three stages of roasted meat: medium rare, rare and "bleu" or very rare. It is important to control the cooking so that the client is served meat to his or her liking.

Trim the meat to remove tendons and excess fat. If needed, tie the meat to keep a uniform shape and sear in a hot pan with a little oil or in a very hot oven. The outside of the meat should brown on contact with the heat to form a crust that locks in flavor and moisture.

Cooked on a spit, beef or chicken can be roasted to perfection. Nothing is better that meat that has turned slowly in front of a blazing hardwood fire. But unfortunately the wood fire has been replaced by gas or electiricity. Whatever the source of heat, spit roasting draws the fat gradually out of the meat which drips to a pan below. The surface of the meat forms a crust, locking in the juices within.

The doneness of the meat can be easily tested by all cooks, whether professional chef or amateur. First check the recommended time to cook the particular size of meat. To confirm the doneness, insert a metal skewer (or meat thermometer) into the center. First observe the juices that exude from the meat. From the color; bright red to light pink, you can tell whether the meat is ready or needs a little more cooking. If only a few drops of pink juice comes to the surface, the meat is ready. Also, the tip of the skewer should be warm to the touch (press to your lower lip). Allow the meat to "rest", so that the juices can "settle" into

the meat before slicing.

Grilled and broiled meats would be included in this category. The method is similar; place the meat on a preheated grill or under a hot broiler.

White meats (veal and pork) and poultry should be cooked "medium" or until the meat juices run clear.

3. Sautéed Meats

The cooking method "sauté" is not just for meats of course. Fish and vegetables can also be sautéed. Meats to be sautéed are usually cut into small pieces and the surface is dried. Butter is then heated with oil and the meat is browned on all sides in the hot fat. (the term "sauté" which means "jump", comes from the heat of the oil which causes a drop of water to jump when it is hot enough.)

To make the dish called "sauté" (a type of stew), the browned meat is removed from the pan and the fat is eliminated. The meat is then returned to the pan and in some cases coated with flour (which later will thicken the sauce). The meat is stirred so the flour cooks then liquid is added to almost cover the meat (stock, wine, Madiera, crushed tomatoes). Seasonings are added along with a bouquet garni, the pan is covered and the dish is cooked in the oven (about 1 hour for veal, 45 minutes for lamb).

"Sauté" can also refer to cooked meats that are rewarmed by pan frying and served with a sauce. "Veal Beauharnais" is a good example: the cooked meat is rewarmed in butter then the pan is deglazed with Madiera and brown sauce with truffles (sauce "Perigeux"). The dish is then served with stuffed mushrooms and sautéed artichoke hearts.

Described at the end of the book:

4. Ragoûts
5. Braised meats

Filet Mignon with Morel Cream

« **La Renaissance** » *(Magny-Cours)*
Chef: Jean-Claude Dray

Ingredient (3 servings)
3 beef filets 200 g (6 1/2 oz) each
50 g (1 2/3 oz) dried morels
50 ml (4 tbls) olive oil
300 ml (10 fl oz) heavy cream
Salt, pepper
1.5 kg (3 lbs) potatoes (for 6-8 servings)
4 tbls each unsalted butter and flour
500 ml (2 cups) whole milk
500 ml (2 cups) heavy cream
100 g (3 1/2 oz) Swiss cheese, grated

Procedure

Chef Dray serves the filets with morels with a creamy potato dish called "Tapinaude Morvandelle". Peel and cut the potatoes into medium slices. Melt the butter and add the flour to make a roux. Whisk in the milk and cream and bring to a simmer to thicken. Add the potato slices, bring the bechamel to a boil; then transfer to a baking dish. Cook at 375 F until the potatoes are tender. Sprinkle grated cheese on the top, and, just before serving, brown under the broiler.
Prepare the meat and the morels.
Soak the morels in water until very soft (this may take 24 hours).
Cut off each stem and cut the top of the morel in half.
Wash the morels thoroughly to eliminate all sand and dirt.
Heat the oil in a heavy pan. Season the filets with salt and pepper. Sear the meat on both sides, then set aside.
Pour the fat out of the pan and add the cleaned morels.
Set the meat on top of the morels, add a little Cognac and flame. Remove the meat. Add the cream to the morels, bring to boil, then simmer 3-4 minutes until the cream thickens.
Just before serving, finish cooking the filets a few minutes at 200 C (400 F).

Plate Presentation

Place the hot filets in the center of heated plates and place a spoonful of morels on top of the meat. Ladle sauce around the meat and serve immediately with the potato gratin passed separately.

Filet Mignon "Paul Cezanne"

« Relais Ste-Victoire »
(Beaurecueil)
Chef : René Bergés

Ingredients
(6 servings)
6 tenderloin steaks
  (150 g (5 oz) each)
2 medium onions, chopped
500 ml (2 cups) red wine
15 garlic cloves, peeled
2 anchovies
3 tbls wine vinegar
1 tbl honey
6 juniper berries
Fresh thyme, rosemary bay leaf
50 g (1 2/3 oz) tampenade
Olive oil

Wild mushrooms, sautéed (for garnish)

Procedure

Sauté the onions in oil. Add the anchovies, juniper berries, bay leaf, rosemary, thyme and 3 garlic cloves. Sprinkle with flour, stir to coat evenly then add the wine, vinegar and honey. Season lightly with salt and pepper and simmer until reduced by about half.
Strain the sauce through a fine-meshed conical sieve and press on the aromatics to extract maximum flavor.
Cut the remaining 12 garlic cloves in half and cook in water until soft but not mushy. Add the garlic and tampenade (black olive and anchovy purée) to the strained sauce.
Heat olive oil and brown the filets on both sides and continue to pan fry to the desired doneness. Pour off the oil in the pan then deglaze the meat juices with a little of the sauce. Stir then add the remaining sauce and bring to a simmer.

Plate Presentation

Arrange the filets on a platter or individual plates.
Spoon the sauce over the meat, distributing the garlic cloves evenly between the portions. Garnish with sautéed wild mushrooms.
Note : This preparation is best made with a high quality red wine. Plan to serve the same wine with the finished dish.

Beef Tenderloin "Pot au Feu" with Foie Gras

"Les Délices du Château" *(Saumur)*
Chef Pierre Millon

Ingredients (4 servings)

2 L (2 qts) beef broth	300 g (10 oz) Brussel sprouts
4 beef filets	8 potatoes, peeled
8 small carrots	1 celeri root
2 thin leeks, cleaned	200 g (6 1/2 oz) duck foie gras
8 small turnips, peeled	Unsalted butter

Meanwhile prepare the sauce and foie gras. Ladle 125 ml (1 cup) broth into a saucepan and reduce by half. Slice the foie gras into four slices and poach in the broth 3-4 minutes. Remove with a slotted spoon and keep warm. Whisk in cold butter to bind the sauce.

Presentations

Remove the meat from the cooking liquid with a slotted spoon. Arrange the vegetables in a circle and place a tournedos in the center with a slice of foie gras on top. Strain the sauce and spoon over the vegetables. Serve very hot.

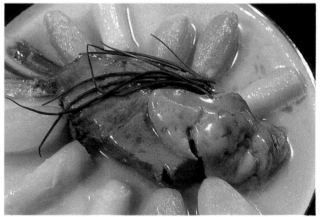

Procedure

Prepare the vegetables: Cut the leeks into 8 pieces and trim the potatoes and celery root into olive-shaped pieces.
Cook the Brussel sprouts (or another seasonal vegetable) about 10 minutes in salted, boiling water.

Bring the beef broth to a simmer, add the carrots, celery root and turnips and cook 10 minutes then add the Brussel sprouts, potatoes and leeks. Simmer 20 more minutes.
Add the beef filets to the simmering broth and cook 7-8 minutes.

Rack of Veal "Margaridou"

Auberge des Cîmes *(St-Bonnet-Le-Froid)*
Chef: Régis Marcon

Ingredients (5 servings)

1 rack of milk-fed veal (5 ribs)
1 lobe sweetbreads
1/2 calve's foot
1 veal kidney
500 g (1 lb) carrots
500 g (1 lb) turnips
500 g (1 lb) potatoes
250 g (8 oz) fresh morels, cooked
250 g 9 8 oz) fresh girolles, cooked

1 kg (2 lbs) fresh cepes
250 g (8 oz) leeks, cooked
250 8 oz) walnuts halves
6 egg whites
Heavy cream
Dry bread crumbs
5 thin slices foie gras
1/2 cup dry white wine

Procedure

"Rack of Veal Mararidou" was created for a culinary competition by Régis Marcon and won him the title "Champion du Monde". This elaborate recipe is prepared in several stages; preparing the veal and the sauce and forming the three decorative garnishes.

To prepare the veal:
Bone the rack of veal and trim the meat. Hollow out a hole through the center of the loin. Purée the meat from the hole and make a mousseline with cream, egg whites, walnuts and cooked girolles (reserve 5 small, cooked girolles).
Pipe some of the mousseline into the hole in the middle of the meat, spread more mousseline over the surface of the veal in an even layer and reserve the remaining mousseline.
Decorate the exterior of the veal with the green portions of cooked leeks, a few cooked morels and slices of cooked carrot. Wrap in caul fat to hold the mousseline in place. (Reserve the white portion of

the leeks (julienned) for making the flower-shaped garnishes.)
Cook the meat at 160 C (325 F) until it reaches 160 C (325 F) in the center, basting occasionally with the stock (recipe follows).

To prepare the stock:
Brown all the bones and veal trimmings. Add the calve's foot and aromatics (onion, thyme, bay leaf and garlic). Add the wine and water to cover and simmer several hours, skimming occasionally. Strain the stock and use to baste the meat.

To prepare the garnishes:
Cut the potatoes into small "trunks" that resemble the thick stem of a cepe. With a small melon baller, hollow out one end. Wrap each in a strip of pork fat, stand them up in a pan, add a little of the stock and bake until tender. Meanwhile, cut the kidney into small dice, sauté until rare, flame with Madeira. Carefully fill the cavity of the cooked potatoes with this mixture. Cook the caps of the cepes in butter and place on top of the potato "stems", keep warm.
In small muffin tins measuring about 4 cm (1 1/2 in), overlap

thin slices of blanched carrots and turnips to form "petals". In the center, place a spoonful of mousseline and cook a few minutes. Top with a small slice of sautéed foie gras. Infuse cardamon into a little stock and glaze the top. Decorate with sautéed girolles and cooked leek julienne.
Blanch the sweetbreads, trim and sauté in browned butter.
Chop the sweetbreads and mix with chopped sautéed morels to form a mixture that can be molded into small sausage shapes. Brush with the cooking juices from the mushrooms. Beat the egg whites to firm peaks and spread on the "sausages". Coat with dried breadcrumbs and deep fry (170 C (340 F)) until golden. Place them on skewers.

Presentation

Cut one neat slice of the veal to show the decorative center. Arrange the meat to one side of the platter. Garnish the platter with the potato and cepe "mushrooms", the carrot and foie gras "flowers" and the "sausages" made with sweetbreads and morels. Pour clarified stock on the base of the platter.

Beef Braised in Red Wine

« Château-Hôtel de Nieuil » *(Nieuil)*
Chef : Luce Bodinaud

Ingredients
(4 servings)

1 kg (2 lbs) beef cheek
  or other tender cut
250 g (8 oz) carrots, cut in
  chunks
150 g (5 oz) pearl onions,
  peeled
1 bouquet garni
1 L (1 qt) red wine
6 peppercorns
2 cloves
2 garlic cloves
150 g (10 oz) button
  mushrooms
1/8 cup Cognac
1 calf's foot, boned
1 L (1 qt) meat broth

Procedure

Trim the nerves from the beef and cut into large dice.
Combine the carrots, onions, bouquet garni and red wine, add the beef chunks, cover and refrigerate for 12 hours.
Remove the meat from the marinade, dry on paper towels. Heat oil and sear the meat. Add the vegetables from the marinade and cook over medium heat to brown for 5-10 minutes.
Flame with Cognac, add the wine from the marinade and the broth.

Bring to a boil and skim all impurities that rise to the surface in the form of a froth.
Add the calf's foot (cut in dice) and the sliced mushrooms.
Lower the heat, season with salt and pepper and simmer gently 2 hours. Season to taste before serving.
Accompany this stew with rice or noodles.
This dish can be made a day in advance and reheated. The flavors will "develop" and the meat will be even more tender.

Veal Shank Braised in White Wine

« Château-Hôtel de Nieuil » *(Nieuil)*
Chef: Luce Bodinaud

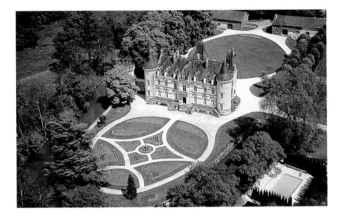

Ingredients (4 servings)

1.5 kg (3 lbs) veal shank
500 ml (2 cups) fruity white wine
1 L (1 qt) chicken broth
Olive oil, flour, salt, pepper
1 kg (2 lbs) carrots

250 g (1/2 lb) onions
125 g (1/4 lb) shallots
2 garlic cloves
1 bouquet garni
Zest of 1/4 lemon & 1/4 orange

Procedure

Slice the vegetables. In a heavy pot combine the vegetables, garlic cloves, bouquet garni, a little butter and season with salt and pepper. Cook over low heat about 20 minutes, stirring occasionally so the vegetables don't brown.

Cut the veal into large chunks. Heat a little olive oil in a heavy pan and sear the meat. Season with salt and peper then add enough flour to coat the meat, stir to coat evenly and cook until browned, about 20 minutes.

Add the wine and chicken broth. Bring to a simmer and cook over low heat 1/2 hour.

Add the cooked vegetables and citrus zest (cut in julienne) and continue to simmer 1/2 hour.

Plate Presentation

Serve the braised veal with a simple garnish of chopped herbs.

Note that this is an excellent dish to make in the spring when "baby vegetables" are available. The French wine that is used in Nieuil is "Pineau des Charentes", a slightly sweet, fruity wine that brings out the sweet taste of small, fresh carrots.

Suckling Pig with Sage, Polenta, Cepes and Foie Gras

« Aux Armes de Champagne » *(L'Epine)*
Chef: Patrick Michelon

Ingredients
(2 servings)

Loin of suckling pig (about 500 g (1 lb))
(with 8 ribs plus the saddle)
400 ml (14 fl oz) water or chicken broth
2 tsp polenta
60-80 g (2-2 1/2 oz) raw foie gras
4 large wild mushrooms
Coarse sea salt, cracked pepper
Fresh sage
200 ml (7 fl oz) peanut oil

Procedure
Bone and trim the pork. Poach for 15 minutes in water or chicken broth. Drain and wipe dry.
Brush the meat with oil, season with salt and pepper and continue cooking in a hot oven (200 C (400 F)) another 10 minutes. The skin should be brown and crisp.
Make a flavorful broth by deglazing the pan with the poaching liquid. Add the meat trimmings and a few sage leaves and simmer to concentrate the flavor. Strain and reserve.
Cook the polenta in lightly salted boiling water. Pan-fry the slices of foie gras, sauté the mushrooms and deep fry 4-6 sage leaves.

Plate Presentation
Place one scoop of polenta on each plate. Add the foie gras and mushrooms in the center. Arrange thin slices of pork around. Ladle the broth over the meat and garnish with fried sage leaves and a sprinkling of coarse sea salt and cracked pepper.

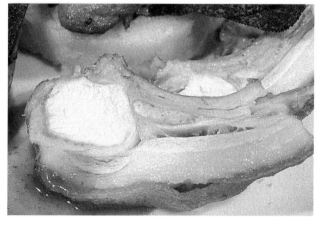

Galette of Pigs' Feet with Potato Crust

« Aux Armes de Champagne » (L'Epine)
Chef : Patrick Michelon

Ingredients
(2 servings)

2 pig's feet
  (preferably back feet)
Chicken or veal broth
150 g (5 oz) foie gras
  (cut into two slices)
2 potatoes
Flavorful salad greens
  (radicchio, arugula, endive)
Walnut vinaigrette
Walnut halves

Procedure

Poach the pig's feet in a flavorful broth for 3 hours. Cut the feet in half and remove the bones. Season lightly with salt and pepper. Lay flat between two trays with a weight on top. Refrigerate over night.

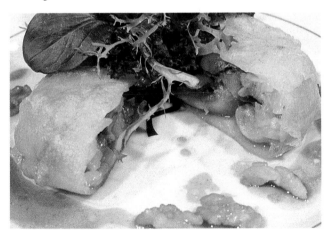

Peel and slice the potatoes thinly. In a buttered ring (10 cm X 2 cm (4 in X 3/4 in)), layer the ingredients. Season each layer lightly. Start with overlapped slices of potatoes in the bottom, next a slice of cooked pressed pig's foot, foie gras in the middle, then pig's foot and a neat layer of potatoes on top.

Drizzle with melted butter and oil and cook at 200 C (400 F) for 15 minutes. The potatoes should be browned and crispy.

Plate Presentation

Toss the greens in vinaigrette and arrange on the plate. Unmold the galette and place on top of the greens and garnish with walnuts.

Lamb Medallions with Morels

« Hostellerie Lenoir » *(Auvillers-Les-Forges)*
Chef : Jean Lenoir

Ingredients (4 servings)

12 lamb medallions
12 dried (or fresh) morels, cleaned
250 ml (1 cup) crème fraîche or heavy cream
Truffle juice, Cognac
4 shallots, chopped
2 tbls unsalted butter
125 ml (1 cup) dry white wine
1 tbl meat glaze
Salt and pepper

Plate Presentation

Arrange the medallions on the plate and spoon the sauce over the meat.
Garnish with vegetables trimmed into even, attractive shapes ("turned") and cooked in a little water with salt and butter.

Procedure

Cook the chopped shallot in butter until soft but not brown. Add the white wine and meat glaze and reduce a little.
If using dried morels, cook a little before adding to the wine sauce, if fresh morels are available, clean them and add directly to the sauce.

Add the crème fraîche (or heavy cream) and reduce by half.

Shortly before serving, add a little Cognac and truffle juice. (The truffle juice may not be needed for extra flavor if using fresh morels.)

Plate Presentation
Arrange the medallions on the plate and spoon the sauce over the meat.
Garnish with vegetables trimmed into even, attractive shapes

104

Panaché of Lamb Provençale

«Le Prieuré» *(Villeneuve-Lès-Avignon)*
Chef : Serge Chenet

Ingredients (4 servings)

2 lamb kidneys
4 lamb chops
4 lamb sweetbreads
   (trimmed and blanched)
4 slices lamb liver
150 g (5 oz) boned saddle of lamb
1 long, thin eggplant
4 zucchini blossoms
300 g (10 oz) tomatoes, chopped,
   cooked,

100 ml (3.5 fl oz) full-flavored
   lamb stock
50 g (1 2/3 oz) unsalted butter
Olive oil, salt , pepper
Fresh thyme
100 g (3 1/2 oz) chicken breast
180 ml (6 oz) light cream
Truffle peelings, chopped

Procedure

Make a chicken mousse to stuff the zucchini blossoms. Purée the chicken in a food processor, transfer to a bowl set inside a bowl of ice. Season with salt and pepper and stir in the cold cream. Use a piping bag to fill the blossoms. (Cut away the stamen of the flowers first.) Slice the zucchini, without cutting through the stem, to cook the squash more evenly. Cover and refrigerate.
Slice the eggplant into 12 slices (about 1 cm (3/8 in) thick). Score the surface with the point of a knife and sprinkle with salt and leave to degorge about 5 minutes. Wipe off the moisture with paper towels and brown both sides in hot olive oil. Transfer the slices to paper towels to absorb excess oil.
Arrange 4 slices of eggplant in a small baking dish. Cover each slice with some cooked, chopped tomato. Top with another sli-

ce of eggplant, more tomato mixture and cover with the remaining eggplant slices. Place in low oven to warm through.
Meanwhile, place the stuffed zucchini blossoms on a plate with a little olive oil, sprinkle with salt and pepper, cover with plastic wrap and steam in a covered pot with a rack and boiling water in the bottom. Keep warm until service.

To cook the meats, heat a little olive oil and butter in a heavy pan. Pan-fry the meats, cooking each one to the desired doneness. Slice the cooked filet and sweetbreads into four pieces and roll the sweetbread slices in the chopped truffles. To make the sauce, pour the fat out of the pan and deglaze the meat juices with a little water. Add the lamb stock and fresh thyme. Reduce until thickened then whisk in a little cold butter. Check for seasonings and keep warm until service.

Plate Presentation

Preheat the plates. Place an eggplant "sandwich" in the center and the cooked zucchini blossom on top. Arrange the meats around the edge and spoon the sauce over the meats. Finish the presentation with a little virgin olive oil drizzled over the meats.

Leg of Lamb
Braised with Garlic

"La Régalido" *(Fontvielle)*
Chef : Jean-Pierre Michel

Ingredients
(4-5 servings)

1 leg of lamb
Peanut oil
3-4 garlic cloves
Olive oil
Fresh thyme
50 g (1 2/3 oz) unsalted butter
Salt and pepper

Procedure

Cook the garlic until softened in the microwave (or oven) with butter, thyme and a little olive oil.

Cut the lamb off the bone and slice into portions about 300 g (10 oz) each. In a large, heavy pot, heat a little peanut oil and sear the lamb on both sides, season with salt and pepper.

Add the garlic, lower the heat and cook until the lamb is medium rare.

Just before serving, turn the heat up, deglaze the pan with a little water, cover and take the pot immediately to the table while the meat is still sizzling.

Plate Presentation

Serve the slices of lamb with the garlic and accompany the meat with sautéed potatoes and a tomato and eggplant gratin.

Lamb Medallions

« Le Vieux Castillon » (Castillon-du-Gard)
Chef : Gilles Dauteuil

Ingredients (10 servings)

3 saddles of lamb (with kidneys)
10 branches fresh thyme
Carrots
2 onions
2 branches of celery
2 cloves of garlic
10 branches fresh rosemary
4 heads of garlic
5 large potatoes
4 basil leaves
50 g (1 2/3 oz) unsalted butter
Salt, pepper
20 baby artichokes, cooked

Procedure

Bone the lamb. Brown the bones and trimmings. Add diced carrots, onions, celery, and 2 crushed garlic cloves and continue

to cook over high heat to brown the vegetables.

Drain off the fat. Cover the bones with water and scrape the bottom to dissolve the meat juices. Simmer 1-2 hours, strain.

Make a garlic purée. Pull apart the the cloves of three heads of garlic. Spread in a single layer in a baking dish, sprinkle with olive oil and cook in a low oven (325 F) for 1 hour. Press through a sieve and mix 1 tbl of the cooking oil into the purée and season with salt, pepper, fresh thyme and rosemary.

Season the lamb filets with salt, pepper, thyme and rosemary. Pan-fry about 3-4 minutes then cut into 1 cm (3/8 in) medallions. Deglaze the pan juices with lamb stock, reduce and whisk in butter to thicken.

To make the «chips»:

Brown the kidneys. Season with salt and pepper and add one chopped shallot and one crushed garlic clove and continue to cook 3-4 minutes. Chop the kidneys and stir in 1 tbl chopped parsley. Peel and cut the potatoes into thin slices. Sandwich a little kidney mixture between two potato slices, press to seal and deep fry until brown and crispy.

Plate Presentation

Arrange the lamb on the plate with a little garlic purée, the artichokes, and the potato kidney «chips». Spoon the sauce over the meat and serve immediately.

Lamb and Spinach «Millefeuille»

"Château de Vauchoux" (Port-sur-Saône)
Chef : Jean-Michel Turin

Ingredients (6 servings)
250 g (8 oz) puff pastry
Rack of lamb (2- 2.5 kg (5-5 1/2 lbs)
100 g (3 1/2 oz) unsalted butter
50 ml (4 tbls) peanut oil
500 ml (2 cups) veal or chicken stock
2 kg (4 1/2 lbs) spinach, washed, trimmed
2 garlic cloves
1 shallot, chopped
200 ml (7 fl oz) dry white wine
2 bay leaves (crumbled), 1 branch thyme, summer savory, 8-10 mint leaves (chopped)
Egg glaze

Plate Presentation

Place the «millefeuille» in the center of heated plates and spoon the sauce around the dish.

Procedure

Roll the puff pasty into thin sheets. Cut into rectangles 6 X 12 cm (about 2 1/2 X 5 in) and chill for 20 minutes. Brush with egg glaze. Bake at 200 C (400 F) 15-20 minutes or until puffed and golden brown. Keep warm.

Heat half the butter in a large pan and add the spinach leaves. Stir as spinach wilts and season with salt and pepper. Keep warm. Bone the rack of lamb and chop the bones. Trim the meat and cut into 6 thick medallions. Rub with garlic.

Heat the remaining butter with oil in a large skillet. Brown the lamb and bones. Add the herbs and shallot and place in a 200 C

(400 F) oven for 4-5 minutes. Transfer the lamb to a plate and keep warm.

Deglaze the pan with white wine. Add the stock and simmer a few minutes then strain. Reduce until the liquid thickens. Taste and season if necessary.

Split the puff pastry rectangles into thirds. On the bottom third place a layer of cooked spinach. Slice the lamb and arrange a few thin slices on the spinach. Add the middle layer of pastry, arrange more lamb slices, then top with final pastry.

Chicken in Chive Cream

"Hôtel d'Espagne" *(Valençay)*
Chef Maurice Fourré

Ingredients (4 servings)

1 chicken (1.1 kg (2 1/2 lbs)
2 tbls. olive oil
50 g (1 2/3 oz) unsalted butter
125 ml (1 cup) dry white wine
500 ml (2 cups) heavy cream
1 bunch chives
2 kg (4 1/2 lbs) fresh spinach
100 g (3 1/2 oz) unsalted butter

Procedure

If using a freshly killed bird, remove the innards and singe the feathers. Cut off the wings and legs, and remove the backbone. Season the pieces of chicken with salt and pepper then heat the oil and butter and brown the meat on all sides.

Deglaze the pan with wine and reduce by one third over low heat. Add the cream and bake in the oven (200 C (400 F)) for about 25 minutes or until the juices in the legs runs clear.

Transfer the chicken to a platter and reduce the sauce until it thickens enough to coat a spoon. Add the chopped chives and season to taste with salt and pepper.

Meanwhile cook the spinach in boiling, salted water for 4 minutes. Drain well and toss in melted butter and season with salt and pepper.

Plate Presentation

Mound the spinach on the plate and arrange a piece of chicken on top. Ladle sauce over the chicken and serve very hot.

109

Chicken Breast with Leeks

"Hostellerie Lenoir" *(Auvillers-Les-Forges)*
Chef : Jean Lenoir

Ingredients
(2 servings)

1 chicken
1/4 cup chicken broth
1/4 cup heavy cream
2 leeks
1 tbl meat glaze
Saffon
Dry white wine
Salt and pepper

Procedure

Remove the legs from the chicken and reserve for another recipe. Season the cavity with salt and pepper, wrap with a sheet of barding fat and tie with kitchen string. Roast in the oven, basting often to keep the meat moist.
Cut the white portion of the leeks into strips and cook with a little wine and butter and season with salt and pepper. Keep warm. Slice the green portion and blanch in boiling, salted water.
To prepare the sauce, reduce the chicken broth by half. Add the cream and the sliced leek greens and the meat glaze.
Season to taste with salt, pepper and saffron.
Simmer a little to infuse the saffron and thicken to a coating consistency. Whisk in a little cold butter just before serving to enrich the sauce and make it shine.

Plate Presentation

Split the chicken down the breastbone. Remove the breastmeat and slice into strips ("aiguillettes").
Fan out the slices of chicken on the plates and ladle the leek infused sauce over the meat. Arrange the leek strips around the chicken. Accompaniments can include carrots, turnips and potatoes cut into even shapes.
The carcass can be used as a dome for the final presentation.

"Pot au Feu" of Chicken with Tarragon Sabayon

"La Belle Époque" *(Bellegarde-sur-Valserine)*
Chef : Michel Sevin

Ingredients (4 servings)

1 fresh chicken (1.7 kg (3 1/2 lbs))
1 bunch fresh tarragon
4 carrots. peeled
4 turnips, peeled
4 small, tender leeks, trimmed
2 medium tomatoes
4 large eggs
1 L (1 qt) chicken broth
100 ml (3.5 fl oz) dry Champagne
Salt and pepper

Procedure

Fill the cavity of the chicken with tarragon stems.
Tie the chicken to hold the shape and steam in a covered pot.
Cut the carrots and turnips into small even shapes as shown and cook until tender in the chicken stock. Keep warm until service.
Clean and cut the leeks into even strips. Cook them in a pot of boiling salted water. Refresh in cold water to keep the bright green color.
When the chicken is almost done, cut the tomatoes in half and add to the pot with the chicken to steam.
To make the sabayon, combine 100 ml (3.5 fl oz) chicken stock and 100 ml (3.5 fl oz) Champagne in a saucepan. Add a large pinch of chopped tarragon leaves, bring to a boil then simmer for 3 minutes.
Whisk the egg yolks in a pan set over another pan with simmering water until they are warmed and very thick. Slowly whisk in the hot tarragon infused liquid.
Add plain salt and freshly ground white pepper to taste.
Spoon the sauce into a bowl and arrange tarragon leaves decoratively on the top.

Plate Presentation

Remove the strings and the tarragon stems from the chicken.
Place the chicken on a heated serving platter.
Arrange the vegetables on the platter to resemble a flower with carrot and turnip petals and stem and leaves made from leeks.
Pass the sabayon separately.

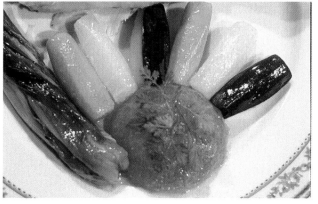

Chicken with Crayfish

"Auberge du Vieux Moulin"
Chef : Élisabeth Mirbey

Ingredients
(4 servings)

1 chicken
3 carrots
2 leeks
2 turnips
1 branch fresh fennel
1 bouquet garni
20 crayfish
3 onions, diced
4 tomatoes, diced
1 red pepper, diced
1 bay leaf
150 ml (5 fl oz) heavy cream
30 ml (1 fl oz) olive oil

Strain the sauce and ladle around the chicken.
If the vegetables are presentable, serve them with the dish.

Procedure

Prepare the chicken. Cut off the wing tips. Bone the breast meat, keeping the wing attached. Remove the legs.

Cut the carcass into three pieces and place with the trimmings in a heavy stockpot. Add the carrots, turnips, leek, fennel, bouquet garni and cover with cold water. Season with coarse salt, cover and simmer 2-3 hours.

Strain the broth and return to the pot. Add the chicken legs and breast and poach for about 20 minutes.

If using live, wild crayfish remove the intestine by twisting the central tail fin and pulling out the bitter-tasting "vein". Rinse the crayfish under cold water.

Heat the oil in a heavy pot and add the crayfish. Stir the crayfish so they cook evenly. When the shells have turned red, remove the crayfish and pour off the oil. Add the diced vegetables, season with salt, pepper and cayenne, cover and cook over low heat. Add the crayfish and cream and simmer a few minutes. Add seasonings to taste.

Plate Presentation

Serve this dish on a large, heated plate.
Place a portion of chicken in the center.
Arrange crayfish around the chicken.

Braised Chicken with Tarragon

"Auberge du Père Bise" *(Talloires)*
Chef : Sophie Bise

Ingredients (4 servings)

1 fresh chicken weighing about 2.2 kg (4 1/2 lbs)
2 bunches fresh tarragon
1/2 cup dry white wine
50 g (1 2/3 oz) unsalted butter
1 shallot, chopped
1/2 L (2 cups) crème fraîche

Procedure

Place 1/2 bunch tarragon in the cavity of the chcken, season with salt and pepper. In a heavy pot just large enough to hold the chicken, heat the butter and brown the chicken on all sides Add the chopped shallot, white wine, 1/2 bunch tarragon and 1/2 cup water.
Bring to a simmer, cover and cook the chicken 10 minutes on the back then 20 minutes on each side. Remove and keep warm. Reduce the liquid by half. Add the cream and the bunch of tarragon (set aside a few leaves for garnish) and reduce until thickened.
Season to taste with salt and pepper and strain the sauce through a conical sieve, pressing on the tarragon to extract the flavor.

Plate Presentation

Ladle the sauce over the chicken, decorate with blanched tarragon leaves. Serve the chicken with boiled Basmati rice with a little butter.

Duck "Gigot" with Whole Grain Mustard

"La Belle Époque"
(Bellegarde-sur-Valserine)
Chef : Michel Sevin

Ingredients
(4 servings)

4 meaty duck legs
100 ml (3.5 fl oz) Port
100 ml (3.5 fl oz) full-flavored
 veal stock
300 ml (10 fl oz) crème fraîche
1 tbl wholegrain mustard (from
 "Meaux")
1 tbl olive or peanut oil
Salt and pepper to taste
1 carrot, peeled, cooked in stock
8 snowpeas, blanched
Parsley

Place 2 snowpeas between slices of meat on each plate and top the presentation with fresh parsley.
Spoon sauce over the tips of the slices.
Pass the remaining sauce separately.
Serve with seasonal vegetables or potatoes puréed with olive oil.

Procedure

Remove any feathers left on the duck legs and trim excess skin.
Remove the bones, season with salt and pepper.
Form and tie each leg to resemble a "gigot" ("leg of lamb").
Heat the oil in a heavy pan and put in the legs, skin side down.

Cook over medium high heat for 10-12 minutes. Lower the heat a little, turn the legs over and continue to cook for 3-5 minutes. The meat should be medium rare.
Remove the legs and keep warm.

Pour off the excess fat from the pan.
Deglaze the pan with Port to release the meat juices stuck to the pan and reduce by half.

Add the veal stock and reduce by half over very low heat.
Add the crème fraîche (or heavy cream) and simmer until the sauce thickens enough to coat a spoon.
Off the heat, stir in the mustard. Season to taste with salt and pepper.

Plate Presentation

Heat the plates. Slice each duck "gigot" lengthwise into 5-6 slices.
Fan out the slices with the wider end of the slices around the rim.
Slice the carrot and place a few slices in the center of each plate.

Rock Cornish Hens with Green Peppercorn Sauce

"Hostellerie Lenoir" *(Auvillers-Les-Forges)*
Chef : Jean Lenoir

Ingredients (2 servings)

2 small rock cornish hens
50 ml (4 tbls) Cognac
125 ml (1/2 cup) white wine
250 ml (1 cup) chicken broth
2 tsps tomato paste
1 tsp green peppercorns in brine
10 g (1/3 oz) unsalted butter
Salt and pepper

Procedure

If using freshly killed birds, remove the innards and singe the feathers.

Salt the cavities and place a few green peppercorns inside.

Rub with butter and roast at 190 C (375 F) about 12 minutes, basting often with broth.

Transfer the birds to a platter and keep warm. Pour off the fat from the roasting pan and flame with Cognac. Deglaze with white wine. Add chicken broth and reduce to concentrate the flavor.

Add the tomato paste and peppercorns, stir and return the chickens to the pot. Simmer to thicken the sauce, season to taste and swirl in the butter just before serving.

Plate Presentation

Place the small hens in the center of the plates and garnish with matchstick fried potatoes.

Pass the green peppercorn sauce separately.

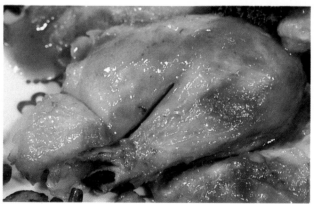

"Demoiselles" of Duck served with Fruit

"La Toque Blanche" *(Pujols)*
Chef: Bernard Lebrun

Ingredients
(4 servings)

16 slices duck breast *
200 ml (7 fl oz) duck stock
Sugar
20 ml (2/3 fl oz) wine vinegar
2 peaches
2 pears
150 g (5 oz) grapes
8 prunes

* *Note:* "Demoiselles" are the thin, tender strips of meat under the breast meat that often remain attached to the carcass. In France they are available by the pound. An acceptable alternative is sliced duck breast (each breast will have one demoiselle attached).

Plate Presentation

Arrange 4 strips of duck on each plate.
Place the warm fruits around the meat and spoon the sauce over the meat.

Procedure

To make the sauce, cook sugar with a little water to a light caramel. Add the vinegar, bring to a boil then add the duck stock. Flavor the sauce with a little peach syrup (from poaching peaches) or peach brandy and reduce until the sauce lightly coats a spoon. Taste and season with salt and pepper. Keep warm.

Peel the peaches and pears, cut in thick slices, brush with sauce and cook in a low oven until warm and slightly softened.
Pit the prunes and plump in warm water.
Warm the grapes in the sauce.
Sprinkle the duck with salt and pepper. Heat unsalted butter until it browns then sauté the meat a minute or two. The strips of duck should remain medium rare.

Duck
with Raspberry Vinegar

"Hostellerie du Coq Hardi" *(Verdun)*
Chef : Patrick Leloup

HOSTELLERIE
du
COQ HARDI
VERDUN

Ingredients
(4 servings)

1 fresh duck (1.5 kg (3 lbs))
100 ml (3.5 fl oz) crème fraîche
 (or heavy cream)
200 ml (7 fl oz) raspberry
 vinegar
2 shallots, chopped
500 g (1 lb) unsalted butter,
 softened

Procedure

Trim the duck, remove the innards.
Salt and pepper the cavity and truss the duck.
Roast at 230 C (450 F) for 20 minutes.
Cook the shallots in a little butter until softened.
Add the raspberry vinegar (and a few fresh raspberries when in season), and reduce by 2/3.
Add the crème fraîche (or heavy cream) to the reduced vinegar, bring to a boil to thicken.
Off the heat, whisk in the butter a little at a time.
Pour the sauce through a conical strainer, keep warm in a water bath.

Plate Presentation

Arrange the duck on a platter and ladle the sauce over the duck. Serve this dish with waffle-cut or very thinly julienned fried potatoes.

Squab with Figs and French Toast

"Auberge du Père Bise" *(Talloires)*
Chef : Sophie Bise

Ingredients (4 servings)

4 squab (500 g (1 lb)) each
4 fresh black figs
1 cinnamon stick, pinch ground cinnamon
16 small round shallots or pearl onions
4 slices of French bread
2 egg yolks
2 tbls sugar
3/4 cup whole milk
500 ml (2 cups) veal stock
1 carrot, chopped
1-2 shallots, chopped
Cognac and Port

Procedure

Split the squab down the backbone. Remove the backbone (reserve for sauce) and flatten the birds. Brush with a little butter, season with salt and pepper and roast in a heavy pan.
To make the cinnamon sauce, brown the bones in a little butter, add the carrots and shallots, cook until softened then deglaze with Cognac and Port. Add the cinnamon stick, a pinch of ground cinnamon and the veal stock and simmer to infuse the cinnamon. Strain and reduce to thicken slightly and concentrate the flavor.
Peel the small shallots (or onions) and cook them over low heat with a little water, butter, salt and sugar until they are softened and lightly caramelized.
Brush the figs with a little melted butter, sprinkle with sugar and cook in the oven (350 F) for 10 minutes.
To make the "French toast", whisk together the egg yolks, sugar, milk.
and a pinch of cinnamon. Soak the slices of bread in this mixture then pan fry in a little butter.

Plate Presentation

Arrange the roasted squab, the slices of toast and the glazed onions on the plates. Spoon a little sauce over the squab and decorate with a cinnamon stick.

Quail Confit with Lentils

"Hôtel d'Espagne" *(Valençay)*
Chef : Maurice Fourré

Ingredients (4 servings)

4 quail
2 kg (4 lbs) coarse salt
1 branch fresh thyme
8 bay leaves
1 head of garlic
2 kg (4 lbs) goose fat
500 g (1 lb) lentils
1 carrot, 1 onion cut in dice
1 bouquet garni
100 g (3 1/2 oz) spring or pearl onions
3 carrots, "turned" into even shapes
Salt and pepper

Procedure

Remove the innards if necessary and truss the quail like a chicken.
Cover the quail with the coarse salt mixed with thyme, bay leaves and the cloves of one head of garlic. Cover and refrigerate 36 hours.
Remove the quail from the salt and wipe them off.
Melt the goose fat, add the quail and cook at 180 C (350 F) for 1 1/2 hours. Reserve in the fat until ready to serve.
Cook the lentils (according to package directions) with the diced carrots and onions and bouquet garni.
Cook the onions and "olive-shaped" carrots separately in salted, boiling water.

Plate Presentation

Spoon lentils on the plate and arrange pieces of boned quail confit on top. Garnish the dish with the onions and carrots.

119

Rabbit with Basil

«Hostellerie Les Bas Rupts» (Gérardmer)
Chef : Michel Philippe

Ingredients (4 servings)

4 rabbit legs
6 garlic cloves, not peeled
2 tomatoes, quartered
100 ml (3.5 fl oz) dry white wine
2 tbls veal stock
1 bunch basil
80 g (2 2/3 oz) butter and oil
60 g (2 oz) cold unsalted butter
2 apples, peeled, cut in half
4 tbls cooked cranberries
4 medium button mushrooms
Salt, freshly ground pepper
Thin green beans, tiny carrots and small turnips, trimmed, cooked

Procedure

Bone the rabbit legs and stuff with basil. Reform the meat in the shape of the leg and sew the opening.
Heat the butter and oil in a skillet and brown the rabbit on all sides.
Season with salt and pepper and add the garlic and tomatoes. Cook for about 12 minutes at 200 C (400 F).
Remove the rabbit, set aside and keep warm.
Deglaze the pan with wine and stock.
Pour through a sieve and press on the tomatoes and garlic.
Add chopped basil to the juices, set over low heat and whisk in the cold butter to thicken the sauce.
Taste the sauce and season if necessary.
Turn the mushrooms and cook with salt, butter and lemon juice.
Bake the apples halves until soft, fill with cooked cranberries.

Plate Presentation

Remove the strings and cut the rabbit legs on the bias in thick slices. Arrange on the plate and coat with sauce. Garnish the plate with the mushrooms, apples and «bouquet» of vegetables.

Saddle of Wild Rabbit Stuffed with Kidneys

«Château de Vauchoux» (Port-sur-Saône)
Chef: Jean-Michel Turin

Ingredients
(4 servings)

4 saddles of wild rabbit
200 g (7 oz) pork loin
30 g (1 oz) shallots, chopped
Salt, pepper
100 g (3 1/2 oz) veal kidneys
200 g (7 oz) onions, chopped
30 g (1 oz) duck fat
100 ml (3.5 fl oz) peanut oil
50 g (1 2/3 oz) unsalted butter
1 bottle Pink Champagne

Procedure

Bone the saddles and cut in half to obtain four portions.
Cook the chopped onions in the duck fat over low heat for 30 minutes.

Cut the pork and the veal and rabbit kidneys into small pieces. Add the chopped shallots, salt and pepper and mix well.

Spread out the boned saddles on the work surface, season lightly and add the stuffing. Roll the meat around the stuffing and tie with string.

In a skillet, heat the butter and oil and brown the rolled rabbit on all sides. Add a «mirepoix» (2 onions, 2 carrots, diced and thyme) and cook at 190 C (375 F) for 10 minutes.

Remove the string from the rabbit and keep warm.

Deglaze the pan with wine and reduce to concentrate the flavor. Pour the sauce through a sieve and season to taste.

Plate Presentation

Spoon cooked onion onto each plate. Slice the rabbit and overlap around the plate. Ladle sauce over the meat and serve very hot.

Salad with Venison Medaillons and Carmelized Apples

"Auberge du Père Bise" *(Talloires)*
Chef : Sophie Bise

Ingredients (4 servings)

700 g (1 lb 6 1/2 oz) saddle of venison	Few juniper berries
1 onion, chopped	1/8 tsp nutmeg
1 branch celery, chopped	1/2 tsp paprika
125 ml (1 cup) red wine	Cognac
1 carrot, chopped	1 kg (about 2 lbs) apples, peeled
1 branch fresh thyme	Peanut oil, unsalted butter
1 small bay leaf	1/2 cup gin
1 tsp peppercorns, coarsely ground	Cranberries, cooked
	Vinaigrette
	Salad greens for 4

trimmings into small dice. Sprinkle the slices with sugar, pan fry in a butter until the sugar lightly caramelizes.

With the remaining apples make a lightly sweetened compote and stir in the reserved diced apples.

Cut thin slices of venison filet (2 cm (3/4 in)) and season with salt and pepper. Pan fry about 2 minutes.

Deglaze the pan with gin, add the reduced marinade liquid, reduce a little and finish with a little vinaigrette.

Plate Presentation

Toss the greens in vinaigrette and mound the salad on the plates. Place three even-sized spoonfuls of compote on each plate. Alternate the slices of venison and caramelized apples and place around the salad. Spoon the sauce over the venison and decorate with a few cooked cranberries.

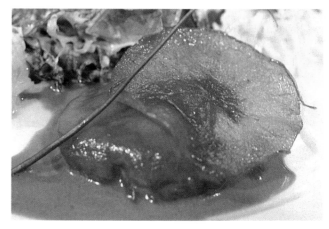

Procedure

Bone and trim the saddle of venison, cover the filets and refrigerate. Place the bones and trimmings in a non-reactive container and add the red wine, onions, carrot, celery, thyme, bay leaf, peppercorns, juniper berries, nutmeg, paprika and a little Cognac. Cover and refrigerate overnight.

The next day, brown the bones and trimmings in a little butter, add the vegetables and marinade liquid and reduce by 3/4. Pour through a conical strainer and set aside.

Cut two apples into round slices, remove core. Cut the apple

124

Venison with Juniper Berries

«Les Chênes Verts» (Tourtour)
Chef Paul Bajade

Ingredients
(10 servings)

1 shoulder of venison
(boned, cut in cubes)
150 ml (5 fl oz) Balsamic vinegar
1 bottle red wine
20 g (2/3 oz) juniper berries,
  crushed
500 g (1 lb) wild mushrooms
50 g (1 2/3 oz) thick bacon
1/2 calf's foot
Carrots, turnips
Bouquet garni. peppercorns,
  carrot, onion

Procedure

Marinate the cubes of venison for 24 hours in red wine with the following aromatics: sliced onion and carrot, peppercorns, juniper berries and a bouquet garni.

Remove the meat with a slotted spoon and pat dry with paper towels. Season with salt and pepper, coat with flour and brown in oil.

Transfer the aromatics to the pan and continue to cook at high heat. Deglaze with Balsmic vinegar then add the marinade liquid. Add the calf's foot and add stock to cover if necessary.

Cook about 1 1/2 hours. Remove the cubes of venison and keep warm. Bone the calve's foot and cut into small dice. Reduce the liquid a little more. Season to taste and strain.

Plate Presentation

Place the cubes of meat in a shallow soup dish. Sprinkle the diced calf's foot on top.

Ladle sauce over the top and garnish with sautéed wild mushrooms and blanched bacon strips («lardons»).

125

Medallions of Game with Two Sauces

"La Tour du Roy" *(Vervins-en-Thiérache)*
Chef: Annie Desvignes

Ingredients (4 servings)

300 g (10 oz) venison
300 g (10 oz) wild boar
30 g (2 tbls) salt
10 g (2 tsp) pepper
1 bottle good red wine
100 g (3 1/2 oz) carrots
50 g (1 2/3 oz) leeks
1 bouquet garni
10 g (1/3 oz) peppercorns
100 g (3 1/2 oz) unsalted butter
100 ml (3.5 fl oz) peanut oil
50 ml (4 tbls) Armagnac
2 tbls currant jelly
1 tbl potato starch

Procedure

Combine the wine, vegetables and aromatics.
Cut the meat in medallions and for at least 24 hours.
Dry the meats on paper towels and season with salt and pepper.
Heat half the butter until nutty brown and sear the meats.
Flame the meats with Armagnac, pour the marinade liquid through a sieve over the meats, bring to a boil and cook 1 minute.
Remove the meats with a slotted spoon, keep warm.
Dissolve the starch in a little cold wine or water. Thicken the sauce by whisking in the jelly and starch.

Plate Presentation

Arrange the medallions on the plates and spoon the sauce over the meat.
For a taste and presentation variation, make a separate sauce of heavy cream simmered with green peppercorns to spoon over the the wild boar medallions.
Choose one or more of the following garnishes to serve with the wild game: sautéed wild mushrooms, pears cooked in red wine, potato pancakes, or celery root purée.

Venison Medallions "à la Normande"

"Hostellerie Lenoir" *(Auvillers-Les-Forges)*
Chef: Jean Lenoir

Ingredients (2 servings)

6 venison medallions
Unsalted butter and oil
125 ml (1 cup) Champagne
50 ml (4 tbls) Port
2 tbls crème fraîche or heavy cream
Salt and pepper
Celery root purée
1 large apple, sliced, sautéed in butter

Procedure

Trim the meat from a rack of venison and cut medallions 2.5 (1 in) thick.
Heat a little butter and oil in a heavy skillet and sear the meat then season with salt and pepper. Continue to cook over high heat 3-4 minutes.
Pour off the fat and deglaze with Champagne. Add Port then transfer the meat to a platter and keep warm. The meat is best when cooked medium rare.
Reduce the sauce by half then add the cream and reduce until the sauce coats a spoon. Season to taste.

Plate Presentation

Arrange the medallions on plates and spoon the sauce over the meat.
Garnish the plate with celery root purée and sautéed apple slices.

Chapter 5 - Desserts

The Crowning Glory of Every Meal

Desserts come in countless flavors, textures and shapes to provide a memorable finale to the meal. At a formal dinner, dessert is served after the cheese and should be as beautiful to look at as it is delicious to eat and impeccably served. This final impression should be perfect in every way.

If something has been amiss during the meal, a fabulous dessert will help the diner "forgive and forget" and leave with an overall good impression of the meal.

Desserts should be neither too light and airy nor heavy. They should be sweet without being sugary amd above all very fresh in appearance and flavor. The arrival of the dessert should be exciting and be further enhanced with a glass of champagne or white wine.

Desserts can be grouped into three categories:

1. Traditional cakes and pastries

This category includes the desserts traditionally prepared by French pastry chefs; sponge cakes layered with various fillings, fruit tarts, cream puff creations, puff pastries and so many more.

For special occasions, the pastry chef can show his talent with stunning "showpiece" desserts decorated with pulled sugar flowers and "satin" ribbons tied in sumptuous bows.

Bite-size pastries and homemade candies are often the highlight of a banquet.

2. "Kitchen" Desserts

Family recipes have been handed down from generation to generation and have become a beloved part of the French dessert reperatory. Many have been refined over time and are a wonderful part of a dessert menu. Even the great chef Carême loved making these simple desserts.

Soufflés flavored with liqueur, chocolate mousse and Bavarian creams molded with ladyfingers to make a charlotte are but a few of the wonderful offerings in this category. Fresh and cooked fruits and custards are served on their own or used as a crêpe filling. The flavors and fillings change with the seasons and mood of the chef. A talented cook will create combinations that please and surprise the clients.

The desserts presented in this book show the variety of wonderful "kitchen" desserts given a personal touch by our talented chefs; puff pastry with pears, tarte tatin, prune soufflé, orange crêpes, chocolate marquise, vanilla bavarian to name a few.

3. Ice creams and sorbets

It is believed that the Chinese invented ice cream by combining honey found in hives in the trunks of trees with fresh fruit juice and snow brought from the mountian tops.

The secret of ice cream then traveled through the Middle East then into Turkey and Grece to end up in Rome where it was refined and became a popular dish.

It was written by Quintus Maximus Gurgus that Nero loved ice cream and always served it to his guests.

Ice cream didn't become part of French cuisine until 1533 when the son of Francois I, King Henri II of France married the Italian princess Catherine de Medicis who brought her many chefs (and the secret of making ice cream) with her to France.

In 1720, the king's chef Francisco Proppio developed "mousse glacée", a frozen confection made with whipped cream that is still very popular in modern cuisine.

In 1774, inspired by a grand ice sculpture, a chef introduced a frozen cream dessert flavored with liqueur, an idea that became instantly popular. Since this time, ice creams made with liqueurs have been served in the famous Café du Caveau in Paris.

Also in Paris, the Italian chef Tortoni created "Biscuit glacé à la Tortoni" which combined layers of genoise (sponge cake) with dried fruits and ice cream.

It is during this time that improvements were made in the texture and flavor of ice cream and the dessert became extremely popular. Many of the refined desserts created during this era are still served today; "parfaits", "baked Alaska" (in French known as "omelette surprise") and frozen soufflés.

Improvements in refrigeration and hygiene have only enhanced the art of ice cream making and brought it to new heights.

Even though frozen desserts have become less fancy over the years, they are more varied and have maintained a high standard of quality.

We now enjoy frozen desserts year round and they are a favorite of young and old alike. Ice creams, sorbets are a wonderful finale to a simple or fancy meal.

French Cheesecake with Candied Angelica

"Château-Hôtel de Nieuil" *(Nieuil)*
Chef: Luce Bodinaud

Ingredients (4-6 servings)

Sweet pie pastry:
125 g (4 oz) flour
75 g (1/3 cup) unsalted butter
20 g (2 tsp) sugar
1 large egg
500 g (1 lb) ricotta, drained

150 g (10 oz) sugar
4 large eggs, separated
150 g (10 oz) flour
50 g (1 2/3 oz) candied angelica, chopped

Procedure

To make the pie pastry, cut the butter into the flour. Add the egg and sugar and mix to make a smooth dough, cover and refrigerate 1 hour. Roll out the dough and press it into a high-sided tart ring or springform pan.

To make the cheese mixture, whisk together the egg yolks and sugar, stir in the ricotta and flour and blend until smooth. Beat the egg whites to form stiff peaks and fold into the cheese mixture. Pour the mixture into the pastry-lined mold, sprinkling the candied angelica throughout the cake.

Cook for 10 minutes at 220 °C (425 F) then lower the heat to 200 °C (400 F) and cook another 30 minutes. The top should be lightly browned.

Plate Presentation

Unmold the cheesecake upside down onto a plate.
When the cake has cooled invert it onto a service platter.
Decorate the top with candied angelica and serve with a sauce of puréed strawberries and/or raspberries.

Note: In France, this dessert is made with "fromage blanc" a fresh cheese similar to whole milk ricotta but smoother and slightly more dense. For best results, drain off a little of the whey of the ricotta (about 1/2 hour in cheesecloth or coffee filter). This cheesecake is much lighter than one made with cream cheese.

Fresh Cheese and Chocolate Napoleons

"L'Etape Lani" *(Bouc-Bel-Air)*
Chefs: Lucien and Joël Lani

Ingredients (4 servings)
300 g (10 oz) bittersweet chocolate

Cheese filling:
300 g (10 oz) ricotta
160 g (5 1/2 oz) sugar
25 ml (2 tbls) water
4 g (1 tsp) unflavored gelatin
5 egg yolks
250 ml (1 cup) cream, whipped
Orange flower water

«Suzette» sauce:
400 g (14 oz) sugar
125 ml (1 cup) water
5 oranges (juice and zest)
250 g (8 oz) apricot jam

Procedure

Cheese filling:
Note: Chef Lani uses a fresh goat's milk cheese called «brousse» for this dessert. Whole milk ricotta, drained in a coffee filter for 1/2 hour can be substituted.
Make a sabayon with the water, sugar (cooked to soft ball stage) and egg yolks. Stir in the softened gelatin and orange flower water. Fold in the cheese and whipped cream. Cover and refrigerate.
Suzette sauce: Cook the sugar and water to a caramel. Deglaze with orange juice. Stir in the zest and jam and bring to a simmer. Strain and set aside.
Chocolate layers: Melt the chocolate and spread in thin layers on flexible plastic forms. Refrigerate to harden then peel away the plastic.

Plate Presentation
Pipe the filling between layers of chocolate. Spoon the Suzette sauce around the «Napoleons».

131

"Délice" of Pineapple with Cointreau

"Hostellerie Lenoir" *(Auvillers-Les-Forges)*
Chef: Jean Lenoir

Ingredients (4 servings)

1 fresh pineapple
Sugar syrup
100 ml (3.5 fl oz) Cointreau
5 egg whites (for meringue)
350 g (12 oz) sugar
100 g (3 1/2 oz) assorted candied fruit, diced,
    macerated in Cointreau
Spongecake
50 g (1 2/3 oz) chopped or sliced almonds, toasted
4 sheets aluminum foil

Procedure

Cut off the top and bottom of the pineapple and reserve.
Cut four thick slices of pineapple and hollow the centers.
Place the rings on sheets of aluminum foil.
Cut circles of spongecake to fit inside the rings and moisten the cake with Cointreau.
Purée the fruit with a little sugar and combine with equal amounts of sugar syrup (equal amounts sugar and water simmered 3 minutes).
Freeze this mixture in an ice cream maker and add 50 ml (4 tbls) Cointreau.
Spread a smooth layer of the sorbet on the cake circle.
Whip the egg whites to stiff peaks and whisk in the sugar to make a Swiss meringue. Flavor with vanilla and stir the candied fruit into 2/3 of the meringue. Cover the sorbet with a smooth layer of meringue. Decorate each portion with the remaining meringue piped with a star tip.
Brown the meringue under the broiler or with a torch (like for a "Baked Alaska"). Sprinkle the top with toasted almonds.

Plate Presentation

Cut a block of ice the size of the serving platter.
Place the top of the pineapple in the center and surround with the "délices" of pineapple.

132

Blueberry Tart

«Hostellerie Les Bas Rupts» *(Gérardmer)*
Chef : Michel Philippe

Ingredients
(8 servings)

Pate brisée:
250 g (8 oz) unbleached flour
125 g (4 oz) unsalted butter
1 large egg
5 g (1 tsp) salt
Cold water

Filling:
800 g (1 lb 10 oz) wild
    blueberries
200 g (1 cup sugar)
4 large eggs
1 tsp cornstarch

Procedure

Make the dough by hand or in the food processor.

Place the flour in a bowl and make a well in the center. Add the eggs, pieces of softened butter and salt and mix until the mixture is crumbly.

Add a little cold water at a time until the dough holds together in a smooth ball. Form into a disk, cover and refrigerate 1 hour.

Lightly grease a heavy baking sheet, sprinkle with water and place a bottomless 25 cm (10 in) tart ring in the center. Roll the dough 3 mm (1/8 in) thick and press the circle into the ring. Cut the dough level with the top of the ring with a paring knife.

Prick the bottom with a fork so bubbles don't form under the crust during baking.

Wash the berries, remove stems, then spread them in the tart mold.

Whisk together the eggs, sugar and cornstarch and pour over the berries.

Bake at 250 C (490 F) about 20 minutes or until the crust is browned and the custard is set. Transfer to a rack to cool.

Plate Presentation

Just before serving, sprinkle the tart with powdered sugar.

133

Warm Chocolate Madeleines

"Restaurant Vidal" *(St-Julien-Chapteuil)*
Chef : Jean-Pierre Vidal

Ingredients

Madeleines:
440 g (15 1/3 oz) sugar
20 g (2/3 oz) trimoline
300 g (10 oz) eggs
250 g (8 oz) heavy cream
25 g (scant 1 oz) baking powder
700 g (1 lb 6 1/2 oz) flour
250 g (8 oz) unsalted butter, melted
50 g (1 2/3 oz) cocoa

Ice cream:
1 L (1 qt) whole milk
250 g (8 oz) sugar
50 g (1 1/2 oz) trimoline
8-10 egg yolks
150 ml (5 fl oz) light cream
3 vanilla beans, split

Procedure

To make the madeleines, whisk together the eggs, sugar and trimoline. Stir in the cream, cocoa and baking powder then gently fold in the flour and melted butter. Fill the prepared madeleine molds and bake at 200 C (400 F) for 15 minutes.

To make the ice cream, bring the milk to a boil with half the sugar, trimoline and vanilla beans. In a bowl, whisk the remaining sugar, egg yolks and cream. Pour the hot milk into the egg mixture, blend then return to the pot and cook over low heat, stirring constantly, until the custard coats the spoon (temperature will be 80 C (180 F)).
Cool the mixture then churn in an ice cream freezer.
Serve the ice cream with the freshly baked madeleines.

Pinenut Tart

"Relais Ste-Victoire" *(Beaurecueil)*
Chef : René Bergés

Procedure

Roll out the dough and press it into a 20 cm (9 in) pastry ring

(or pie pan) and place on a moistened baking sheet.
Cream the butter and blend with the powdered sugar and almonds.
Beat in the egg then the sugar and whisk until light. Add the pastry cream and stir to blend.
Fill the tart shell with this mixture and sprinkle the pine nuts evenly over the top. Bake at 350 F about 20-25 minutes or until the crust is lightly browned and the filling is set.

Ingredients (6 servings)

250 g (8 oz) sweet pie pastry	50 g (1 2/3 oz) sugar
25 g (scant 1/4 cup) powdered sugar	50 g (1 2/3 oz) unsalted butter
25 g (scant 1/4 cup) ground almonds	1 large egg
	100 g (3 1/2 oz) pastry cream
	100 g (3 1/2 oz) pine nuts

Banana "Delice" with Creole Sauce

"Le Grand Ecuyer" *(Cordes)*
Chef : Yves Thuriès

Ingredients (4 serving)

Banana "Delice"
1 kg (about 2 lbs) bananas
Butter, sugar, rum
300 ml (10 fl oz) grapefruit juice
200 ml heavy cream
10 large eggs, separated
100 g (3 1/2 oz) sugar
50 g (1 2/3 oz) flour
1 package unflavored gelatin
300 g (10 oz) sugar

Creole Sauce
400 g (14 oz) bananas
Juice of 2 lemons
500 ml (2 cups) crème fraîche
750 g (1 1/2 lbs) sugar
200 ml (scant 1 cup) water
150 ml (5 fl oz) rum

Creole Sauce

Purée the bananas with the lemon juice in a food processor. Bring the crème fraîche to a boil and add the mashed bananas. Cook the sugar with the water to the light caramel stage, add the banana mixture and simmer for a few minutes. Pour the sauce through a conical strainer and stir in the rum.

Keep in a water bath, or make in advance and warm the sauce just before serving.

If it becomes too thick, thin with a little water or hot milk.

Plate Presentation

Serve the "Banana Delice" warm with Creole Sauce and a few slices of uncooked bananas.

Procedure

Peel the bananas and cut in half lengthwise. Cook the bananas in butter until slightly softened, turning them once to cook evenly.

When they are almost done, add sugar, cook to caramelize the sugar and flame with rum. Remove with a slotted spoon and set aside.

Make the grapefruit mousse.

First step is to make a grapefruit flavored pastry cream. Bring the juice and crème fraîche to a boil. Meanwhile, whisk the egg yolks with the 100 g (3 1/2 oz) sugar until light and stir in the flour. Stir the cream into the eggs then pour the mixture back into the pot, bring to a boil, whisking constantly. Cook about 1 minute to thicken, remove from heat, add the softened gelatin and mix well.

Meanwhile, make an Italian meringue. Beat the egg whites to firm peaks. Simultaneously, cook the 300 g (10 oz) sugar with 1/3 cup water to the soft ball stage. With the mixer on medium speed, pour the cooked sugar into the eggs in a steady stream, continue to beat a little until smooth and glossy. Immediately combine the warm meringue and the hot pastry cream. To form the "delice", place parchment paper on a tray and place a bottomless tart mold (rectangular is best) on the paper. Spread the mousse on the bottom and sides of the the mold. Place the cooked bananas down the center and cover with the remaining mousse, cover with plastic wrap and place in the freezer.

Remove the pastry ring, cut thick slices, sprinkle with powdered sugar, transfer to a heat proof plate and caramelize the top under the broiler. Finally, warm the dessert in a hot oven for 12-15 minutes.

Strawberries and Kiwis in Flaky Pastry

« Le Grand Ecuyer » *(Cordes)*
Chef : Yves Thuriès

Ingredients (12 servings)

3 eggs
Icing sugar
1 k (2 lbs) light cream
24 strawberries
12 kiwis

Make the puff pastry.
Make a dough with 500 g (1 lb) flour, 10 g (2 tsp) salt, 50 g (1 2/3 oz) unsalted butter and 250 ml (1 cup) cold water.

Procedure

After the dough has rested in the refrigerator, roll out into a thick circle, enclose 350-450 g (12-14 oz) unsalted butter in the center and roll into a long rectangle. Fold into thirds. Repeat the rolling and folding process 4 times, resting the dough between "turns".

Cut rectangles from the dough, brush with egg glaze and score the top with the tip of a knife. Bake at 200 C (400 F) 15-20 minutes. Just before the pastries are done, sprinkle with powdered sugar which will carmelize on the top.

Plate Presentation

Split the freshly baked, cooled pastries in half and spread the bottom with flavored whipped cream or pastry cream blended with whipped cream. Arrange the fruits in an attractive pattern. Serve immediately.

137

Strawberry Gratin with Monbazillac

« Le Cyrano » *(Bergerac)*
Chef : Jean-Paul Turon

Ingredients
(4 servings)

100 g (3 1/2 oz) sugar
3 egg yolks
300 ml (10 fl oz) Monbazillac
150 g (5 oz) strawberry coulis
60 medium strawberries, hulled

Note : that the strawberry coulis can be passed separately rather than being spooned on the bottom of the plate.

Procedure

In a non-reactive saucepan over a water bath, whisk together the egg yolks and sugar. Continue whisking as the eggs and sugar become warm and thick. Add the Monbazillac or other sweet wine a little at a time as the sauce thickens.
The sabayon is done when the mixture is light yellow and thick and holds a "ribbon" when the whisk is lifted.

Plate Presentation

On each heat-proof plate, spoon some of the strawberry sauce ("coulis") in the bottom then arrange 15 strawberries, pointed end up, on the plate.
Ladle sabayon over the strawberries and immediately brown the sauce under the broiler or with a torch.
Serve immediately.

Prune Bavarian Cream

"La Toque Blanche" *(Pujols)*
Chef : Bernard Lebrun

Ingredients (8 servings)

350 ml (12 fl oz) whole milk
4 egg yolks
125 g (4 oz) sugar
1 tbl. powdered gelatin

200 ml (7 fl oz) whipping cream
200 g (7 oz) pitted prunes
Ladyfingers, sugar syrup
40 ml (1 1/3 fl oz) Armagnac or
  prune "eau de vie"

Procedure

Split the ladyfingers (depending on size) and brush them with sugar syrup. Place a circle of parchment paper in the bottom of a round cake mold and line the mold with the ladyfingers. Soften the gelatin in a little water.

To make the crème anglaise which is the base of the bavarian cream, heat the milk to a simmer in a heavy saucepan and in a bowl whisk together the egg yolks and sugar until light. Off the heat, stir the gelatin sponge into the hot milk, then whisk the hot

milk into the egg mixture. Return the custard to the saucepan and cook over very low heat, stirring constantly until the mixture coats the back of the spoon. Strain and cool the mixture in a wide open bowl.

Purée the prunes with the liquor in a food processor.
Whip the cream to soft peaks in a cold bowl.
When the crème anglaise is cooled (but not set), mix with the prune mixture then gently fold in the whipped cream. Fill the lined mold with the bavarian cream, cover the top with ladyfingers and chill in the freezer 2 hours or in the refrigerator overnight.

Plate Presentation

Serve slices of the Prune Bavarian cream with a little crème anglaise or a sauce made with puréed prunes mixed with Armagnac. A late harvest, sweet dessert wine would be delicious with this dessert.

French Toast "Ardennais"

"Hostellerie Lenoir" *(Auvillers-Les-Forges)*
Chef : Jean Lenoir

Hostellerie Lenoir
Auvillers-les-Forges

Ingredients
(4-5 servings)

1/2 loaf stale French bread
4 large eggs
150 g (5 oz) sugar
500 ml (2 cups) whole milk
Vanilla extract

Note: Fancy versions of French toast or "pain perdu" have appeared recently on the menus of French bistrots. This comforting dessert is a delicious use for day old baguettes.

Plate Presentation

Place the toast on plates with a doilie and sprinkle liberally with powdered sugar and serve immediately.

Procedure

Cut the bread into 1.5 cm (1/2 in) slices.
Separate the eggs and whip the egg whites to firm peaks with a pinch of salt.

Whisk the egg yolks with a little vanilla and 1/3 of the sugar until thick, then gently fold into the egg whites.

Warm the milk with the remaining sugar and flavor with a little vanilla. Dip the slices of bread into the milk to absorb the liquid without getting too soggy.

Allow the excess milk to drip from the slices without pressing on them then cover both sides with the egg mixture.

Heat butter and peanut oil in a heavy skillet and pan fry the bread on both sides until golden brown.

Walnut "Fondant"

"Le Moulin du Roc" *(Champagnac-de-Belair)*
Chef: Solange Gardillou

"Fondant" means "melting" in French which describes this melt-in-your-mouth dessert. The walnut fondant is traditionally served with a chocolate sauce.

Ingredients (10 servings)
300 g (10 oz) walnuts
250 g (8 oz) unsalted butter
150 g (5 oz) sugar

Pastry cream:	Chocolate sauce:
1 cup whole milk	250 g (8 oz) bittersweet chocolate
4 egg yolks	400 ml (14 fl oz) strong coffee
4 tbls. suhar	2 tbls. heavy cream
1 tsp. cornstarch	2 tbls. sugar
1 tsp. flour	75 g (2 1/2 oz) unsalted butter
2 tbls. Kirsch	

Procedure

To make the pastry cream, whisk together the sugar and egg yolks until light and thick. Stir in the cornstarch and flour then the Kirsch.

Bring the milk to a simmer in a heavy saucepan. Pour the hot milk over the egg mixture, whisk to blend then return to the saucepan. Stirring constantly, cook the pastry cream over medium heat until it bubbles and thickens. Transfer to a clean bowl to cool.

In a food processor, chop the walnuts very finely (not powdered). Cream the butter and sugar until light and creamy.

Mix the finely chopped walnuts and the butter mixture then stir in the cooled pastry cream.

Line a charlotte or cake mold with parchment paper and gently spoon the walnut fondant into the mold. Tap the mold on the counter to eliminate air pockets without deflating the mixture. Cover and refrigerate at least 12 hours.

To make the chocolate sauce, warm the coffee and add the chocolate. When the chocolate is melted, add the sugar and stir to blend. Stir in the cream. While the mixture is still slightly warm, stir in the butter to make a smooth, shiny sauce.

Plate Presentation

Unmold the walnut fondant and cut into slices.
Decorate each plate with walnut halves. To add a splash of color, top the slices with "sprinkles".
Serve the warm chocolate sauce on the side in individual dishes.

Caramel Meringues with Rich Chocolate Sauce

Hôtel d'Espagne *(Valençay)*
Chef : Maurice Fourré

Ingredients
(8 servings)

6 egg whites
250 g (8 oz) sugar
1 tsp gelatin, softened
Peanut oil

Chocolate sauce:
1 L (1 qt) whole milk
250 g (8 oz) semi-sweet
   chocolate
3 large eggs plus 3 egg yolks
400 g (14 oz) sugar

Plate Presentation

Unmold the chilled meringues and coat with the chocolate sauce.

Procedure

Whip the egg whites to stiff peaks and whisk in half the sugar.
Dissolve the remaining sugar in a little water and cook until it
_____. Stop the cooking with a little water, dissolve the
gelatin in the warm caramel and blend the caramel
meringue. Spoon the mixture into 8 oiled molds and
__.

Make the chocolate sauce. Bring the milk to a boil and add the
chocolate.
Whisk together the eggs, egg yolks and sugar.
Combine the milk and chocolate mixture into the eggs and cook
in a heavy saucepan, stirring constantly, over medium heat until
the mixture thickens. Cool the mixture before serving.

Lentil and Chestnut Gâteau

« La Cognette » *(Issoudun)*
Chef : Alain Nonnet

Ingredients (8 servings)

2 round chocolate genoise layers	100 g (3 1/2 oz) sugar
50 ml (4 tbls) rum	1 vanilla bean
200 g (6 1/2 oz) pastry cream	150 g (5 oz) cooked, peeled
150 g (5 oz) green lentils	chestnuts
500 ml (2 cups) whole milk	Chocolate glaze

Procedure

Combine the milk, sugar and lentils and cook over low heat until the lentils are soft.

To assemble the cake, moisten the bottom layer of chocolate genoise with rum and spread with pastry cream.

Cover the layer of pastry cream with the cooked chestnuts and lentils.

Place the second layer of genoise on top.

Coat the entire cake with chocolate glaze (or ganache).

143

Golden Delicious Apples in Truffle Cream

« Les Chênes Verts » *(Tourtour)*
Chef : Paul Bajade

Ingredients
(10 servings)

15 Golden Delicious apples,
   peeled, halved, seeded
4 tbls ground almonds
8 tbls powdered sugar
200 ml (7 fl oz) heavy cream
100 g (3 1/2 oz) unsalted butter
50 g (1 2/3 oz) fresh truffles,
   cleaned, cut in thin julienne
10 small tulip cookies filled
   with red fruits (garnish)
3 tbls truffle juice

les Chênes Verts
Tourtour

Paul BAJADE, Chef de Cuisine

Procedure

Place the apple halves on a baking sheet and sprinkle with the powdered almonds, half the powdered sugar, and place a bit of butter on each.
Bake at 150 C (300 F) about 15-20 minutes.
Meanwhile reduce the cream by half. Add the truffle juice. Over very low heat whisk in the remaining powdered sugar and butter.

Plate Presentation

Place three apple halves on each plate and the tulip filled with red fruits in the center.
Ladle sauce over the apples and garnish with truffle julienne.
Serve immediately.

Chocolate Marquise

«Château de Vauchoux» (Port-sur-Saône)
Chef: Jean-Michel Turin

Ingredients (12 servings)

Sponge cake:
6 eggs, separated
200 g (7 oz) sugar
150 g (5 oz) unbleached flour
60 g (2 oz) cocoa powder
200 ml (7 fl oz) Cognac

Chocolate mousse:
4 eggs separated
150 g (5 oz) sugar
100 ml (3.5 fl oz) water
240 g (scant 8 oz) bittersweet
covering chocolate
60 g (2 oz) unsalted butter

Procedure

To make the sponge cake: Separate the 6 eggs. Beat the yolks with 2/3 of the sugar until very thick and lemon-colored. The mixture will fall from the whisk in a ribbon.
Beat the whites to stiff peaks, then whisk in the remaining sugar to «tighten» the whites and keep them from getting grainy.

Sift the flour and cocoa together over the egg yolk mixture and gently fold in until mixed. Fold in the beaten egg whites, taking care not to deflate the mixture.
Butter and flour two round cake pans and fill each halfway with batter. Bake at 220 C (425 F) about 20-30 minutes or unil the cakes spring back in the center.
Unmold and transfer to a rack to cool.
To make the chocolate mousse: Combine the sugar and water in a heavy saucepan and cook to the «thread» stage; 106 C (230 F). Beat the egg whites to soft peaks. With the mixer on medium speed, pour the hot sugar syrup into the egg whites in a steady stream. Beat the meringue until completely cool.

Melt the chocolate in a waterbath or over very low heat. The temperature should not exceed 35 C (98 F). Whisk in the butter, then the egg yolks.

Gently incorporate the meringue into the chocolate mixture, being careful not to deflate the mousse.
To assemble the Marquise: Cut a cake in half and place each piece, cut side up in the bottom of a springform pan. Fill the mold to the top with mousse. Smooth the top with a metal spatula dipped in hot water. Refrigerate for 12 hours.
Run a knife around the mousse and unmold the cakes. Cover the top with a generous dusting of cocoa powder.

Plate Presentation

Slice generous portions of the marquise and place on plates just before serving.
Ladle vanilla or pistachio crème anglaise around the cake.

145

Caramelized Apple "Gâteau"

"Le Moulin du Roc" *(Champagnac-de-Belair)*
Chef: Solange Gardillou

Ingredients
(4 servings)

1.8 kg (3 lbs 10 oz)
    Golden Delicious apples
200 g (1 cup) sugar
20 g (2/3 oz) unsalted butter
Juice of 1 small lemon
1 tsp vanilla sugar

Plate Presentation

This dessert is best when served warm accompanied with crème anglaise (warm or cold) and a large scoop of vanilla ice cream.

Procedure

Peel the apples, remove the core and cut in thick slices.
Cover the bottom of a heavy saucepan (24 cm (10 in)) with the sugar, butter, lemon juice and vanilla sugar (or 1/2 tsp vanilla extract).
Place the apples in the pan and press down to compact them.
Cover the pan and cook the apples over low heat until soft.
Remove the cover, turn the heat to high to cook the liquid exuded by the apples.

When the liquid has caramelized, press on the apples to coat them well with caramel. Let cool slightly.
To unmold, place a plate on top and with one hand firmly pressing on the plate, flip the "gâteau" out of the pan.

146

Caramelized Apples

"Auberge du Vieux Moulin" *(Aubigney)*
Chef: Elisabeth Mirbey

Ingredients
(4 servings)

8 apples
200 g (6 1/2 oz) sugar
150 g (5 oz) unsalted butter
Cinnamon
Vanilla ice cream

Procedure

Peel the apples, cut each into 6 pieces and remove the core. Toss the apples in half the sugar with a pinch of cinnamon.

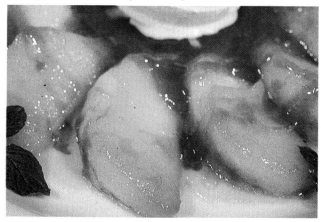

Heat the butter in a non-stick pan. When the butter bubbles, add the apples in a single layer and cook over medium heat until golden brown. Turn the slices over to caramelize the other side.

Plate Presentation

Serve this dessert on a large, warm plate.
Fan the apples slices around the plate.

Put the remaining sugar into the pan that the apples cooked in and cook the sugar until it caramelizes, stirring frequently.
Place a scoop of vanilla ice cream in the center of the apples and drizzle the caramel sauce over the apples and ice cream.
Serve immediately.

Wine-Poached Pears with Cassis Sorbet

« Le Jardin Gourmand » *(Sartrouville)*
Chefs : Régis Ligot and Christian Gipteau

Ingredients
(4 servings)

4 large pears (ripe, firm)
500 ml (2 cups) good red wine
250 g (8 oz) sugar
Cinnamon stick
200 g (7 oz) cassis in syrup
1/2 L (1 pint) cassis sorbet
16 fresh mint leaves
Baked meringues

With a spoon or piping bag, fill the cavity inside the cooled pears with cassis sorbet and place in the center of the plates.

Garnish around the edge of each plate with 4 small scoops of sorbet decorated with mint leaves.

Place the snow-white meringue on the magenta coulis and serve immediately. Pass the remaining sauce separately.

Procedure

Peel the pears and core them from the bottom to keep them whole.

Combine the wine, sugar and cinnamon stick in a non-reactive pot large enough to hold the pears.

Add the pears to the wine, bring to a simmer and cook until the pears are just tender (test with the point of a knife). Remove the pot from the heat and allow the pears to cool completely in the liquid.

Drain the black currants («cassis») and purée in the food processor. Add enough of the poaching liquid to make a thin sauce («coulis»). Make small baked meringues that are crisp but not browned.

Plate Presentation

Trim the bottoms of the pears to make them flat so they will stand up on the plates.

Fruit «Minestrone» with Almond Raviolis and Cheese Ice Cream

« Aux Armes de Champagne » *(L'Epine)*
Chef : Patrick Michelon

Ingredients
(2 servings)

Ripe, seasonal fruit salad:
(in autumn for example)

1 apricot
1 fig
6 small, yellow plums
2 red plums
1 peach
Small bunch grapes

Wash and cut the fruits into neat slices. Refrigerate.

"Raviolis":
2 sheets filo pastry
Unsalted butter, melted

Almond cream («frangipane»):
150 g (5 oz) each unsalted butter, powdered sugar and powdered almonds, 30 g (1 oz flour), 1 large egg.
Cream butter, sugar and egg. Stir in flour and a drop of rum.

Brush the sheets of dough with butter. A ravioli mold can be used to form these pastries. Place spoonfuls of almond cream at even intervals cover with the second sheet of dough and press to seal. Cut the «raviolis» and bake at 180 C (360 F) for 5 minutes.

Cheese Ice Cream (yield 1 L (1 qt)):
500 g (1 lb) cheese

Note: Chef Michelon uses a rich local cheese «Chaource». St André or whole milk ricotta cheese (drained 1 hour) can be substituted.
400 ml 14 fl oz sugar syrup:
1 L (1 qt) water/1.7 kg (3 1/3 lbs) sugar
60 ml (2 fl oz) lemon juice

Mix all ingredients until smooth and churn in an ice cream freezer.

"Beggar's Purse" with Pears Cooked in Spiced Wine

"Le Prieuré" *(Villeneuve-Lès-Avignon)*
Chef : Serge Chenet

Ingredients (4 servings)

4 pears
1 bottle red wine
500 ml (2 cups) orange juice
1 orange, 1 lemon, sliced
4 strips of orange zest, candied
100 ml (3.5 fl oz) sugar syrup
2 cinnamon sticks
1 vanilla bean, split
5 juniper berries
4 star anise, 2 cloves
1/2 tsp peppercorns
Filo dough, clarified butter
Candied orange peel (long strips)

Fresh Vanilla Ice Cream:
500 ml (2 cups) whole milk
100 ml (3 1/2 fl oz) light cream
125 g (4 oz) sugar
8 egg yolks
2 vanilla beans, split

Heat the milk and cream
with the vanilla beans.
Whisk the eggs and sugar.
Whisk hot milk into the eggs.
Return mixture to the heat.
Cook over low heat, stirring
constantly until mixture coats
the spoon.
Strain through a conical sieve.
Process in ice cream freezer.

Procedure

Peel and core the pears and rub with lemon.
Combine the spices, lemon and orange slices, orange juice, sugar syrup and wine in a large, non-reactive pot. Bring to a boil, cover and let aromatics infuse, off the heat, about 30 minutes. Add the pears, bring to a simmer and poach until just tender. Remove the pears with a slotted spoon and reduce the poaching liquid to concentrate the flavor. Return pears to the reduced liquid and spoon it over to coat well.
Cut filo dough into long 1 inch strips, brush with clarified butter and arrange the strips in a star, overlapping in the center. Place a pear in the center, pull the strips of dough up and over the pear to form a "beggar 's purse" and "tie" the top with a strip of candied orange peel.
Bake at 375-400 F about 5 minutes or until golden brown.

Plate Presentation

Whisk a little unsalted butter into the reduced poaching liquid and spoon the sauce on the plates.
Place the pear in pastry on the plate with a scoop of vanilla ice cream and decorate with fresh mint leaves.

Frozen Soufflé with Batavia

" Le Bourbon"

(Yssingeaux)

Chef: André Perrier

Ingredients

10 egg yolks
300 ml (10 fl oz) sugar syrup (60 degrees)
100 ml "Batavia" or Kirsch
Chopped, candied orange zest
1 L (1 qt) whipping cream
Crème anglaise

Procedure

Pour the hot sugar syrup into the egg yolks and beat until thick and cool.
Whisk in the Batavia liqueur (fresh cherry juice can be substituted for the liqueur) and the chopped orange zest.
Whip the cream to soft peaks and fold into the egg yolk mixture.
Fill individual molds (or pastry circles set on a baking sheet) and place in the freezer until frozen.

Plate Presentation

Ladle crème anglaise on the plates.
Unmold the frozen soufflés and place on the plates.
Decorate with a tulip cookie filled whipped cream, candied orange peels and candied cherries.

Thyme «Craquelins» with Lavender Honey Ice Cream and Chocolate

« Le Vieux Castillon » *(Castillon-du-Gard)*
Chef: Gilles Dauteuil

Orange Butter

125 ml (1 cup) orange juice
40 g (1 1/3 oz) unsalted butter
1 tsp powdered sugar

Reduce the orange juice by 3/4. Whisk in the butter a little at a time. Return to a simmer, remove from the heat and stir in the sugar.

Chocolate «Velouté»

500 ml (2 cups) light cream
90 g (3 oz) sugar
4 egg yolks
350 g (12 oz) covering chocolate, chopped

Whisk the yolks and sugar until thick and lemon-colored. Boil the cream, stir it into the yolk mixture. Return to the pot and cook over very low heat, stirring constantly, until the custard thickens enough to coat a spoon. Off the heat, stir in the chopped chocolate. Cover and refrigerate 12 hours. Use a melon baller dipped in hot water to form marble-sized balls of the chocolate.

«Craquelin» with thyme

50 g (1 2/3 oz) sugar
40 g (1 1/3 oz) unsalted butter
40 ml (3 tbls) heavy cream
50 g (1 2/3 oz) chopped almonds
1 branch fresh thyme

Combine the sugar, butter and cream and bring to a boil. Stir in the almonds and crushed thyme leaves. Spread the batter in thin circles on a parchment paper-lined baking sheet and bake at 180 C (375 F) until brown and crisp.

Honey ice cream

500 ml (2 cups) whole milk
500 ml (2 cups) light cream
8 egg yolks
25 g (2 tbls) sugar
175 g (6 oz) lavender honey

Whisk together the yolks, sugar and honey until thick and lemon-colored. Bring the milk and cream to a boil and stir into the egg yolk mixture. Return to the pot and cook over very low heat, stirring constantly, until the mixture thickens enough to coat a spoon. The temperature should not exceed is 84 C (185 F).

Chocolate «Chiffonade»

125 ml (1 cup) whole milk
4 large eggs
65 g (2 oz) sugar
25 ml (2 tbls) peanut oil
10 g (1/3 oz) cornstarch
20 g (2/3 oz) flour
100 g (3 1/2 oz) covering chocolate, chopped

Whisk together the yolks and sugar until thick and lemon-colored and stir in the cornstarch and flour. Bring the milk and oil to a boil and stir into the egg yolk mixture. Return to the heat and cook like a pastry cream. Pour the custard over the chopped chocolate and stir until smooth. Spread the mixture in thin bands on a sheet of parchment. Bake at 180 C (360 F) until set. Remove from the baking sheet and cool.

152

Chestnut Dome with Frozen Coffee Parfait

"Auberge du Père Bise" *(Talloires)*
Chef : Sophie Bise

Ingredients (8 servings)

8 domes made from covering chocolate

Coffee Parfait:
4 egg yolks
125 g (4 oz) sugar
50 ml (1 2/3 fl oz) strong coffee
500 ml (2 cups) whipping cream

Crème Anglaise:
500 ml (2 cups) whole milk
125 g (4 oz) sugar
6 egg yolks

Chestnut Mousse:
Candied chestnuts
(more for decoration)
Whipping cream
Cognac
Candied chestnuts

Procedure

To make the coffee parfait, cook the sugar with a little water to the soft ball stage. Beat the yolks until thickened. With the mixer running, pour the sugar syrup over the eggs, then the coffee. Beat

until cool. Whip the cream and fold into egg mixture.
Spoon into the parfait molds and place in the freezer 2 hours. To make the crème anglaise, heat the milk, whisk together the egg yolks and the sugar. Stir the hot milk into the eggs, return the mixture to the pot and cook low heat, stirring constantly until the custard coats the spoon. Strain and cool quickly over a bowl of ice. To make the chestnut mousse, puree candied chestnuts with a little cream and Cognac to make a smooth mixture. Fold in a little whipped cream and with a spatula, line the chocolate domes with the mousse.

Plate Presentation

Unmold the coffee parfaits in the center of the plates.
Place the chocolate domes over the parfaits.
Spoon crème anglaise around the dome and decorate with a few candied chestnuts.

153

Roasted Figs with Sabayon

"Les Délices du Château" *(Saumur)*
Chef: Pierre Millon

Ingredients (4 servings)

12 large fresh figs
50 g (1 2/3 oz) unsalted butter
125 ml (1 cup) white wine (see note)
3 egg yolks
4 tbls sugar
4 scoops coconut ice cream

Note: Chef Millon uses "Coteaux du Layon" for this dish, a rich white
wine from the Loire.

Procedure

Trim the stem of the figs and make a small criss-cross incision
in the top. Place in a heat-proof baking dish and sprinkle half the
sugar on the figs and place a little piece of butter on top.
Add the wine, bring to a simmer and poach for 15 minutes.

Meanwhile, whisk the egg yolks and remaining sugar over a
water bath until the mixture thickens.
When the figs are cooked, transfer them to a plate and whisk the
hot wine into the egg yolks.

Plate Presentation

Cover the bottom of the plates with the sabayon.
Arrange the figs on the plate and serve with a scoop of coconut
ice cream.

154

Frozen Nougat "Bûche" with Raspberries

"La Tour du Roy" *(Vervins-en-Thiérache)*
Chef: Annie Desvignes

Ingredients (4 servings)

Nougat:
100 g (3 1/2 oz) sugar
50 g (1 2/3 oz) honey
2 egg whites
100 g almond brittle
30 g (1 oz) raisins, soaked in rum
250 ml (1 cup) whipping cream
Orange blossom water

Raspberry sorbet

Baked meringue:
2 egg whites
125 g (4 oz) powdered sugar
50 g (1 2/3 oz) powdered almonds
Zested rind of 2 lemons

Procedure

To make the nougat, cook the sugar and honey to the soft ball stage (120 C (238 F). Meanwhile, beat 2 egg whites to soft peaks. Beat the the hot sugar syrup into the whites and beat on low speed until the meringue cools.
Beat the cream to soft peaks in a cold bowl. Fold the whipped cream, raisins and chopped almonds into the cooled meringue.

To make the meringue, beat 2 egg whites to stiff peaks with half the powdered sugar. Gently stir in the remaining sugar, powdered almonds and lemon zest.
Pipe out a band of meringue the width of the log shaped mold.
Bake at 200 C (400 F) about 10-12 minutes or until browned and crispy.
Fill the mold with alternating layers of frozen nougat and raspberry sorbet.
Top with the layer of baked meringue, cover and firm up the filling in the freezer.

Plate presentation. Turn out the dessert onto a platter and decorate with chocolate curls, candied fruits or candied chestnuts.

"Bouzy Rouge" Granité

"Hostellerie Lenoir" *(Auvillers-Les-Forges)*
Chef: Jean Lenoir

Ingredients

200 g (6 1/2 oz/1 cup) sugar
250 ml (1 cup) water
Juice of 2 oranges
Juice of 1 lemon
Cinnamon
1 bottle Bouzy rouge
   (see note)

Plate Presentation

Scoop "chunks" of this icy granité into large Burgundy wine glasses ("ballons").
Decorate the dessert with chilled slices of white peach poached in jasmine tea and honey.

Note: Bouzy is the only still red wine produced in the Champagne region. Choose a good quality red wine for this granité.

Procedure

Combine the sugar and water in a saucepan, bring to a boil. Skim the surface and cool the syrup.

Add the fruit juices and a pinch of cinnamon to the sugar syrup. Stir in the wine and freeze in an ice cream maker.

Muscadet Sorbet with Mint

"La Châtaigneraie" *(Sucé-sur-Erdre)*
Chef : J. Delphin

Ingredients (6-8 servings)

250 g (8 oz) sugar
250 ml (1 cup) water
1 bottle Muscadet
Mint leaves

Procedure

Bring the water and sugar to a boil and simmer a few minutes to completely dissolve the sugar. Pour the hot syrup over the mint leaves, cover and leave to infuse until the syrup is cooled.

Purée the leaves with the syrup in a blender or food processor and strain the liquid through a fine-meshed conical sieve or a paper filter.

Add the Muscadet and freeze in an ice cream maker according to manufacturer's directions.

Plate Presentation

Scoop irregular, "rock-like" shapes of the sorbet and serve them in attractive glasses.

Decorate with two pretty mint leaves on the top.

Note: This sorbet does not contain a stabilizer so it will crystalize if left frozen too long. It is recommended to serve it the day it is made.

Ratafia Sorbet

"Hostellerie Lenoir" *(Auvillers-Les-Forges)*
Chef: Jean Lenoir

Ingredients

200 g (6 1/2 oz/1 cup) sugar
500 ml (2 cups) water
Juice of one lemon
500 ml (2 cups) Ratafia de Champagne

Procedure

Combine the sugar and water in a saucepan and bring to a boil.
Skim the surface and cool the syrup.
Stir in the lemon juice and Ratafia.
Freeze in an ice cream maker.

Note: Ratafia is a combination of unfermented grape juice and brandy.

Plate Presentation

Decorate the rims of champagne flutes by dipping in water (or beaten egg whites) then in a bowl of granulated brown sugar. Note that the egg whites combine with the sugar to make a more even rim of sugar which doesn't melt like the water and sugar.

Garnish the scoops of sorbet with peeled (and seeded) grapes that have been macerated in "Marc de Champagne" and serve with a crispy cookie (the traditional accompaniment is "langue de chat" or "cat's tongue").

Frozen Nougat Swans with Blue Curaçao

"La Belle Époque" *(Bellegarde-sur-Valserine)*
Chef : Michel Sevin

Ingredients (4 servings)

500 ml (2 cups) light cream
3 egg whites
125 g (4 oz) sugar
200 g (6 1/2 oz) candied fruits, chopped
300 g (10 oz) praline, chopped

250 g (8 oz) white covering chocolate
(to form the neck and wings)
10 g (1/3 oz) dark chocolate

(for eyes)
200 ml (6.5 fl oz) blue Curaçao
Seasonal fruits, peeled, sliced

Procedure

Form 12 necks and 24 wings with melted white covering chocolate and 12 eyes with melted dark chocolate.
Make an Italian meringue with the egg whites and sugar (cooked to the soft ball stage). Beat until cooled.
In a cold bowl, whip the cream to stiff peaks.
With a spatula, gently fold together the meringue and whipped cream then fold in the chopped praline and candied fruits.
Place this mixture in the freezer for two hours.

Plate Presentation

Form 12 "football-shaped" scoops ("quenelles") of the frozen nougat and insert the chocolate "necks" and "wings" to make the swans.
Pour 50 ml (4 tbls) of the Curaçao on one half of each plate.
Arrange seasonal fruits on the other side. Place 3 swans on the blue "pool" of sauce on each plate. Serve at once.

159

Apple «Mille Feuille» with Frozen Calvados Soufflé

« Hôtel du Dauphin » *(L'Aigle)*
Chefs: Michel Bernard and Jean-Philip Fulep

Ingredients (4 servings)

Apple slices and garnish:
4 Golden Delicious apples
1 Granny Smith apple
50 g (about 3 tbls) sugar syrup
50 g (3 tbls) unsalted butter
25 g (2 tbls) sugar
20 ml (2 1/2 tbls) Calvados
200 ml (7 fl oz) crème anglaise

Frozen souffle mixture:
meringue: 2 egg whites with
    100 g (3 1/2 oz) sugar
sabayon: 2 egg yolks with
    15 g (1/2 oz) sugar
50 ml (4 tbls) Calvados
25 ml (2 tbls) heavy cream

Procedure

To make the frozen Calvados soufflé:
Make an Italian meringue with the egg whites and 100 g sugar.
Make a sabayon with the yolks, 15 g sugar and half the Calvados.
Whip the cream to stiff peaks, stir in the remaining Calvados.
Gently fold in the meringue and sabayon. Transfer to a shallow
dish cover and place in the freezer 24 hours.

To prepare the apples:
Peel and core the Granny Smith apple and cut into 16 thin
slices.
Dip the slices in the sugar syrup then lay flat on a parchment paper-
lined baking sheet and bake at 80 C (150 F) for 2 1/2 hours.
Peel and core the Golden Delicious apples and cut each into 5-
6 sections. Melt the butter and sugar, add the apples and cook
over medium-high heat until lightly caramelized. Flame with
Calvados.

Plate Presentation

For each serving, stack four candied apple slices with frozen
soufflé in between. (Use a flat ice cream scoop or spatula to
form flat, round portions of the soufflé; these «slices» could be
portioned ahead and frozen for quicker assembly.)
Place the «millefeuille» in the center, arrange the caramelized
apples around and spoon crème anglaise on the plate. Serve
immediately.

Chapter 6 - Additional Recipes and Information

In this chapter, we present 83 additional recipes classified by courses. Although these recipes are not accompanied by photographs, the original ideas will tempt you to try them. On page 185 is a list of the chefs who have contributed the recipes in this chapter.

Starting on page 186 is a list of the names and information about the 37 chefs who contributed recipes in the first five chapters.

Here you will find:

1. Restaurant address, telephone and fax.
2. An introduction to the restaurant and messages from several of the chefs to colleagues, apprentices and customers.
3. Author Pierre Paillon has added a few comments on particular recipes, pointing out special techniques or ingredients.

Before visiting one of these restaurants, it is recommemded to consult an up-to-date guide for commentary on the menus and general information on days and hours of service, etc.

At the end of this book is a "Glossary of Professional Terms" which explains many of the specific culinary terms used in the recipes.

Additional Recipes

Introduction to « Meat Dishes » p. 95 : the end.

4. Râgouts

In France, there are many types of stews or «ragouts» and these are named according to the methods used to cook the meat and thicken the sauce. Although the differences are sometimes subtle each has its own unique flavor.

«Sauté» for example starts with meats that are «sautéed» in fat the flour is added which blends with the fat to make a «roux». Liqui is added which thickens when it heats with the roux.

«Blanquette» is a ragout of veal, poultry or lamb in which cubes of meat are cooked in water or stock «à blanc» (white) which keeps the meat whiter in color. The sauce is simmered to concentrate the flavor with mushrooms and a squeeze of lemon juice adds a a touch of needed acidity.

«Civet» of rabbit or wild boar always indicates a stew with a blood thickened sauce. «Matelote» is a ragout of eel with red wine, «fricassée» is usually made with chicken, «salmis» with game birds and «daube» is a beef ragout.

5. Braised Meats

The original pot for braising meats was made of cast iron, which was set in the embers of the fire and glowing coals were placed on top so that the meat cooked slowly from above and beneath.

Today we have to settle for the modern «braisière», which is a heavy gauge aluminium or tin-lined copper pot with a tight fitting lid. Meats to be braised are usually large cuts which are well trimmed the cooked at a moderate temperature for a long time. Beef and mutton, meats with dard red flesh are excellent choices for this cooking method (beef ribs and leg and shoulder of mutton are the cuts most often used). The French braise other meats as well, such as veal loin or lamb shank.

A thick slice from the ham with the rind attached (adds flavor and a rich gelatinous texture), braised slowly then served with glazed chestnuts and Brussel sprouts is a favorite dish.

To braise the meats, they are first seared on all sides in a little hot fat to scal in juices, then liquid is added to cover about halfway. The cooking vessel is covered and the dish is cooked in a moderate oven.

Dublin Bay Prawns with Creamy Herb Sauce

Ingredients (4 servings)

16 large prawns, shells removed
250 ml (1 cup) chicken stock
2 egg yolks
100 m (3.5 fl oz) heavy cream
Small bunch fresh chervil, chopped
Juice of 1 lemon
2 tomatoes
Salt, pepper

Procedure

Combine the stock and egg yolks in a bowl over a water bath. Whisk constantly as the mixture cooks and thickens. Transfer this sabayon to a bowl over ice and whisk as it cools slightly to stop the cooking.

Whip the cream to firm peaks and fold into the sabayon along with the chopped chervil. Season to taste and keep warm (not hot) in a water bath.

Peel and seed the tomatoes and cut into julienne. Pan fry the prawns in hot olive oil until golden, cut in half lengthwise.

Plate Presentation

Spoon equal amounts of sauce on four heated plates. Arrange the prawns in a star and mound the tomato julienne in the center.

(J.L. Martin)

Violet Soufflé

Ingredients (4 servings)

200 ml (7 fl oz) whole milk
3 eggs, spearated
50 g (1 2/3 oz) sugar
50 g (1 2/3 oz) flour

1 pinch salt
3 tbls chrystalized violets
Fresh violets (organically grown)
Powdered sugar

Procedure

Bring the milk to a boil.

Whisk together the egg yolks and sugar until thick and light, then blend in the flour.

Stir the hot milk inot the eggs, return to the saucepan and cook until thepastry cream bubbles and thickens.

Beat the egg whites to firm peaks and fold into the pastry cream and add the candied violets.

Butter a large soufflé dish and coat with sugar. Fill with the soufflé mixture and bake at 220 C (425 F) until puffed, about 20-25 minutes.

Presentation

Sprinkle the top of the baked soufflé with powdered sugar and decorate with fresh violets (which are edible if organically grown). Place on a platter and serve at once.

(L. Piguet)

Salmon Paupiettes with Oysters

Ingredients (6 servings)

1 dozen oysters
1 kg (2 lbs) salmon fillets
1/2 cup dry white wine
Fresh herbs, chopped
250 g (8 oz) unsalted butter
125 ml (1/2 cup) heavy cream
2 large eggs
4 shallots, chopped

1 cup fish stock
Olive or peanut oil
Salt, pepper, nutmeg and Cayenne pepper

Procedure

Remove the skin from the salmon, rinse under cold water and trim 150 g (5 oz) of flesh for the filling.

Butterfly the fillets and cut into 6 thin pieces. Marinate 1 hour with 1/4 cup white wine, salt, pepper and chopped herbs.

Purée the reserved salmon and blend in 75 g (2 1/2 oz) softened butter, 75 ml 2.5 fl oz) cream and 2 eggs. Season with salt, pepper, nutmeg, and Cayenne pepper.

Open the oysters and strain the liquid into the fish stock.

Lay out the marinated salmon fillets on the work surface and spread with salmon mousseline. Place two oysters in the center and roll the fillet around the oysters to form "paupiettes".

Place, seam side down, in a shallow baking dish and cover with the fish stock. Bring to a very low simmer and gently poach 10-12 minutes.

Meanwhile make the butter sauce. Cook the shallots in a little butter then add the remaining white wine and a little white wine vinegar; reduce until the liquid is evaporated.

Add the cream, then whisk in the remaining butter. Season to taste with salt and freshly ground white pepper.

Plate Presentation

Place the paupiettes in the center of heated plates and cover with butter sauce. Decorate the dish with chopped chives and a puff pastry "fleuron", a bite-size pastry cut in a pretty shape and baked until golden.

(S. Letrone)

Onions "Auxonnaise"

Ingredients (8 servings)

8 large onions, peeled
200 ml (7 fl oz) oil
1 bottle dry white wine
2 tbls tomato paste
500 ml (2 cups) chicken stock
200 g (7 oz) unsalted butter
50 g (1 2/3 oz) flour
50 ml (4 tbls) Cognac
8 medium eggs
8 small slices ham
8 slices sandwich bread
1 kg (about 2 lbs) potatoes
100 ml (3.5 fl oz) heavy cream
Salt, pepper, bouquet garni, fresh coriander

Procedure

Combine the wine, stock and tomato paste in a large baking dish with a cover. Place the onions in the dish with the bouquet garni in the middle and season with salt, pepper and chopped coriander. Cover and cook in a low oven for 1 1/2-2 hours until the onions are tender.
Strain the liquid and keep the onions warm. .
Make a roux with 3 tbls each butter and flour. Whisk in enough cooking liquid to make a velouté. Finish the sauce with Cognac and cream. Bring to a simmer then season to taste. Pour the sauce over the onions and keep warm.
Peel the potatoes and cut into small even shapes. Steam or boil.
Trim the crusts of the bread, spread with butter and toast until golden in the oven.
Poach the eggs in simmering water, remove with a slotted spoon, and place on the toasted bread. Place a slice of ham on each egg and transfer to heated plates.

Plate Presentation

Place an onion next to each egg and spoon sauce over the onions. Arrange two potatoes next to each onion.
Sprinkle chopped parsley over the eggs and onions and serve immediately.

(J. Houbron)

164

Sardine Tart with Tomato Basil Sauce

Ingredients (4-6 servings)

150 g (5 oz) pie pastry
20 sardines
5 tbls heavy cream or crème fraîche
4-6 spinach leaves
6 ripe tomatoes
1 branch fresh basil
1 tbl olive oil
Salt, pepper

Procedure

Rinse the sardines under cold water and remove the fillets. Set aside 24 fillets and purée the rest with the cream.
Roll out the dough and press into a tart ring. Line with foil or parchment, fill with pie weights and bake about 10-15 minutes at 200 C (400 F).

Cool the tart shell and spread the sardine purée in the bottom. Dip the trimmed spinach leaves in boiling water and lay on top of the purée. Arrange the sardine fillets on top in a star pattern and bake the tart 10 minutes.

Meanwhile, peel and seed the tomatoes. Purée in the food processor and press through a sieve. Heat the «coulis» without cooking. Add a little chopped basil and olive oil.

Plate Presentation

Cut the tart into 6 portions and decorate with basil leaves.
Serve the hot tomato sauce separately.

(D. Lecadre)

Cepe Gratin

Ingredients (4 servings)

4 large, fresh cepes
150 g (5 oz) lean pork
30 g (1 oz) caul fat
40 g (1 1/3 oz) unsalted butter
Salt, pepper, parsley, garlic

Procedure

Trim and wash the cepes. Cut off the caps and set aside. Chop the stems coarsely. Sauté in butter with garlic, season with salt and pepper and toss with chopped parsley. Grind the pork and mix with the mushrooms.
Fill the cepes with the pork fillling and wrap with caul fat. Place the cepes in a buttered heat-proof baking dish. Cook in a hot oven 15-18 minutes.

Plate Presentation

Place each mushroom in the center of a heated plate and garnish with deep-fried parsley. Serve immediately.

(M. Prades)

French Andouille with Sorrel

Ingredients (1 serving)

3 thick slices French andouille
(about 100-120 g/scant 4 oz)
120 g (scant 4 oz) sorrel
30 g (1 oz) unsalted bbutter
50 ml (4 tbls) heavy cream or creme fraiche
Salt, freshly ground pepper

Procedure

Trim and wash the sorrel.
Melt the butter, add the sorrel and lightly season with salt and pepper. When the sorrel is wilted, add the cream and cook over very low heat 5-6 minutes. Meanwhile, grill or pan fry the slices of andouille.

Plate Presentation

Mound the sorrel in the center of the plate nad arrange the slices of andouille on top.
Serve with small or "turned" boiled potatoes.
Serve very hot.

(Hotel de la Poste - Domfront)

Snail Beignets

Ingredients (1 serving)

6-8 snails
30 g (1 oz) unsalted butter
1 tbl chopped shallots
Crushed garlic
Salt and freshly ground pepper
Beignet batter:
100 g (3 1/2 oz) sifted flour
2 tbls walnut oil
1 egg yolk and 2 egg whites
200 ml (7 fl oz) warm milk or beer
1 tbl chopped chives
1 small bunch fresh parsley
Peanut oil for frying

Procedure

Rinse the snails under cold water and dry. Sauté in butter with shallots and garlic. Season with salt and pepper and keep warm.

To make the beignet batter, whisk oil, egg yolk and liquid into the flour. Season with salt and pepper and add chopped chives. Just before serving, beat the egg whites to firm peaks and fold into the batter.

Heat oil in a shallow pan. Coat the snails in the batter and deep fry until golden brown. Transfer to a paper towel to absorb excess oil. Wash and thoroughly dry the parsley. Deep fry by plunging into the oil and removing as soon as the parsley is crisp but still green.

Plate Presentation

Place the beignets on a folded napkin on a plate, garnish with fried parsley and serve immediately.

(L. Piguet)

Kidney Omelette

Ingredients (2-4 servings)

1 veal kidney
6-10 eggs
Unsalted butter
Salt, freshly ground pepper
Brown sauce with chopped truffles, cream and chopped tomatoes
Chopped herbs

Procedure

Trim the kidneys, remove the fat in the center and slice thinly. Season lightly and sauté medium rare in butter.
Whisk the eggs with a little salt and pepper. Heat butter in a pan, add the eggs and cook until almost set. Arrange the slices of kidney on top and transfer to a heated plate. Spoon sauce over the kidneys and sprinkle with chopped herbs.

(F. Laustriat)

Eggplant Stuffed with Rice "Arlesienne"

Ingredients (4 servings)

200 g (7 oz) rice
1 1/2 cups chicken broth
1 kg (2 lbs) clams, rinsed
4 medium eggplant
2 onions, sliced
1 garlic clove
50 g (1 2/3 oz) grated parmesan
Salt, pepper, saffron
Fresh breadcrumbs
4 tsps unsalted butter

Procedure

Cook the onions in 2 tsps butter. Add the rice and sauté briefly. Heat the broth and add the rice. Season with salt and pepper, cover and cook very low heat, about 15 minutes or until all the liquid is absorbed.
Open the clams over high heat and lift from the pot with a slotted spoon, remove the shells. Strain the clam liquid though a coffee filter or cheesecloth.
Cut the eggplants lengthwise. Cook in salted boiling water until tender. Scoop out the flesh without tearing the skin. Chop the eggplant, then stir in the rice, clams, garlic and season with salt, pepper and a pinch of saffron. Spoon the filling into the eggplant skins and place in a baking dish. Cover with breadcrumbs and grated cheese, sprinkle with melted butter and brown in a hot oven.

(P. Paillon)

Veal Sweetbreads in Puff Pastry with Morels and Truffles

Ingredients (8 servings)

500 g (1 lb) veal sweetbreads
800 g (1 lb 10 oz) prepared puff pastry
150 g (5 oz) button mushrooms, sliced
100 g (3 1/2 oz) unsalted butter
4 tbls flour
60 g (2 oz) dried morels
40 g (1 1/3 o z) canned truffles (chopped)
1 L (1 qt) Madiera
500 ml (2 cups) dry white wine
1 cup chicken or veal stock
3 tbls heavy cream or crème fraîche
2 carrots, 3 shallots, thyme, bay leaf
Juice of 1 small lemon
1 egg yolk
Salt, pepper

Procedure

Soak the morels and rinse several times to eliminate all sand and dirt. Cover with stock and simmer until tender. Trim and wash the button mushrooms and cook over high heat with a little butter and lemon juice.

Degorge the sweetbreads under cold running water. Blanch in simmering salted water for 5 minutes then cool. Remove the thin skin, nerves and fat.

Braise on a bed of sliced carrots and shallots (cooked in butter) and season with salt and pepper. Remove the sweetbreads and cut into dice, set aside.

To the pot, add the Madiera, wine, stock and cooking liquid from the mushrooms. Simmer for 1/2 hour then strain.
Prepare a roux with 4 tbls each butter and flour.

Whisk in braising liquid and simmer to make a velouté. Stir in the cream and liquid from the can of truffles and simmer a few minutes. Season to taste.

Combine the sauce with the diced sweetbreads, chopped truffles and cooked mushrooms and cool.

Roll out the puff pastry and cut two large circles. Place one circle on a baking sheet and prick with a fork. Spoon the sweetbreads mixture onto the pastry, leaving a 1 inch border.

Brush egg glaze around the edge and place the second circle of puff pastry on top. Press the edges to seal then make a neat design around the outside edge with the back of a paring knife.

Brush egg glaze over the top and score a crisscross design with the point of a paring knife. Make a small hole in the top for steam to escape during cooking.

Start cooking at 240 C (475 F) for 5 minutes, then lower the heat to 180 F (375 F) for about 30 minutes or until the pastry is golden.

(J. Rogliardo)

Lamb Sweetbreads with Crayfish

Ingredients (pour 6 servings)

1.5 kg (3 1/3 lbs) lamb sweetbreads
1 kg (2.2 lbs) crayfish
150 g (5 oz) unsalted butter
100 ml (3.5 fl oz) heavy cream or crème fraîche
50 ml (4 tbls) olive oil
100 ml (3.5 fl oz) crayfish (or fish) stock
250 ml (1 cup) dry white wine
75 ml (1/3 cup) Cognac
50 g (1 2/3 oz) morels, cooked
1 onion, 1 carrot, 2 shallots, 1 branch celery
4 tomatoes (chopped), 1 stem tarragon
1 bouquet garni, 2 garlic cloves (crushed)
1 tsp tomato paste

Procedure

Clean the crayfish and set aside 6 of them. Heat olive oil in a large heavy pot and add the remaining crayfish. Cook over high heat a few minutes, stirring constantly. Remove the shells from the tails and place the shells and crayfish heads in a large pot with sliced onion, shallots, carrot and celery.

Add salt and pepper and cook over high heat 10 minutes. Add half the Cognac and flame. Add the tomatoes, tomato paste, garlic cloves, tarragon and bouquet garni. Season with a little Cayenne pepper and add the white wine and crayfish stock. Simmer for 40 minutes. Strain the liquid, pressing on the ingredients to extract all the flavor.

Cook the reserved crayfish in court boullion (to keep them bright red).

Degorge the sweetbreads under cold running water. Blanch in lightly salted water, cool in cold water then remove the thin skin, nerves and fat.

Season with salt and pepper. Heat 3 tbls of the butter and brown the sweetbreads five minutes on each side.

Transfer the sweetbreads to a plate and deglaze the pot with the remaining Cognac. Add the crayfish sauce and reduce, adding the cream a little at a time. When the sauce thickens, remove from the heat and whisk in the remaining butter. Season to taste and keep warm in a water bath.

Plate Presentation

Slice the sweetbreads into 6 portions and overlap in the center of a platter. Garnish with the crayfish tails and morels. Ladle sauce over the sweetbreads and decorate the platter with the whole crayfish.

(P. Pomarède)

Lamb's Tongue with Crayfish and Tarragon

Ingredients (6 servings)

1 kg (2.2 lbs) crayfish
2 tbls tarragon leaves
1/2 cup dry white wine
250 ml (1 cup) heavy cream or crème fraîche
3 tbls olive oil
3 tbls unsalted butter
3 tomatoes
1 shallot, chopped
1 tbl tomato paste
Salt, pepper, Cayenne

12 lamb's tongues
1 truffle
1 onion, 1 carrot, 1 shallot
1 stem tarragon
Parsley, thyme, bay leaf
Salt, pepper

Procedure

To prepare the crayfish:
Clean the crayfish. Heat the oil in a large heavy pot. Add the crayfish, shallots and tarragon and stir until the shells become red. Add the wine and simmer 3 minutes. Season with salt and pepper and Cayenne. Remove the crayfish and separate the tails from the heads. Pull the shells off the tails, reserve the meat. Strain the cooking liquid, add cream and reduce by half.

To prepare the lambs' tongues:
Degorge the tongues under cold running water for 2 hours. Make a full-flavored court bouillon with carrot, onion, tarragon, shallot and bouquet garni. Season lightly with salt and poach the tongues for 40 minutes. Cool and pull off the skin. Slice lengthwise.
Heat the sauce, add the truffle juice and season to taste. Warm the tongues and crayfish tails in the sauce.

Plate Presentation

Ladle sauce on the bottom of the plates. Arrange four slices of tongue in a star pattern on each plate. Garnish with the crayfish tails and decorate each plate with a whole crayfish, truffle julienne and chopped tarragon.

(L. Piguet)

166

Veal Kidney Fricassé with "Gaillarde" Sauce

Ingredients (4 servings)

2 veal kidneys
500 ml (2 cups) heavy cream or crème fraîche
2 tbls Dijon mustard
60 ml (2 fl oz) Cognac
3 tbls unsalted butter

Procedure

Trim the kidneys and remove the thin skin that covers them. Cut into large dice (2 cm (3/4 in)).
Season with freshly ground pepper. Do not salt them before cooking, which would make them tough.

Heat oil and pan fry about 5 minutes to cook the diced kidneys medium rare.
Pour off the cooking oil and flame with Cognac. Remove the kidneys and keep warm.

To make the "Gaillarde" sauce:

Deglaze the pan with cream and reduce 2 minutes. Add the mustard and season to taste with salt and pepper. Whisk in the butter to enrich the sauce and make it shine.

Plate Presentation

Mound the diced kidneys on heated plates and ladle the sauce over them. Garnish with slices of sandwich bread, cut in a decorative shape and pan fried in butter until crisp and golden.
(C. Bex)

Fish Dishes

Pike with Walnuts

Ingredients

1.2 kg (2 1/2 lbs) pike fillets
250 g (8 oz) unsalted butter
500 ml (2 cups) heavy cream
24 walnut halves, coarsey chopped
Juice of 1 lemon
Salt, pepper
1 lemon, sliced
Parsley, chopped

Procedure

Check the pike fillets for bones and remove the skin. Season with salt and pepper and coat lightly with flour. Heat butter until it browns and pan fry the fish. Set aside and keep warm. Pour off the fat from the pan and deglaze with cream. Simmer until the cream thickens then, off the heat, whisk in about 3 tlbs butter. Stir in the lemon juice and walnuts and season to taste.

Plate Presentation

Ladle half of the sauce on plates or a platter.

Arrange the fish fillets on the sauce and garnish with lemon slices and chopped parsley. Pass the remaining sauce separately.

(F. Laustriat)

Pike "Chop" with Eel "Tenders"

Ingredients (4 servings)

1 pike (about 1 kg (2.2 lbs))
500 g (1 lb) eel
2 large eggs
600 ml (2 1/4 cups) heavy cream
325 g (11 oz) unsalted butter
50 ml (4 tbls) Cognac
2 leeks, 2 carrots, 1 celery root
6 shallots
300 g (10 oz) sorrel
500 g (1 lb) button mushrooms
500 ml (2 cups) dry white wine
Salt, pepper

Procedure

Clean the pike, remove the skin and check the fillets for bones. Make a mousseline: Puree the fish in a food processor and add the eggs, 2 cups cold cream and 3 tbls softened butter. Add the Cognac and season to taste with salt and pepper. Transfer to a bowl, cover and refrigerate.

Mold the chilled mousseline in "cutlet" molds (sold in France to make cutlet shaped preparations from chopped meat). Alternatively, mold the mousseline by hand or bake in a terrine. Individual portions will take about 10 minutes to cook. The texture of the mousseline is best if cooked shortly before serving.

Clean the eel (or other firm fish) and cut the flesh into strips (to resemble the "tenders" attached to chicken or duck breasts). Pan fry in clarified butter and keep warm.

Cut the leeks, carrots and celery root into julienne. Combine the vegetables with 1 tbl butter, 1/4 cup wine and 1 tbl chopped shallot, season with salt and pepper and cook about 10 minutes or until tender and glazed.

Wash and coarsely chop the mushrooms. Cook them over high heat with 1/4 cup white wine, 2 tbls chopped shallots and salt and pepper (to taste) until the mushrooms are soft and have rendered all their liquid. Stir in 2 tbls cream and spoon the mixture into a buttered mold. Press on the top to compress the mushrooms and set in a water bath to keep warm.

Make a butter sauce by reducing to a glaze: 1 cup fish stock with 1/4 cup white wine and 2 tbls chopped shallots Add 2 tbls cream and bring to a simmer. Season to taste. Just before serving, whisk in 200 g (7 oz) softened butter.

Plate Presentation

Arrange the (cutlet-shaped) portions of pike mousseline in a circle on a platter. Surround with the glazed vegetables and unmold the mushroom "cake" in the center. Arrange the strips of eel around the platter and ladle sauce over the fish.

(P. Paumel)

Salmon with Red Wine Sauce

Procedure

This lovely dish combines a fillet of salmon with a hearty wine sauce made with red Sancerre and a delicate butter sauce made with puréed lettuce.
Prepare salmon fillets about 140 g (scant 5 oz) per person. Remove the skin and all bones and rinse under cold water.
Just before serving, lightly season the salmon fillets with salt and pepper and pan fry in butter. To make the red wine velouté: Make a "mirepoix" (small dice) of 100 g (3 1/2 oz) each carrots and onions, season with salt and pepper and a bouquet garni and cook in a little butter. Add the salmon bones and trimmings, cover with red wine and simmer 20 minutes. Add chicken, veal or fish stock and continue to simmer about 20 minutes. Skim the surface as the fumet cooks then strain through a fine-meshed sieve.
Make a light roux (2 tbls each butter and flour for each cup of fumet). Whisk in the fumet and just before serving, enrich the velouté with a little butter.

To make the lettuce sauce (4 servings):

Separate the leaves of one large Boston lettuce and rinse well. Cook the leaves in butter and season lightly with salt. When the leaves are wilted, press on them to extract the maximum amount of liquid and set them aside for the presentation. Reduce the liquid and add cream and stock and reduce to a light coating consistency. Just before serving, whisk in a little butter to enrich the sauce.

Plate Presentation

Mound a little cooked lettuce in the center of the plates and lay the salmon fillet on top.
Spoon a ribbon of red wine velouté around the fish.
Serve the remaining red wine sauce and the lettuce butter sauce in two separate sauce boats.

(F. Laustriat)

167

Stuffed Trout "Saint Walfrid"

Ingredients (4 servings)

4 salmon trout (about 500 g (1 lb) each))
2 garlic cloves, chopped
30 g (1 oz) shallots, chopped
130 g (4 1/3 oz) chopped tomatoes
130 g (4 1/3 oz) button mushrooms, sliced
100 g (3 1/2 oz) fennel bulb, julienned
10 g (1/3 oz) tomato purée
1 L 1 qt) dry white wine (and/or fish stock)
60 ml (2 fl oz) heavy cream
2 egg yolks (optional)

For the filling:

100 g (3 1/2 oz) cooked ham
100 g (3 1/2 oz) onions
100 g (3 1/2 oz) button mushroms
30 g (1 oz) fennel bulb
Salt, pepper

Procedure

Scale the fish and clean through the gills. Rinse under cold running water.
Grind the filling ingredients, stir together and season to taste. Stuff the trout through the gill opening.
Arrange the fish in a baking dish and add the white wine (or stock), tomato purée, shallots, tomatoes, mushrooms, garlic and fennel.
Bring to a simmer on top of the stove then braise in the oven about 30 minutes.
Pour the cooking liquid through a sieve and reduce to a glaze. Add the cream and simmer to thicken. Just before serving, whisk the 2 egg yoks into the hot sauce to enrich it.

Plate Presentation

Remove the skin from the trout and place in the center of the plates. Ladle the ivory-colored sauce over the fish and sprinkle with chopped parsley.
Serve the trout very hot accompanied by boiled potatoes or rice pilaf.

(J.C. Schneider)

168

Lemon Sole with Pasta

Ingredients (4 servings)

4 lemon sole filllets
400 g (14 oz) fresh noodles
50 g (3 tbls) unsalted butter
2 ripe tomatoes
2 shallots
80 ml (1/3 cup) dry white wine
125 ml (1 cup) heavy cream or crème fraîche
1 1/2 tbls Bearnaise sauce
Salt, pepper, Cayenne pepper

Procedure

Remove the skin from the fish fillets, check for bones and rinse under cold running water.
Peel and seed the tomatoes and chop coarsely.
Peel the shallots and chop finely.

Cook the pasta in boiling salted water, drain and mound on a platter, keep warm.
Heat butter and pan fry the sole without browning. Arrange on top of the pasta, cover and keep warm.

Cook the shallots and tomatoes in a little butter then add the wine. Simmer a few minutes, add the cream and reduce to a light coating consistency. Whisk in the bearnaise sauce to enrich the sauce.

Plate Presentation

Spoon sauce over the fish fillets then brown under the broiler.
Serve the remaining sauce separately.

(Hotel de la Poste - Domfront)

Sole "Vaugrain"

Ingredients (4 servings)

4 soles (300 g (10 oz) each)
Filling:
250 g (8 oz) button mushrooms
30 g (1 oz) unsalted butter
1 lemon
10 g (1/3 oz) chopped parsley
1 garlic clove, chopped
3 shallots, chopped
3 slices sandwich bread
80 ml (1/3 cup) heavy cream or crème fraîche
1 large egg

Sauce:
1 L (1 qt) dry white wine (Sancerre)
250 ml (1 cup) fish stock
250 ml (1 cup) heavy cream or crème fraîche
50 g 3 tbls unsalted butter
20 g (2 tbls) toasted bread crumbs

Procedure

Remove the bones of the sole keeping the head and tail in tact. Make a slit down the middle of the white side. Glide the knife along the bones to release the top fillets. Cut around the sides of the bones and at the top and bottom of the backbone.

Slide the knife under the bones to detach them from the lower fillets. Pull out the bones in one piece. Rinse under cold running water.

Cook the mushrooms over high heat wth a little butter, lemon juice and salt and pepper.

Reserve the liquid exuded from the mushrooms. Chop the mushrooms and combine with finely chopped shallots, garlic and parsley. Stir in the breadcrumbs and cream and cook about 15 minutes over low heat. Season to taste and bind the filling with beaten eggs.

Lightly season the fish and fill the cavities with the stuffing. Arrange in a shallow baking dish. Pour the wine, fish stock and mushroom liquid over the fish. Bring to a simmer on top of the

stove then bake at 200 C (400 F) about 8-10 minutes. Trim the edges of the cooked fish. Reduce the cooking liquid by half, add cream and reduce to a light coating consistency. Whisk in butter to enrich the sauce and season to taste with salt, pepper and lemon juice.

Plate Presentation

Place the stuffed fish in the center of the plates and coat with sauce then sprinkle with bread crumbs.
Garnish the dish with puff pastry decorations ("fleurons") and dill sprigs.
Accompany the sole with boiled potatoes, cut in small even shapes ("turned") and colorful vegetables.

(F. Desroys du Roure)

Sole "Paternoise"
(4 servings)

Procedure

Clean and scale one large sole. Soak in cold milk for 15 minutes. Pat dry, season with salt and pepper and coat lightly wth flour. Heat butter and oil and brown the sole on both sides, lower the heat and cook a few more minutes.
Slice 250 g (8 oz) potatoes and blanch in boiling salted water (2 minutes). Cook one finely sliced onion in butter. Combine the potatoes and onions, season and finish cooking in the oven.
Slice 125 g (4 oz) mushrooms, season with salt and pepper and cook in a little butter. Add the cooked potatoes.

Plate Presentation

Mound the potatoes with onions and mushrooms on an oval platter or on four plates. Place the browned sole on top (whole or cut in portions). Pour a little browned butter over the fish. Garnish the platter or plates with lemon slices (cut in half, zest trimmed with a channel cutter).
Serve very hot.

(P. Paillon)

Sole with Cream Sauce Served on Rice

Ingredients (4 servings)

300 g (10 oz) rice
Fish stock (fumet)
1 sole (750 g (1 1/2 lbs))
100 g (3 1/2 oz) unsalted butter
1/2 cup dry white wine
125 g (4 oz) button mushrooms
2 tbls breadcrumbs
5 tbls heavy cream or crème fraîche
1 tsp flour
Bouquet garni, 1 onion with cloves
1 shallot, finely chopped
Paprika, chopped parsley, lemon juice
Salt, pepper

Procedure

Bone the sole, set aside the fillets and make a fumet with the bones and trimmings.

Cook the rice briefly in the butter, season and add 2 1/4 cups fish fumet. Bring to a simmer, cover and cook over low heat or in a 375 F oven 15 minutes.

Place the fish fillets in a shallow baking dish. Season lightly with salt, pepper and paprika.

Top with a bit of butter and chopped parsley, add the white wine. Cover the dish with buttered foil and cook at 375 F for 15 minutes.

Meanwhile, slice the mushroom stems (keep the caps whole). Season with salt and pepper and cook with a little butter and lemon juice. Spoon the mushroom stems on top of the fish, sprinkle with breadcrumbs and return to the oven, uncovered, about 10 more minutes.

Stir the flour into the cream. Bring the cooking liquid to a boil and whisk in the cream/flour mixture and simmer until the sauce thickens.

Plate Presentation

Form mounds of the cooked rice the same size and shape as the fish fillets.

Pose a fillet on each bed of rice and coat with sauce.

Divide the mushroom caps evenly between the portions to garnish the plates.
Decorate with small puff pastries cut in fish shapes.

(P. Paillon)

Sole Papillottes with Leeks

Ingredients (1 serving)

4 small sole fillets
2 small leeks, white portion
30 g (1 oz) duck foie gras
Salt, pepper, paprika

Procedure

Cut each fillet diagonally into 3-4 strips ("goujonettes"). Poach in a mixture of milk and water. Slice the leeks, season with salt and cook in a little butter until tender.

Cut a large square of aluminum foil (20 cm (8 in)) and brush with butter. Make a bed of cooked leeks, place the fish on top and finish with the foie gras. Season wth salt, pepper and a little paprika.

Fold the edges of the foil to seal. Put the papillotte into a hot oven and cook until it expands, about 10 minutes.

Plate Presentation

Place the papillotte on a large plate, open the foil package a little and serve at once.
The plate can be decorated with a few "sprigs" of the leek greens, cut thin and fanned out.

(C. Seysalles)

Red Mullet with Seaweed

Ingredients (4 servings)

5 large mullets
2 carrots, 1 onion, 2 shallots, 1 branch celery (diced)
1 sprig parsley, 1 sprig tarragon
1 bay leaf, 1 sprig thym
100 g (3 1/2 oz) button mushrooms, diced
2 tbls heavy cream
2 tsps unsalted butter
Juice of 1 lemon
1 pinch sugar
1 turnip, 2 leeks, 2 carrots (julienned)
1 egg plus 1 egg white
500 ml (2 cups) dry white wine
1 cup seaweed (dulse)

Procedure

To prepare the sauce:
Scale the fish and clean. Rinse under cold running water. Remove the fillets and reserve. Sauté the diced vegetables in butter. Add the aromatics, fish bones, wine and 1 L (1 qt) water. Bring to a boil, skim the impurities that rise to the surface. Lower the heat and simmer 20-30 minutes. Strain the hot fumet over the seaweed (dulse), which has been trimmed, rinsed and spread in a shallow baking dish. Soften the seaweed in the hot fumet for five minutes then remove. Reduce this liquid then add the cream and reduce to a light coating consistency. Season with lemon juice, chopped chives, a few leaves of chopped seaweed and a little salt and pepper (remember the seawweed is salty).

To prepare the fish mousseline:
Cook the mushrooms with butter, chopped shallots and tarragon.
Drain and cool. Purée in a food processor with two of the mullet fillets and the egg and egg yolk. Season to taste. Spread this mixture on the mullet fillets and bake in the oven.

To prepare the garnish: Cook the julienned vegetables in a little stock and butter. Season with salt and pepper.

Plate Presentation
Just before serving, ladle sauce over the fish and brown under the broiler.
Serve the souffléd fillets of mullet in the center of heated plates surrounded by julienned vegetables.

(M. Derbane)

Bass with Braised Lettuce and Tomato Sauce

Procedure

Scale the bass, clean and rinse under cold running water. Cut into thick steaks (1 1/2 in). Place close together in a buttered baking dish. Season with salt and pepper, cover with fish fumet, add a little olive oil. Set the pan over very low heat and cook gently.
Melt a little butter and add the lettuce leaves seasoned with salt. Cook over low heat until tender. Drain and chop finely.
To prepare the sauce, combine chopped shallots, mushrooms and white wine. Simmer to evaporate all the liquid. Add cooking liquid from the fish and reduce by half. Add cream and reduce to a coating consistency.
Enrich the sauce with butter, stir in the chopped lettuce and keep warm in a water bath.
Make a tomato sauce with peeled, seeded tomatoes, chopped coriander, basil vinegar, olive oil, parsley and salt and pepper.
Peel an apple, cut in half and cut into thin slices. Fan out the slices, sprinkle with salt and pepper and bake in the oven until tender.

Platter Presentation

Ladle the lettuce sauce on the platter (or plate). Arrange the fish side by side and garnish with the cooked apple slices fanned out on each end of the platter. Spoon a little tomato sauce between the fish and the apples.
Serve the remaining lettuce sauce separately.

(M. Vessat)

Pike Perch "Marianne"

Ingredients (4 servings)

1 pike perch 1-1.25 kg (2-2 1/2 lbs)
500 g (1 lbs) fresh spinach
50 g (1 2/3 oz) unsalted butter
50 g (1 2/3 oz) chopped parsley
250 ml (1 cup) dry white wine
250 ml (1 cup) fish fumet
4 shallots, chopped
100 ml (3.5 fl oz) heavy cream
Nutmeg, salt, pepper

Procedure

Trim and wash the spinach and blanch a few minutes in boiling salted water. Drain well and combine with the butter. Season with salt, pepper and nutmeg and cook over very low heat.

Fillet the fish, remove the skin and check for bones. Rinse under cold running water, wipe dry. Cut each fillet in half and arrange in a buttered shallow baking dish, cover and refrigerate. Make a fumet with the bones.

Shortly before serving, season the fish fillets with salt and pepper and add the white wine and fumet to the baking dish. Add a bit of butter on top of each fillet, bring to simmer on top of the stove and poach until the flesh is white and firm (in the oven or on top of the stove).

Transfer the cooking liquid to a saucepan and reduce, add the cream, bring to a simmer to thicken and season to taste.

Plate Presentation

Mound the spinach in the center of the plates and place a fillet of pike perch on top. Spoon sauce over the top and brown uuder the broiler. Serve at once.

(R. Moser)

170

Brandade with Zucchini

Ingredients (4-5 servings)

1 kg (2.2 lbs) salt cod
750 ml (3 cups) whole milk
400 g (14 oz) zucchini
150 ml (5 fl oz) virgin olive oil

Procedure

Use a thick piece of salt cod that is very white and pliable. Soak in cold water 26-48 hours to remove excess salt. (Change water twice a day.) Remove the bones and skin and cut into 1 inch cubes.

Combine the cod and milk and bring to a boil. Drain (reserve the milk) and keep the cod warm. Cut the nicest zucchini (without peeling) into thick slices. Just before serving, dip in the milk, then in flour and pan fry in olive oil until golden.

Peel the remaining zucchini. Cut into pieces and steam until very tender. Press through a sieve then dry out the purée over low heat. When the zucchini purée is quite firm and dry, stir in the olive oil a little at a time.

Stir the cod to break up the cubes then stir in the zucchini purée. Over very low heat, stir until the brandade is very smooth and light. Season to taste.

Plate Presentation

Mound the zucchini brandade on plates or on a platter and garnish with then fried zucchini slices. Serve very hot with toasted slices of French bread.

(P. Beekes)

Turbot with Saffron

Ingredients (4 servings)

1 turbot (1.5-2 kg (3-4 lbs))
2 tomatoes
200-300 g (7-10 oz) green beans
250 g (8 oz) fresh noodles
50 g (3 tbls) unsalted butter
Chopped parsley

Saffron butter sauce:
4 g (1/16 oz) saffron powder
2 tbls finely chopped shallots
1/2 cup dry white wine
100 ml (3.5 fl oz) heavy cream or crème fraîche
300 g (10 oz) unsalted butter
Salt, pepper
1 tbl lemon juice

Procedure

Fillet the fish and make a fumet with the bones. Poach the fillets in the fumet for about 8-9 minutes. Transfer the fish to a platter and keep warm. Save the fumet for a soup or other dish. To make the butter sauce: Cook the shallots in 1 tbl butter until soft but not brown. Add the wine and reduce until all the liquid is evaporated.

Stir in the cream and saffron, bring to a simmer to thicken. Off the heat, whisk in the butter a little at a time. Season to taste with salt, white pepper and lemon juice. Keep warm in a water bath.

Peel and seed the tomatoes and cut into dice. Cook the noodles and green beans (separately) in boiling salted water.

Plate Presentation

Arrange the turbot fillets on the plates with the noodles and diced tomato.
Spoon the sauce over the fish and noodles and decorate with green beans.
Sprinkle the dish with chopped parsley.
Saupoudrer de persil haché.

(O. Ruellan)

Turbot with Spring Vegetables

Ingredients (4 servings)

800 g (1 lb 10 oz)
2 young leeks, 2 small carrots, 1 small celery root
250 ml (1 cup) dry white wine
250 ml (1 cup) heavy cream or crème fraîche
2 egg yolks
1 tbl flour
100 g (3 1/2 oz) unsalted butter
2 tbls olive oil
Fresh sorrel
Salt, pepper

Procedure

Choose a very fresh turbot. Clean and rinse the fish then remove the fillets.
Make a flavorful fumet with the bones and head.

Cut the vegetables into julienne, season and cook in butter.

Place the turbot fillets on top of the vegetables and cook in a moderate oven.

Make a veouté sauce with fumet and white wine. Stir in the cream, simmer to thicken. Off the heat whisk the egg yolks into the hot sauce. Transfer the fish to a heatproof dish and spoon the julienned vegetables on top. Ladle sauce over the turbot and brown under the broiler.

Plate Presentation

Place a portion of fish in the center of each heated plate.
Cut the (uncooked) sorrel into thin strips and arrange around the fish. Serve at once.

(R. Moser)

Turbot Soufflé

Ingredients (10 servings)

1 turbot 2.5 kg (5 1/2 lbs)
250 g (8 oz) whiting fillets
100 g (3 1/2 oz) unsalted butter
125 g (4 oz) flour
250 ml (1 cup) whole milk
6-8 egg whites
Barding fat
1/2 bottle fruity white wine
(Sancerre, Muscadet or Riesling)
10 large button mushrooms
3 tbls heavy cream or crème fraîche
1/2 cup fish velouté
1/2 cup hollandaise sauce
Toasted bread
Chopped shallots
Fish fumet (stock)
1 truffle (canned or fresh)
Puff pastry decorations (in form of fish)

Procedure

Clean the turbot, scrape the skin and cut off the spiny fin. Rinse under cold running water. Cut down the center of the white side, glide the knife under the bones, detach at each end then pull out the central bone.

Make a delicate filling for the boned turbot with whiting and a classic «panade» (similar to «chou» or cream puff pastry). Begin by combining the milk and butter and bringing to a boil with a pinch of salt and nutmeg. Off the heat, add the flour to the hot liquid, stir then return to the heat to dry out the mixture a little. Off the heat, stir in 6 egg whites, one at a time, and blend until smooth. Transfer to a bowl, cover and refrigerate.

Remove the skin from the whiting fillets and rinse under cold running water. Check for bones, then purée in a food processor. Blend in the «panade» until smooth then the cream. Poach a spoonful of the mixture to check for seasoning and to make sure the texture is good.

If the «soufflé» doesn't hold together well enough, stir in 1-2 more egg whites.

Season the turbot lightly and pipe this mixture into the cavity. Season the outside of the fish and lay the barding fat on the top.

Transfer the fish to a large shallow baking dish and add the wine, chopped shallots and mushroom trimmings (from «turning» the mushrooms which gives the caps a decorative look; cook caps in butter and lemon juice).

Braise the fish at 220 C (425 F) about 1 hour, basting often.

Carefully transfer the fish to a serving platter and keep warm.

Reduce the braising liquid a little, whisk in some velouté and cream and simmer to thicken. Just before serving, stir in 1/2 cup hollandaise and season to taste.

Plate Presentation

Cut the turbot into portions, remove the skin and coat with sauce.
Garnish the plate with mushrooms caps.
The plates can also be garnished with individual tart shells filled with diced shrimp or lobster combined with the same the sauce.
Serve this dish very hot.

(S. Letrone)

Seafood Choucroute

Ingredients (6 servings)

1.5 kg (3 1/3 lbs) saurkraut
500 ml (2 cups) Muscadet
203 shallots
4 tbls goose fat
1 kg (2/2 lbs) monkfish, cut in slices
1 kg (2.2 lbs) haddock
Fish fumet
12 juniper berries
12 shrimp
12 mussels
6 small slices smoked salmon
6 slices smoked halibut

Procedure

Rinse the saurkraut in cold water and squeeze dry.
Peel and cut the shallots into thin slices.
Heat the goose fat and cook the shallots without browning.
Add the saurkraut, wine, fumet, and juniper berries. Season with a little salt and pepper. Cook in a low oven for 3 hours.

Flatten the surface of the saurkraut and arrange the monkfish, haddock and mussels on top. Cover and return to the oven a few minutes. Combine 100 ml (3.5 fl oz) heavy cream, 100 g (3 1/2 oz) unalted butter, juice of 1/2 lemon. Simmer to thicken a little, then season to taste.

Plate Presentation

Spoon the «choucroute» onto heated plates. Place a slice of each fish and the opened mussels on top. Place a warm shrimp inside the empty mussel shell.
Arrange the smoked fish on the choucroute and cover with sauce. (*Note* if the halibut is too salty, soak in milk.) Sprinkle the dish with chopped parsley and serve with boiled, "turned" potatoes.

(F. Robadey)

Seafood "Meli-Melo"

Ingredients (5 servings)

200 g (7 oz) salmon fillets
200 g (7 oz) monkfish
200 g (7 oz) snapper
5 large Dublin Bay prawns
10 crayfish
10 oysters
5 clams, 5 sea urchins
50 ml (4 tbls) olive oil
30 g (1 oz) chopped shallots
2 garlic cloves
200 ml (7 fl oz) dry white wine
500 ml (2 cups) fish fumet
300 ml (10 fl oz) heavy cream or crème fraîche
3 carrot, 3 turnips, 1/2 cucumber
Pinch saffron
Fresh parsley
Salt, freshly ground pepper

Note: This dish should be made with the freshest fish at the market. Choose an assortment of colors and textures.

Procedure

Peel the carrots and turnips and cut into small, even olive-shaped pieces. Do not peel the cucumber; cut into small shapes so one side is green with skin. Cook each vegetable separately with a little butter, water, salt and pepper over medium heat until they are lightly glazed and tender but not too soft.

Keep warm.

Prepare each of the seafoods.

Trim the spines of the sea urchins. Remove the intestines from the crayfish, if necessary. Clean the fish and remove the fillets.

Heat the olive oil in a large pan. Add the fish fillets and cook briefly without browning. Add the shellfish, chopped shallots and garlic and a little chopped parsley. Add the white wine and bring to a simmer. Add the fish stock and cream and simmer gently 8-10 minutes.

Remove all the seafood with a slotted spoon. Add saffron to the cooking liquid and reduce over high heat to thicken. Season to taste.

Plate Presentation

Arrange the fish fillets on a platter and place the shellfish on top.

Open the sea urchins and oysters and place around the fish.

Ladle hot sauce over the fish and garnish the platter with vegetables.

To keep the dish hot during service, place on a warming tray.

(T. Larique)

Skate in Cream Sauce with Raspberry Vinegar

Ingredients (4 servings)

4 wings of skate
4 shallots, chopped
200 g (7 oz) shelled shrimp
2 tbls raspberry vinegar
100 g (3 1/2 oz) unsalted buter
100 ml (3.5 fl oz) heavy cream or crème fraîche
200 g (7 oz) rice
12 fresh raspberries
1 small head raddichio
Chopped parsley
Salt, pepper

Procedure

Cook the rice («pilaf») and spoon it into buttered ramekins. Press on the rice to mold it and keep warm until service.
Trim the skate and make a fumet with the trimmings. Poach the fish in this stock for a few minutes. Keep warm.
Cook the shallots in a little butter until soft but not brown. Add the vinegar and reduce by half.
Whisk the butter then the cream into the vinegar reduction to make a light, creamy sauce. Pour through a fine-meshed sieve, pressing on the shallots to extract flavor. Season to taste.

Plate Presentation

Place one portion on each plate and unmold a rice "timbale" next to it. Decorate the top of the rice with a few fresh raspberries.
Garnish the plate with warm shrimp and a few raddichio leves. The magenta lettuce contrasts beautifully with the white fish.
Ladle a little sauce over the fish and pass the remaining sauce separately.
Sprinkle chopped parsley over the fish.
(O. Ruellan)

Stuffed Cabbage with 5 Fish

Ingredients (5 servings)

200 g (7 oz) smoked salmon
200 g (7 oz) turbot fillets
200 g (7 oz) monkfish
200 g (7 oz) sea scallops
200 g (7 oz) bass fillets
200 g (7 oz) unsalted butter
100 g (3 1/2 oz) button mushrooms, chopped
50 g (1 2/3 oz) chopped shallots
20 g (2/3 oz) chopped parsley
500 ml (2 cups) heavy cream
5 leaves green cabbage
5 leaves red cabbage
300 dl (10 fl oz) red wine
10 g (1/3 oz) chopped coriander
Salt, freshly ground pepper

Procedure

Choose firm, whole cabbage leaves. Blanch them in boiling salted water. Refresh in cold water to stop the cooking, drain and dry on paper towels.
Trim the fish fillets, check for bones, remove the skin and rinse under cold water. Cut the turbot, monkfish and bass into 1 inch dice, slice the salmon into pieces and cut the scallops in half. Mix all the fish together and stir in 200 ml (7 fl oz) cream. Season with salt, pepper and chopped coriander.
Lay the cabbage leaves on the work surface with a red leaf on top of a green leaf. Spoon the fish mixture into the center of the leaves. Pull the egdes up to cover the fish and overlap to form small spheres. Tie kitchen string around the balls to keep their shape and steam or poach for 20-25 minutes.
Combine the wine, shallots, parsley and mushroooms and simmer until the liquid is reduced by 2/3. Add the remaining cream and simmer to thicken.
Off the heat, whisk in the butter to enrich the sauce. Pour through a sieve, pressing on the ingredients to extract flavor. Season to taste and keep warm in a water bath.

Plate Presentation

Ladle sauce on the bottom of the plates. Remove the kitchen string and place a cabbage and seafood «bundle» in the center. Decorate with a fresh parsley sprig.

(T. Larique)

Sardine Bouillabaise

This variation on bouillabaise is a traditional specialty of the Varois region. The dish is best when prepared with sardines caught in the morning which are more flavorful than sardines caught in the evening.

Procedure

Slice one large onion and the white portion of a leek. Peel and seed a large tomato and chop coarsely. Heat olive oil in large pot and cook these vegetables without browning. Season lightly and add 1 L (1 qt) water.

Bring to a boil and add a bouquet garni made with thyme, bay leaf, fresh fennel and orange peel. Add a pinch of saffron, 2 crushed garlic cloves, and a few peppercorns.
Peel 1 kg (2 lbs) potatoes and cut into quarters and add to the pot.
Clean 1 kg (2 lbs) fresh sardines. Scrape the scales, remove the bones and heads.

When the potatoes are about half cooked, place the sardines on top of the ingredients in the pot. Lower the heat so that the liquid is barely simmering and cook until the potatoes are tender.
Season to taste with salt and pepper.

Plate Presentation

Lift the sardines off the top without breaking them up and arrange them in the bottom of shallow serving bowls.
Arrange potatoes around the sardines.
Sprinkle chopped parsley over the fish and potatoes.
Pour the liquid though a sieve then ladle it over the fish.
Fish soups in France are traditionally served with slices of toasted French bread rubbed with garlic and grated Parmesan or gruyere.

(D. Lecadre)

Bass with Green Cabbage and Smoked Salmon

Ingredients (4 servings)

1 bass (about 1.2 kg (2 1/2 lbs))
Olive oil
1 small green cabbage
8 slices smoked bacon
2 slices smoked salmon
150 g (5 oz) unsalted butter
1 onion
Salt, pepper

Procedure

Fillet the bass and remove all bones. Rinse under cold running water and cut each fillet in half. Coat the fillets with olive oil, season with salt and pepper and set aside.

Separate the leaves of the cabbage and cut out the thick, central rib. Blanch 3 minutes in boiling salted water, drain and set aside.

Finely chop the onion and bacon and cook together with the butter in a heavy pot without browning. Slice the cabbage into thick strips and add to the pot. Cover and cook over low heat about 8 minutes.

Place the fish fillets on top of the cabbage, cover and cook over low heat about 4 minutes. Remove the fish with a slotted spatula and keep warm between two plates.

Cut the smoked salmon into strips and stir into the cabbage.

Plate Presentation

Mound the cabbage on four plates and place a fillet of bass on top of the cabbage. Serve immediatley.

The chef recommends serving this dish with a Hermitage blanc.

(H. Pautard)

Meat Dishes

Filet Mignon and Foie Gras with Cider

Ingredients (4 servings)

4 beef tournedos
4 slices (each 150 g (5 oz)) foie gras
12 apples, peeled, cored
200 ml (76 fl oz) Calvados
400 ml (14 fl oz) light duck stock
500 ml (2 cups) hard cider
150 g (5 oz) unsalted butter, clarified

Procedure

Slice 8 of the apples and marinate in the Calvados and cider for 12 hours (refrigerated). Make a duck stock with walnut wine (see recipe «Duck Breast with Walnut Wine»). Cook the macerated apples in the stock, cider and Calvados until very soft. Stir to break up the apples into a purée which will thicken the liquid slightly. Reduce to concentrate the flavors and consistency. Season to taste and keep warm.

Season the slices of foie gras. Pan fry in clarified butter over high heat to brown each side, the foie gras should remain rare. Sear the beef in hot clarified butter and pan fry to desired doneness. Cut the 4 remaining apples into round slices and sauté in clarified butter until golden but still firm.

Plate Presentation

Transfer the tournedos to the center of heated plates and place a slice of foie gras on top of each. Spoon the apple-thickened duck sauce around the meat.
Garnish with the apple slice overlapped around the plate.
Serve immediately.

(A. Parveaux)

Beef Filet with Honey

(8 servings)

Trim a 1.5 kg (3 lbs) beef filet and place it in an oval casserole.

Prepare a marinade with 1 bottle of red wine 200 g (7 oz) honey, 1 large sliced onion, 1 large sliced carrot, thyme, bay leaf, 5-6 juniper berries, cracked pepper, and a pinch of salt. Bring to a boil then cool completely before pouring over the meat.

Cover and marinate in the refrigerate 3-4 days. To make the sauce, prepare a «mirepoix» of diced carrots and onions and cook in a little oil without browning. Deglaze with a little honey vinegar, add 1/2 bottle red wine, 2 cups of the marinade and 300 ml (10 fl oz) brown sauce.

Cover and simmer for 2 1/2 hours. Add more wine and marinade as the sauce cooks.
Pour the liquid through a sieve. Bring to a simmer and thicken with beurre manié (equal amounts flour/softened butter blended together). Season to taste.

Wipe off the meat to dry the surface, sear in oil then roast in the oven or grill.

Prepare a chestnut purée and a celery root purée. Prepare a very lightly sweeteened compote of blueberries.

Plate Presentation

Slice the meat and place on heated plates. Ladle sauce over the meat.
Garnish with 2 separate purées of chestnut and celery root piped out with a star tip.
Drizzle a little juice from the blueberry compote over the purées and pass the compote in a sauceboat.

(P. Paillon)

Filet of Beef with Wild Mushrooms

Ingredients (1 serving)

200 g (7 oz) trimmed beef filet
10 g (1/3 oz) dried morels
10 g (1/3 oz) fresh morels
10 g (1/3 oz) black trumpet mushrooms
1 g (pinch) chopped truffle
3 large chestnuts
1 eggs yolk
10 ml (scant tbl) wine vinegar
10 g (13 oz) cured ham, julienned, sautéed
20 g (2/3 oz) unsalted butter, softened
Salt, pepper

Procedure

Wash and trim the mushrooms and sauté in a litlle oil. Chop them very finely (the chef uses a mini processor). Peel the uncooked chestnuts and cut into tiny dice, finely chop the truffle and stir all these ingredients together

Spread this mixture over the entire surface of the meat. Heat a little oil in a heavy pan and pan fry the meat until medium rare, carefully transfer to a plate and season with salt and pepper.

Pour the fat out of the pan then deglaze with vinegar. Whisk in the egg yolk and over low heat continue whisking until thick and light (sabayon). Whisk in the butter a little at a time to make an emulsified sauce. Gently stir in the julienned ham and season to taste (the ham is salty, so don't overseason).

Presentation

Place the meat in the center of the plate.
Spoon the sauce over the meat ans serve at once.

(P. Laripidie)

Fresh Ham in Aspic

Ingredients (4 servings)

Small fresh ham with foot attached
1 leek, 1 onion, 1 carrot, 1 garlic clove
1 stem tarragon
1 bottle white wine
1 egg white (to clarify the aspic)
Salt, pepper

Procedure

Bone the ham and split the foot.

Season the inside of the meat with salt and pepper. Roll the boned ham into a cylinder and tie secruely with kitchen string.

Make a court bouillon with the wine, vegetables and the pig's trotter. Poach the ham in this liquid, adding water during cooking to keep the ham completely immersed (about 1 hour at 180 C (350 F).

Remove the cooked ham from the liquid and set on a rack to cool.

Strain the poaching liquid and bring to a boil. Skim all impurities that rise to the surface. Lower to a simmer and continue to skim as the liquid reduces to concentrate the flavor and color.

Strain the liquid again through a fine-meshed sieve and return to a clean pot and bring to a simmer.

Beat the egg white until foamy, then whisk it into the simmering liquid. When the egg white and fat come to the surface, skim then pour the liquid through a cheesecloth.

Cool the aspic until slightly thickened and coat the cooled ham.

(R. Moser)

173

Grandmother's "Hochepot"

This traditional slow-cooking beef stew is updated here with Port and Cognac and served with sliced mushrooms.

Ingredients (6 servings)

600 g (1 1/4 lbs) beef shoulder
600 g (1 1/4 lbs) beef flank
6 slices oxtail
300 g (10 oz) lean smoked bacon, diced
3 large onions, finely chopped
3 garlic cloves, crushed
300 g (10 oz) carrots, cut in matchsticks
300 g (10 oz) celery root, sliced
500 g (1 lb) button mushrooms, sliced
1 bouquet garni
2 stems fresh sage
2 L (2 qts) good red wine
200 ml (7 fl oz) Cognac
200 ml (7 fl oz) Port
Salt, freshly ground pepper
Chopped parsley

Procedure

In large heavy pot with a cover, cook the diced bacon in a little oil, set aside.
Brown the meats in a little oil, season lightly and set aside.
Cook the chopped onions, garlic, leeks, carrots and celery root until softened a little.
Return the meats and bacon to the pot. Add the red wine, Cognac, Port and 2 cups of water. Bring to a boil and skim all impurities that rise to the surface.
Season with salt and pepper, add the bouquet garni and sage leaves.
Lower the heat, cover the pot and simmer about 4 hours, skimming the surface occasionally.
When the meats are cooked, cool the stew overnight.
Remove the fat from the chilled stew and discard. Take out the pieces of meat and cut into slices or cubes.
Melt a little butter in large pot and cook the mushrooms with a little salt. Add the meats to the pot. Strain the liquid and pour over the meats and simmer 25-30 minutes. Heat the cooked vegetables separately.

Plate Presentation

Ladle the stewed meats into heated shallow bowls. Sprinkle with a little red wine.
Arrange the cooked vegetables around the edge of the dish.
Sprinkle chopped parsley over the meats.
Serve with pasta or braised cabbage.

(D. Ducroux)

Traditional Cassoulet from Castelnaudray

Cassoulet, a flavorful stew of beans, sausage and pork, is a pillar of good French regional cooking. This hearty fare from Southwest France is appreciated throughout the country. Each cook who has added his or her personal touch to the stew proudly gives a special name to their version. The variation described here was developed by «une Grande Dame de Fourneau» of the «Pair de la Grande Confrerie du Cassoulet de Castelnaudary»!
Each chef carefully chooses the type of bean for their cassoulet. For this version, the creator recommends «lingots de Vendée». White «navy» beans or greenish «flagelots» can be used. Look for dried beans that are not old and shriveled.
Rinse 1 kg (2 about 2 lbs) beans well in cold water then leave them to soak 6-8 hours in spring water (a good tasting water). The water should be changed several times during soaking. If your tap water is good, the beans are best when left to soak under cold running water.
Meanwhile, make a flavorful broth with ham and smoked pork bones, pork rind, bouquet garni, onion stuck with cloves, and sliced carrots. Simmer several hours, then strain. Chill, then skim the fat that solidifies on the top. You will need 4 L (4-5 qts) of broth for every kilo (2.2 kbs) of dried beans plus another quart for the final cooking.
Cover the soaked beans with broth, season lightly (remember the broth ingredients were a little salty). Bring to a boil and skim the surface.
Lower the heat, cover and simmer 2 hours (or the beans can be cooked in a 350 F oven).
Halfway through the cooking, make a combination of finely chopped

garlic (10-12 cloves) and chopped fatback (200 g (7 oz)). Sprinkle this on top of the beans and continue cooking. The authentic version also uses some strong-tasting yellowish rind from aged fatback.
When the beans are soft enough to be crushed easily, remove the pot to a warm place and hold overnight. (American health laws would prohibit this practice in a restaurant –, alternatively, refrigerate overnight and slowly bring to room temperature the next day.)
Prepare the meats that will be served with the beans. The selection for this cassoulet is Castelnaudary sausage (350 g (12 oz)) (similar to «Toulouse sausage – lean and peppery), pork loin, pork shoulder (1 kg (2 lbs) of each) and 8-10 portions goose confit (goose legs cooked several hours in a «bath» of goose fat and cooled in the fat). Heat goose fat and cook the pork loin and shoulder until well done. Cut the loin into 1 inch cubes and pull the pork shoulder off the bones and shred. Slice the sausage and heat in goose fat and pan fry the confit, skin side down, until golden and heated though. For extra flavor, poach pork rind in broth. Deglaze the cooking pans with broth.

In a large casserole, alternate layers of the various meats with 1 inch of beans in between. Pour the deglazing liquid over the beans and add more broth to the top to moisten all the ingredients. Bring the cassoulet to a boil on top of the stove, then drizzle melted goose fat over the top, This will keep the beans from drying out during cooking and also creates a glaze on the top that is typical of the Castelnaudary cassoulet. Continue cooking in a 350 F oven (to maintain a low simmer) for about 2 hours, adding a little broth if needed.
The cassoulet should be served bubbling hot. It can also be cooled, refrigerated several days and reheated.

Plate Presentation

A serving of beans should be accompanied by a little of each of the meats. By spooning straight down through the layers, it's usually easy to find the various ingredients.

(Mme Gouttes)

Veal Shoulder «Bayonnaise»

Ingredients (4 servings)

400 g (14 oz) veal shoulder
300 g (10 oz) rice
Cured ham, sliced thinly
Veal or chicken broth
12 pearl or spring onions, peeled
50 g (about 1/2 cup) grated parmesan or gruyere
Unsalted butter, salt, freshly ground pepper

Procedure

Bone the veal shoulder and trim the cartilage.
Spread it out on the work surface (you may need to butterfly the meat a little to make a piece of an even thickness). Cover the surface of the meat with thin slices of cured ham (the chef uses Bayonne ham from his region).
Heat a little butter and brown the meat on all sides. Remove the meat and put the onions in the pan. When the onions are lightly browned, put the meat back into the pan, deglaze with 1/2 cup broth, cover and cook over very low heat about 1 hour.
While the meat is cooking, prepare the rice. Melt 1-2 tbls butter, add the rice (1 1/2 cups or 300 g (10 oz)) and stir over low heat until the rice absorbs the butter without browning. Add one and half times the volume of the rice in water or broth (2 1/4 cups). Add a little salt (amount depends on the flavor of the broth), bring to a simmer, cover, then cook gently 17 minutes or until all the liquid is absorbed. Gently stir the grated cheese into the cooked rice with a fork.

Presentation

Slice the meat and overlap the slices in the center of a platter. Surround the slices of meat with rice and garnish with the onions.
Alternatively, the rice can be molded in a ring mold with the slices of meat overlapped around the rice with the onions in the center.
Strain the meat juices and pass separately in a sauce boat.

(P. Paillon)

174

Veal Blanquette with Pearl Onions

Ingredients (6 servings)

1.5 kg (3 1/4 lbs) veal shoulder
Unsalted butter
3 carrots, 1 leek, 1 garlic clove
1 large onion studded with a clove
1 bouquet garni with celery
300 g (10 oz) button mushrooms
1/2 cup dry white wine
150 g (5 oz) pearl onions, peeled
18 Brussel sprouts, braised
5 Belgian endive, braised
1 bunch chervil, chopped

Sabayon sauce:
2 egg yolks
2 tsps unsalted butter
1 tbls heavy cream
Juice of 1/2 lemon
1/2 cup dry white wine

Procedure

To prepare the blanquette:
Bone the veal shoulder, trim fat and cartilage and cut into 5 cm (2 inch) cubes. In a large heavy casserole, melt a little butter and cook the meat a little over medium heat to sear the outside without browning. Pour off the fat and add water to cover and season with salt and pepper.

Bring a boil and skim all impurities that rise to the surface in the form of a froth. Lower the heat and add the bouquet garni, onion with clove and sliced carrots, leeks and garlic. Simmer for about 1 1/2 hours or until the meat is tender. Remove the meat with a slotted spoon and place in a large shallow bowl, keep warm.

Use cooking liquid from the meat to braise the endives and Brussel sprouts. Simmer the mushrooms in 1/2 cup white wine, 1 cup veal broth and 1 tlb butter until the liquid is reduced and the mushrooms are glazed. Cook the onions in broth and butter until glazed.

To prepare the sabayon:

Shortly before serving the blanquette, combine 1/2 cup white wine and 2 egg yolks in a saucepan. Whisk over a water bath until the the mixture becomes warm and thick. Remove from the heat and whisk to increase the volume. Whisk in the butter a little at a time and the cream, then season with lemon juice, salt and white pepper.

Presentation

Heat the remaining broth and strain over the meat. Garnish with braised vegetables. Ladle sabayon over the top of the dish.

(M. Derbane)

Veal Sweetbreads Blanquette with Cepes and Foie Gras Sauce

Ingredients (4 servings)

2 large veal sweetbreads
500 ml (2 cups) veal stock
250 ml (1 cup) heavy cream or crème fraîche
2 tbls puréed foie gras
5-6 fresh cepes
1 onion, 1 carrot, 1 bouquet garni
Salt, white pepper

Procedure

Degorge the sweetbreads in cold water for 12 hours.
Remove the thin skin, blanch 15 minutes in simmering salted water, then stop the cooking in ice water.
Separate the lobes of the sweetbreads and place in a casserole with the onion, carrot, bouquet garni and seaon with salt and pepper. Cover with veal stock and simmer 1 hour. Remove the cooked sweetbreads with a slotted spoon. When cooled slightly, cut into thick slices and keep warm.
Meanwhile, thoroughly wash the cepes and cut into thick slices. Sauté in butter and season with salt and pepper, set aside.
Make a roux and cook without letting it brown. Whisk in the cooking liquid from the sweetbreads to make a velouté. Strain, then add cream. Simmer this sauce to make it smooth and rich. Shortly before serving whisk in the foie gras. To further enrich the sauce (this step is optional), whisk in 1 egg yolk (stir a little hot sauce into the yolk, then whisk into the sauce. Add the cooked cepes to the finished sauce.

Plate Presentation

Arrange the warm slices of sweetbreads on plates and ladle the foie gras sauce over the meat. Chef Cazalis decorates this sumptuous dish with tiny golden croissants made with puff pastry.

(M. Cazalis)

Stuffed Saddle of Lamb «en Croûte» with Mandarine Liqueur

Ingredients (8 servings)

1 saddle of lamb (1.5 kg (3 1/4 lbs))
800 g (1 lb 10 oz) leg of lamb
400 g (14 oz) small mushrooms*
1/2 cup mandarine liqueur
1/2 cup heavy cream or crème fraîche
1 sprig rosemary
200 g (7 oz) barding fat
Unsalted butter
Salt, pepper
*The chef uses small, mild «mousserons», known as St George's mushrooms.

Procedure

Cut the leg of lamb into small dice. Heat a little butter and sear the lamb over high heat. Lower the heat, add the mushroms and cook until the juice exuded from the mushrooms is evaporated. Add the liqueur, cream and rosemary and simmer gently until the liquid is reduced and thickened. Set aside to cool.

Meanwhile, bone the saddle of lamb and trim the fat. Lay the meat flat on the work surface, season lightly and spread the cooled lamb and cream mixture over the center of the meat. Roll the boned saddle around the filling, tie with kitchen string and wrap the ends with barding fat.
Spread a layer of lamb bones and sliced carrots and onions in a roasting pan and brown in a hot oven. Place the stuffed meat on top of the bones and return to a very hot oven 230 C (450) to brown for 5 minutes. Set on a rack to cool.

Roll out the puff pastry, place the meat on top and seal the edges. Brush the top with egg glaze and return to a 200 C (400 F) oven for 15-18 minutes. The pastry will be golden and the meat will be medium rare.
A sauce can made with the bones and served with slices of the lamb.

(C. Parrain)

Pheasant with Grapes and Oranges

Procedure

Brush with butter (do not wrap in barding fat) and roast in a hot oven, basting often with the cooking juices.
Cook 2 tbls sugar with a little water to a very light caramel. Deglaze with the juice of 3 oranges and 1 cup of reduced chicken broth.
Bring the liquid to a boil. Dissolve potato starch in Port and whisk into the broth to thicken.

Peel and seed 20 large green grapes and add to the sauce. Just before serving, whisk in 50 g (3 tbls) butter and add a few walnut halves and sections from 3 oranges.
Clean and prepare a large pheasant. Truss the bird and season with salt and pepper.

Plate Presentation

Cut the pheasant into four portions.
Place each in the center of heated plates and coat with sauce, dividing the elements of the sauce evenly between the servings.

(M. Cazalis)

Rabbit Stuffed with Chevre and Mint

Ingredients (6 servings)

2 large rabbits
6- 20 cm (8 inch) squares caul fat
8-10 oz fresh goat cheese («chevre»)
2 bunches fresh mint
300 ml (10 fl oz) heavy cream or crème fraîche
Salt, pepper
Fresh pasta (egg and spinach), cooked

Procedure

Bone the rabbits and separate the legs from the saddles.
Blend 2/3 of the chevre with 1 small bunch finely chopped mint leaves. Make a slit in each piece of rabbit to form a pocket and stuff with the cheese. Season with salt and pepper, then cover each portion with caul fat. Roast in a 230 C (450 F) oven about 45 minutes. Baste from time to time with the meat juices, use a little water or stock if needed to keep the meat moist.

Meanwhile infuse the second bunch of mint into 2 cups of water. Strain then whisk in the cheese and stir as the mixture simmers and becomes smooth. Stir the cream into the simmering sauce and continue to whisk until it is thick and smooth. Season with freshly ground pepper.

Transfer the cooked rabbit pieces to a plate and keep warm. Pour off the fat from the roasting pan and deglaze with the sauce. Bring to a simmer then strain.

Plate Presentation

Mound cooked flat noodles on each plate (egg and spinach noodles combined). Place a portion of rabbit on top and ladle sauce over the meat.

(D. Ducroux)

178

Saddle of Rabbit with Blackberries

Ingredients (4 servings)

2 saddles of rabbit
250 ml (1 cup) dry white wine
250 g (8 oz) thick sliced bacon or pork fat
150 g (5 oz) blackberries
1/4 cup Cognac
2 tbls each oil, unsalted butter
2 carrots, 1 onion, 1 bay leaf, 1 thyme sprig
Juice of 1 lemon
2 tbls red currant jelly
1 tsp tomato paste
Salt, freshly ground pepper
250 g (8 oz) sandwich bread, unsliced

Procedure

Trim the saddles of rabbit. Insert matchstick-size pieces of the bacon or pork fat into the rabbit flesh to baste the meat from within during cooking. Place the rabbit pieces and trimmings on a bed of sliced carrots and onions with aromatics and cover with Cognac and white wine. Season very lightly with salt and add a few black peppercorns to the marinade, cover and refrigerate 24 hours.
Remove the saddles of rabbit from the marinade and pat dry. Roast in a hot oven with a little oil until medium rare. Remove the carrots, onions and rabbit trimmings from the marinade and brown in butter. Add the marinade liquid and simmer one hour, skimming the surface occasionally.
Strain through a fine-meshed sieve and whisk in the currant jelly and tomato paste. Season to taste with salt, pepper and lemon juice.
Cook the blackberries a few minutes in their own juices, then add to the sauce.
Cut the bread into large croutons and pan fry in butter.

Plate Presentation

Cut the saddles in half to obtain 4 portions. Place each portion of rabbit on a crouton. Serve with potaotes Dauphine (croquettes). Spoon a little sauce on the meat and pass the rest separately.

(R. Moser)

Haunch of Wild Boar Spit Roasted with a Golden Crust

This is a very special recipe which won the «Concours Eugenie Lacroix» in Frankfurt in 1953.

An entire haunch of wild boar (available in Europe during fall hunting season) is slow roasted on a spit then encrusted with a thin batter which is poured over the meat during the final stage of cooking. It takes a practiced technique to achieve good results.

Cooking the wild boar «ham»:

Choose a short meaty haunch and remove the bone, working from both sides to the middle to keep the meat intact. Trim tendons and silverskin and remove most of the fat, leaving a 1/4 inch layer.

Make a classic wild game marinade (red wine, aromatics, including juniper berries) and marinate the boned meat for four days in the refrigerator.

Truss the meat if necessary to keep it in a solid piece and place on the spit before a hot fire made from hard woods. Count about 20 minutes per pound.

Place a pan below the meat to catch the drippings. Add a good white wine to the juices and use this liquid to baste the meat as it turns on the spit. Place 2 kilos (4 1/2 lbs) blanched chestnuts in the flavorful basting juices to finish cooking.

The batter for the crust:

While the meat is cooking, prepare a thin batter made with 500 g (1 lb) flour, 200-250 g (7-8 oz) sugar, 400 g (14 oz) unsalted melted butter, 1 tsp salt, 1/2 cup fruity white wine and 9 large eggs (separated).

Beat together the yolks and sugar until thick and light. Stir in the flour and melted butter, then stir in the wine. Beat the egg whites to stiff peaks and fold them into the mixture. The batter should fall from the spatula in a thick ribbon; if it is too firm, thin out with a little wine.

Covering the meat with the pasty crust:

Before adding the batter, allow the meat to cook without basting so the surface is dry. Remove the pan with the meat drippings and chestnuts and set aside. Place another pan beneath the meat to catch the excess batter. As the meat continues to turn on the spit, drizzle the batter over the meat. As each thin layer cooks, continue to add batter until the crust is about 2 cm (3/4 in) thick and is golden brown.

This very fancy «ham en croûte» provides meat for a large group.

Presentation

Carefully remove the meat from the spit and transfer to a large oval platter without breaking the crust.

Place the cooked chestnuts around the meat. Also garnish with small braised onions and individual portions of braised cabbage about the size and shape of an egg.

Place the platter on a cart to transport it to the dining room and slice just before serving.

Make a sauce with cranberry jelly or relish blended with some of the cooking juices, pass separately.
(
P. Paillon)

Wild Boar Medallions with Chestnut and Celery Root Purées

Ingredients (4 servings)
1.5 kg (3 lbs) young wild boar (bone in)
200 g (7 oz) prepared pie pastry
600 g (1 lb 3 1/2 oz) chestnut purée
400 g (14 oz) celery root purée
250 ml (1 cup) blood (thickener)

Procedure

Remove the bone and trim the meat. Keep the bone and trimmings for the sauce.
Cut the meat into thick slices (2 cm (3/4 in)) with a weight of about 60-75 g (2-2 1/2 oz) each.
Make a marinade with 1 sliced carrot, 1 onions with two cloves, 1 sliced shallot, 1 pinch cracked peppercorns, 1 crushed garlic clove, 1 parsley sprig, 1 thyme sprig, 1 bay leaf, 1/2 cup vinegar, 1 bottle red wine, and a little salt and pepper. Add the meat, cover and refrigerate 24 hours.
Roll out the pastry dough and make individual «barquette» shells (boat-shaped tartlette), prick the base with a fork then bake.
Prepare the chestnut and celery root purées (with cream).
Shortly before serving, using a star tip, pipe the purées into the baked tartlette shells. The chef serves 1 celery root and 2 chestnut tartlettes per person.

Poivrade sauce:

Brown the meat trimmings and the vegetables from the marinade in oil. Deglaze with 50 ml (4 tbls) wine vinegar and reduce completely. Add 250 ml (1 cup) each veal stock and marinade liquid and 12 crushed peppercorns and simmer gently 1 hour.
Pour the liquid through a fine-meshed strainer. Bind the sauce with the blood (same procedure as thickening a sauce with eggs) and stir in 1 tbl currant jelly. Season to taste and keep warm without bringing to a simmer which would curdle the blood in the sauce.

Presentation

Dry the marinated medallions of boar and pan fry in butter over high heat.

Place three slices of meat per person on heated plates and arrange the tartlettes in between. Spoon sauce over the meat and serve the rest separately.

(M. Prades)

Filet of Wild Boar with Cream

Ingredients

1 fresh boar filet
1/2 bottle red Burgundy
Unsalted butter
Aromatics (carrot, onion, etc.)
250 ml (1 cup) heavy cream or crème fraîche
250 ml (1 cup) «poivrade» sauce
2 fl oz Cognac
Chestnuts and/or fresh pasta
Sandwich bread

Procedure

Trim the filet, leaving a thin layer of fat.
Make a marinade with sliced carrots, onions, parsley, thyme, bay leaf and wine. Add the meat, cover and refrigerate 3-4 days.
Pat dry the marinated filet in a dish towel. Heat butter over high heat in a roasting pan and add the meat and drained vegetables from the marinade. Turn the meat and brown on all sides. Finish roasting in a hot oven about 35 minutes, basting occasionally.
Remove the meat and keep warm.
Deglaze the roasting pan with Cognac, flame, add the cream and reduce.
Stir in the poivrade sauce and reduce to thicken and concentrate the flavors. Season to taste then bind the sauce with blood and enrich with butter.
Trim sandwich bread into croutons the diameter of the filet and pan fry in butter.

Presentation

Slice the filet, place the meat on the croutons and coat with sauce.
Surround the meats with chestnuts glazed in butter. Mound fresh cooked pasta, tossed in butter, in the center.

(J. Rogliardo)

Desserts

«Ressurection» Cream

This old recipe from the Bourbonnais has been enjoyed by the farmers of that region on holidays for many years. It is a rich sabayon made with dry white wine and «Marc» a strong liqueur distilled from the skins of crushed grapes.

This invigorating dessert has been aptly named «crème de la résurrection».

Ingredients (6 servings)

12 egg yolks
100 ml (3.5 fl oz dry white wine
125 g (4 oz) sugar
50 ml (4 tlbs) «marc»
Juice and zest of 1 lemon

Procedure

Whisk together the yolks and the sugar in the top of a double boiler. As the mixture becomes warm and thick, continue to beat to achieve a light, foamy sabayon.

Whisk in the wine and lemon juice and continue to cook over the water bath until the mixture is warm and thick and forms a ribbon when the whisk is lifted.

Remove from the heat and whisk constantly as the sabayon cools. Stir the «marc» and lemon zest into the cooled «crème».

Presentation

Spoon the dessert into champagne glasses. Sprinkle crumbled nougatine on top and accompany with freshly baked vanilla-flavored ladyfingers.

(F. Laustriat)

Tarte Tatin «Bonne Auberge»

Ingredients (8 servings)
2
00 g (7 oz) unsalted butter
400 g (14 oz) sugar
250 g (8 oz) prepared pie pastry
1.5 kg (3 1/4 lbs) apples (Reinettes or Golden Delicious)

Procedure

The traditional pan for this upside down tart is a heavy copper pie plate. Use an oven-proof pan that conducts heat well so that the sugar does not burn.
Roll out the dough and form a circle about 30 cm (12 in) in diameter. Cover and reserve in a cool place.
Peel the apples, cut into quarters and remove the core.
In a 28 cm (10 inch) pan, melt the butter, then stir in the sugar. Cook until the mixture becomes a dark caramel. Remove from the heat and cool a few minutes. Arrange the apple quarters on end in circles, starting on the outside. They should be packed tightly into the pan.
Bake the apples in a hot oven (220 C (425 F) until very soft and their juices have blended with the caramel.
Remove the tart from the oven and place the circle of pastry on top, tucking the ends around the edge to completely cover the apples.
Brush with egg glaze and score a design wth a fork. Cut a small hole in the center and insert a «chimney» made with foil or parchment paper to allow steam to escape.
Bake another 10 minutes to cook the pastry.
Set the baked tart on a cooling rack until just warm. Place a large plate on top and invert the pie onto the service plate.

Presentation

Sprinkle powdered sugar over the warm tart and flame with Calvados at the table.

(J. Rogliardo)

Caramelized Peach in Crispy «Feuilleté»

Ingredients (4 servings)

500 g (1 lb) prepared puff pastry
or prepare fresh with:
250 g (8 oz) unbleached flour
15 g (3 tsps) salt
100 ml (3.5 fl oz) cold water
200 g (7 oz) unsalted butter

Mango «coulis»:
100 ml (3.5 fl oz) water
100 g (3 1/2 oz) sugar
1 large ripe mango

Garnish:
250 g (8 oz) wild strawberries
1 pint pistachio ice cream
4 ripe peaches
100 g (3 1/2 oz) sugar

Procedure

Make the puff pastry in advance so that it has time to rest before rolling out. Roll out a rectangle 3 mm (1/8 in) thick. Sprinkle cold water on a heavy baking sheet and transfer the pastry to the sheet.

Prick the entire surface with a fork and trim the edges.

Cut the pastry into 8 even squares (be sure your serving plates are large enough to hold the «feuilletés»). Chill the dough, then bake in a 200 C (400 F) oven about 20-25 minutes or until golden and crisp.

Make a simple syrup; combine the water and sugar, simmer two minutes and skim the surface and cool. Peel the mango and purée in a food processor, adding sugar syrup to make a smooth sauce or «coulis».

Plunge the peaches 3 seconds into boiling water to loosen the skins. Peel, cut in half and remove the stone.

Place, rounded side up, on a baking sheet and sprinkle copiously with powdered sugar. Caramelize the sugar under the broiler.

Presentation

Spoon the mango sauce onto 4 plates. Sprinkle each pastry with powdered sugar then place a peach half on top of each. Place one pastry in the center of each plate and carefully position a second pastry square on top. Garnish the mango sauce with the wild strawberries.

(D. Simunic)

Banana Crêpes with Pineapple and Rum

Ingredients (6 servings)

1 large ripe pineapple (750 g (1 1/2 lbs))
400 g (14 oz) ripe bananas
400 ml (14 fl oz) whole milk
3 large eggs
Sugar
150 g (5 oz) unbleached flour
100 ml (3.5 fl oz) corn oil
200 ml (7 fl oz) rum
100 ml (3.5 fl oz) heavy cream
1 vanilla bean

Procedure

Make the crêpe batter in a large bowl. Whisk together the milk, eggs, 1 1/2 tbls sugar, a pinch of salt, 20 ml (2/3 fl oz) rum and 1 tbl oil. Place the flour in the bowl, then stir the wet ingredients into the flour. If the batter is not perfectly smooth, pour it through a fine-meshed sieve and press on the lumps. Cover and refrigerate.

Make a simple syrup with 500 ml (2 cups) water and 300 g (10 oz) sugar. Bring to a boil, skim, add a split vanilla bean and simmer 2-3 minutes. Skim the surface again and keep warm.
Peel the pineapple and cut into thick slices 1-1.5 cm (3/8-1/2 in). Cut out the core of each slice with a round cutter.

Poach the pineapple slices in the syrup, then carefully, without breaking the slices, transfer them to a rack to drain.
Peel the bananas and cut into thick slices. Poach them in the syrup used to poach the pineapple. Purée the cooked bananas in a food mill, then stir in the cream and 20 ml (2/3 oz) rum.
Cook the crêpes (12 total). Spread them on the work sorface and sprinkle with rum. Spread the banana compote on the crêpes and fold in quarters.
Arrange two crêpes on each (heatproof) plate and place in a warm oven.

Presentation

Place a slice of pineapple on top of each crêpe, sprinkle generously with powdered sugar and caramelize under the broiler.
Flame with rum at the table and serve while still warm.

(J. Houbron)

Souffléd Crêpes with Grand Marnier

Ingredients (8 servings)

Crêpe batter:
250 ml (1 cup) whole milk
100 g (3 1/2 oz) unbleached flour
70 g (2 1/3 oz) melted butter
2 eggs and 3 egg yolks

Crème patissière (pastry cream):
250 ml (1 cup) whole milk
300 g (10 oz) unbleached flour
70 g (2 1/3 oz) sugar
1 vanilla bean, split
5 egg yolks

Soufflé additions and flavorings:
150 g (5 oz) sugar
8 egg whites
100 ml (3.5 fl oz) Grand Marnier
4 large oranges
Powdered sugar, unsalted butter

Sauce: crème anglaise with Grand Marnier

Procedure

To make the crêpes, begin by whisking together the milk, eggs and melted butter then stir into the flour. If not perfectly smooth, pour through a strainer. Thin with a little milk if necessary. Cook 16 crêpes, 15 cm (6 in) in diameter. Remove the zest of the oranges with a vegetable peeler and chop finely. Combine the zest with the Grand Marnier and the juice of the 4 oranges and macerate 15 minutes.

To make the crème patissière, bring the milk to a boil with the vanilla bean. Whisk together the sugar and egg yolks until thick and lemon-colored. Stir in the flour until blended in with no lumps.
Whisk the hot milk into the egg mixture then transfer it all back to the pot and cook over moderate heat, stirring constantly, as the custard thickens.
Off the heat, stir in the orange zest, orange juice and Grand Marnier.
Beat the 8 egg whites to firm peaks, whisk in 150 g (5 oz) sugar and fold this meringue into the pastry cream.
Spoon some of the soufflé mixture onto one half of each crêpe and fold over the other half to cover. Transfer carefully to a buttered and lightly floured baking sheet. Sprinkle the crêpes with powdered sugar and bake at 200 C (400 F) until puffed, about 10 minutes.

Presentation

Arrange two crêpes on each plate and flame with Grand Marnier at the table. Serve immediately.
Pass the crème anglaise with Grand Marnier in a sauceboat.

(C. Parrain)

«Beggars' Purses» with Mandarine Soufflé

Ingredients (10 servings)

Crêpe batter:
4 large eggs
5 g (1 2/3 oz) sugar
2 tbls oil
200 g (7 oz) sifted unbleached flour
50 g 1 2/3 oz) melted unsalted butter
50 ml (4 tbls) mandarine liqueur
250 ml (1 cup) whole milk
1 tsp vanilla extract
1 tsp orange flower water

Soufflé mixture:
500 ml (2 cups) whole milk
8 large eggs, separated
150 g (5 oz) sugar
60 g (2 oz) flour
100 ml (3.5 fl oz) mandarine liqueur

Soufflé flavoring::
100 g (3 1/2 oz) sugar
250 ml (1 cup) water
10 mandarine oranges

Sabayon sauce:
8 egg yolks
100 g (3 1/2 oz) sugar
250 ml (1 cup) brut Champagne
2 drops grenadine syrup
Mandarine julienne and syrup (from filling)

Procedure

To make the crêpes:
Whisk together the eggs and sugar until light and thick. Stir in the flour until the mixture is smooth. Stir in the melted butter and oil a little at a time. Add the milk a little at a time, then stir in the orange flower water, liqueur and vanilla. The batter should be very smooth and fluid (like heavy cream).

Cover and set aside in a cool place for 15 minutes.
Cook 10 crêpes in a 20 cm (8 in) pan, set aside.

To make the soufflé flavoring:
Peel the mandarine oranges and cut the peel of five of them into very thin julienne. Cover with cold water in a saucepan, bring to a boil, strain then refresh in cold warer.
Make a syrup with the sugar and water, add the julienned peel and simmer to candy the peel and concentrate the syrup.
Remove the candied peel with a slotted spoon and add the mandarine orange sections. Simmer for 5 minutes, remove the sections and cool.

To make the soufflé mixture:
Bring the milk to a boil. Meanwhile, whisk together the egg yolks and sugar until thick and lemon-colored. and stir in the flour until well blended. Whisk the hot milk into the egg mixture. Return it to the pot and continue cooking about 2 minutes until the mixture bubbles and becomes very thick, stirring constantly so the custaard doesn't stick.
Transfer to a bowl to cool.
Beat the egg whites to firm peaks and gently fold them into the pastry cream.

To fill the «beggars' purses»:
Spoon soufflé mixture into the center of the crêpes and add a few poached mandarine sections and candied peel to each. Pull the edges of the crêpes up over the filling and gather them at the top to resemble a small purse. Keep the top closed with two toothpicks inserted at right angles.
Place the purses on a buttered and lightly floured baking sheet. Sprinkle with powdered sugar, cover with a sheet of parchment paper and bake for 15 minutes at 190 C (375 F).

To make the sabayon sauce:
Whisk together the yolks and sugar over a water bath until thick. Whisk in the Champagne a little at a time.
When the mixture is hot (but not hot enough to cook the eggs), remove from the heat and continue beating until the sabayon is cool and thick. Stir in the genadine syrup, remaining zest and mandarine syrup (from cooking the zests).
Keep the sauce warm in a water bath until service.

Presentation

Spoon the sauce on the plates and place a filled crêpe in the center.
Garnish with the remaining mandarine sections and fresh mint leaves.

(P. Paumel)

Crispy Almond Cookies with Two Chocolates

Ingredients (8-10 servings)

Frozen Mousse
300 g (10 oz) bittersweet chocolate
3 egg whites
750 ml (3 cups) heavy cream
100 g (3 1/2 oz) powdered sugar
1 pint mint or raspberry sorbet
75 g (2 1/2 oz) white chocolate

Cookie batter:
65 g (2 oz) powdered sugar
2 egg whites
1/2 tsp vanilla extract
50 g (1 2/3 oz) sifted flour
50 g (1 2/3 oz) unsalted butter, melted
75 g (2 1/2 oz) sliced almonds
1 pinch salt

Sauce:
Crème anglaise with candied orange peel

Procedure

To make the frozen mousse:
Chop the chocolate and melt over a water bath. Keep slightly warm to keep it melted.

Beat the egg whites to firm peaks and whisk in half of the powdered sugar.

Beat the cream to firm peaks (in a cold bowl) and beat in the remaining sugar.

Fold the meringue into the slightly warm chocolate, then the whipped cream.

Transfer the mixture to a rectangular mold (or loaf pan), cover and place in the freezer at least 5 hours.

To make the cookies:
Stir together the egg whites and powdered sugar until smooth. Blend in the vanilla, salt, flour, then stir in the melted butterto obtain a smooth batter.

With a pastry brush, spread paper-thin rectangles (5 X 10 cm (2 X 4 in)) of the batter on buttered baking sheets. Sprinkle sliced almonds on each rectangle of batter.

Bake for 3-4 minutes at 200 C (400 F) or until the edges are browned and the center of the cookies is cooked but not browned.

Transfer the cookies immediately to a flat surface to cool.
You will need two cookies per serving.

Presentation

Unmold the frozen mousse and slice it into 8-10 portions.
Place a cookie in the center of each plate and postition a slice of mousse on top. Top the mousse with a slice or scoop of sorbet.

Place a second cookie on top and cover with white chocolate shavings.
Serve with crème anglaise flavored with candied orange peel.

(M. Derbane)

181

Pear «Gargouilleau»

This simple pear cake comes from northeast France where it is enjoyed at informal dinners. This is an easily prepared variation on the classic cherry «clafoutis» which is usually served warm from the oven.

Ingredients (6 servings)

12 pears
75 g (2 1/2 oz) sifted flour
100 g (3 1/2 oz) sugar
2 large eggs
200 ml (7 fl oz) whole milk
100 ml (3.5 fl oz) heavy cream
Coarse sugar

Procedure

Mix the flour and sugar. Stir in the eggs, then thin the batter with milk and cream.
The mixture is very similar to a crêpe batter with a texture like heavy cream. If not perfectly smooth, pour through a sieve.

Peel the pears and remove the seeds from the top or bottom with a corer. Cut into round slices and arrange in a heavily buttered earthenware or glass dish and pour the batter over the pears.

Sprinkle the surface with coarse sugar and place a few bits of butter on top.
Bake at 220 C (425 F) about 45 minutes.

(F. Laustriat)

Pear Surprise

For each serving, peel one large, ripe pear and cut in half. Remove the core with a melon baller and slice thinly. Fan out the slices in a circle on a dinner plate.

Place a double mint leaf in the center of the pears and pose a bright red raspberry in the center of the leaves.
Spoon a red fruit coulis around the edge of the plate.

(To make 1 L of red coulis bring 300 ml (10 fl oz) red wine to a simmer with 200 g (14 oz) sugar, stir in 300 ml (10 fl oz) each puréed raspberries and black currants and simmer 2-3 minutes. Strain and cool.)

Pipe a little crème fraîche through a paper cone to make small decorations in the red sauce. Use the point of a knife to «pull» the cream through the sauce to elaborate the design.

Between the decorations place a small scoop of pear sorbet, a small pear charlotte decorated with red currants and a bite size pear-filled turnover. (For the latter, sauté diced pears in butter with honey and chopped almonds, cool and fill circles of puff pastry, fold in half and bake until golden brown.)
Make the elements of the «Pear Surprise» in advance and assemble just before serving.

(M. Vessat)

Pear «Flognarde»

Ingredients (4 servings)

200 g (7 oz) flour
1/2 tsp baking powder (optional)
5 large eggs
50 g (1 2/3 oz) unsalted butter, melted
70 g (2 1/2 oz) powdered sugar
1 pinch salt
500 ml (2 cups) whole milk
2 pears

Procedure

Butter a jelly roll pan or baking sheet with sloping sides.

Mix the wet ingredients into the dry ingredients like for a crêpe batter. Blend until smooth without working the batter too much. Pour through a sieve if necessary.

Spread the thick batter onto the pan, smoothing the surface to make an even layer. Arrange the pear slices in rows, overlapping the edges slightly. Bake in a 200 C (400 F) oven until the flan is puffed and golden around the edges. Sprinkle with granulated sugar and serve warm.

(A. Parveaux)

«Flaune Millavoise»

Ingredients (6 servings)

Pie pastry:
250 g (8 oz) sifted unbleached flour
125 g (4 oz) unsalted butter
1 egg
1 tbl oil
1 pinch salt
1 pinch sugar

Filling:
1.25 kg (2 1/2 lbs) ricotta*
6 large eggs
200 ml (7 fl oz) orange flower water
8 tbls sugar
*This dessert is traditionally made with «recuite», a soft, low fat cheese made from recooked whey.

Procedure

Prepare the pie pastry. Form a well in the flour and place the softened butter, egg, salt and sugar in the center. Blend the wet ingredients into the flour until smooth without over working the dough. Roll out and line a tart pan. Trim the edges and prick the bottom with a fork.
In the mixer, blend the cheese, eggs, orange flower water and sugar until smooth. Fill the tart with this filling and smooth the surface. Bake at 200 C (400 F) for 30 minutes or until the filling is set.
Sprinkle with powdered sugar and serve warm or cold.

(P. Pomarède)

Peaches with «Marc de Gewurztraminer»

Ingredients (4 servings)

4 very large peaches poached in syrup
Sliced almonds, toasted

Vanilla ice cream:
230 ml (1 cup whole milk
250 ml (1 cup) heavy cream
5-6 egg yolks
1 vanilla bean
100 g (3 1/2 oz) sugar

Sabayon with Marc de Gewurztraminer:
6 egg yolks
200 g (7 oz) sugar
500 ml (2 cups) whipping cream
(half of the whipped cream is for decoration)
50 ml (4 tbls) Marc de Gewurztraminer
(«Marc» is a very strong, clear liqueur distilled from the crushed skins of grapes)

Procedure

To make the ice cream:
Whisk the yolks and sugar until thick and light. Whisk in the milk and cream and transfer the mixture to a saucepan. Add a split vanilla bean and cook the crème anglaise over low heat, stirring constantly until it thickens enough to coat a spoon. Strain, cool and freeze in an ice cream maker according to manufacturer's instructions. Spoon into a decorative mold (which will fit in the center of the service platter) and store in the freezer.
Marc sabayon:
Whisk the yolks and sugar together over a water bath until thick and lemon-colored. When the mixture holds a «ribbon» when the whisk is lifted, remove from the heat and continue to whisk until cooled.
Beat the cream and fold half of it into the sabayon, alternating with spoonfuls of «marc». Work carefully without deflating the sauce.

Presentation

Unmold the ice cream onto the center of the platter. Decorate with the remaining whipped cream piped with a star tip.
Arrange 8 peach halves around the ice cream (rounded side up). Spoon the sauce over the peaches and sprinkle toasted almonds on top. Serve immediately.
(R. Moser)

Prune Ice Cream with Macaroons

Ingredients (5 servings)

Ice cream:
1 L (1 qt) whole milk
8 egg yolks
300 g (10 oz) sugar
2 vanilla beans, split
100 g (3 1/2 oz) prune purée
50 ml (4 tbls) prune «eau de vie»

Garnish:
300 g (10 oz) pitted prunes
100 ml (3.5 fl oz) prune «eau de vie» or Armagnac
200 ml (7 fl oz) raspberry coulis
Caramel made with 200 g (7 oz) sugar

Macaroons:
100 g (3 1/2 oz) ground almonds
100 g (3 1/2 oz) grated coconut
300 g (10 oz) powdered sugar
3 egg whites

Procedure

To make the ice cream:
Infuse the split vanilla beans into the milk.

Whisk the egg yolks with the sugar until thick and light. Stir the simmering milk into the egg yolks, then return the mixtue to the saucepan. Cook over low heat, stirring constantly, until the crème anglaise thickens just enough to coat a spoon. Strain through a fine-meshed sieve and cool.

Mix the prune purée and prune liqueur into half of the crème anglaise and freeze in an ice cream maker according to manufacturer's instructions. Store in the freezer.

To make the macaroons:
Mix together the almonds, coconut and sugar. Stir in the egg whites one at a time to make a firm mixture. Form 15 macaroons by hand or with a piping bag and place on a baking sheet lined with parchment paper.

Brush the tops of the macaroons with water which makes them shiny. Bake at 200 C (400 F) for 6-8 minutes or until lightly browned on the outside and still moist on the inside.

To make the caramel cage:

Add enough water to the 200 g of sugar to dissolve it. Cook the sugar until it becomes a clear, golden caramel. Stop the cooking by placing the pot in a pan of cool water, then transfer to a pan of hot water to keep the caramel fluid.

Oil the back of a 10 cm (4 in) ladle. With a spoon, pour thin, crossing lines of the caramel over the ladle to form a «cage. Cool, unmold carefully and store in a dry place. Make 5-6 cages all together (or one large one for a platter presentation).

Chop the prunes and macerate in the liqueur and make the raspberry coulis.

Plate Presentation

Spoon the remaining crème anglaise on the plates. Place three macaroons in the center and cover each with a scoop of prune ice cream. Cover the ice cream with a spoonful of macerated chopped prunes.

Drizzle a circle of raspberry coulis through the crème anglaise and use the point of a knife to «pull» the coulis into the crème to make a pretty design.
Place the caramel cage over the ice cream in the center and serve at once.

(T. Larique)

Chocolate Fondant with Mandarine Liqueur

Ingredients

250 g (8 oz) bittersweet chocolate
250 g (8 oz) powdered suagr
250 g (8 oz) unsalted butter, softened
4 large eggs
Mandarine liqueur
Vanilla crème anglaise
Candied clementine slices

Procedure

Melt the chocolate over a water bath. Off the heat, stir in the powdered sugar and mandarine liqueur and blend well. Stir in the softened butter and stir until smooth.

Beat the eggs over a water bath until warm, thick and light (like the first step in making a genoise). Fold the beaten eggs into the chocolate mixture to make a smooth, light mousse.

Spoon the mixture into buttered ramekins, and cook in a water bath at 350 F until set.

Plate Presentation

Spoon crème anglaise on the plates. Unmold the «fondants» («melt-in-your-mouth») and place in the center. Top each dessert with a slice of candied clememtine.

Serve each guest a small glass of chilled mandarine liqueur with the dessert.

(F. Robadey)

Prune Soufflé with Armagnac

Ingredients (6 servings)

1.5 L (1 1/2 qts) whole milk
50 g (1 2/3 oz) sugar
30 g (1 oz) sifted flour
20 g (2/3 oz) unsalted butter
4 large eggs, separated
60 g (2 oz) prune purée
1 pinch salt
6 pitted prunes, macerated in Armagnac
2 fl oz Armagnac

Procedure

Bring the milk to a boil. Whisk together the yolks, sugar and salt until thick and light, then stir in the flour. Stir the hot milk into the eggs, return to the saucepan and cook until the pastry cream bubbles and thickens.

Remove from the heat and stir in the butter, prune purée and Armagnac.
Beat the egg whites to firm peaks and fold into the pastry cream.

Butter 6 large ramekins and sprinkle with sugar. Fill the molds halfway with the soufflé mixture, place a macerated prune in the center and fill to the top.
Smooth the surface with a spatula and bake in a 220C (425 F) oven.

Presentation

When the soufflés are about half done, sprinkle with sugar, which will caramelize while the soufflés finish cooking.
Serve the soufflés immediately.

(F. Laustriat)

Frozen Soufflé with Green Walnut Liqueur

(8 servings)

Procedure

Whisk together 8 egg yolks and 125 g (4 oz) sugar over a water bath (like for a genoise). When the mixture is thick, light and forms a ribbon, remove from the heat and beat until it is completely cooled.

Beat 500 ml (2 cups) heavy cream to stiff peaks with 150 ml (5 fl oz) walnut liqueur. Keep chilled.
Beat 8 egg whites to stiff peaks and whisk in 250 g (8 oz) sugar to make a firm meringue.

Fold the meringue into the beaten egg yolks, then gently fold in the whipped cream along with 50 g (1 2/3 oz) of chopped toasted walnuts. Transfer the soufflé mixture to a rectangular mold, cover and place in the freezer overnight.

Plate Presentation

Unmold the soufflé.
Cut thick slices and place in the center of the plates. Pour a little walnut liqueur over the slices and serve.

The liqueur can be flamed at the table (warm the liqueur flame then pour over the dessert).

(A. Parveaux)

Vanilla Ice Cream

At home or in a restaurant, good vanilla ice cream is a welcome dessert. Rich "French" vanilla ice cream, made with eggs, combines well with toppings of any flavor.

For a divine pleasure, place a scoop inside a warm crêpe flamed with rum. For a fancy dessert, top a scoop with crushed almond cookies and spoon melted raspberry jam over the ice cream and pipe whipped cream all around!

Fresh fruit "coulis", ladled around a scoop of golden vanilla ice cream, provides color and flavor contrast.

Making the crème anglaise, the base for traditional ice cream, is not difficult. The recipe can be adapted for restaurant service so that it will maintain a creamy texture for more than one day.

Ice cream freshly churned at home is usually served at once without storing in the freezer at all. This, of course, is the very best way to enjoy ice cream, while it is creamiest and most flavorful.

But in a restaurant, making fresh ice cream daily is not always possible. By adding a portion of evaporated skim milk powder, the amount of ice crystals is reduced when the ice cream is frozen and it remains creamy for a longer period of time.

Of course, the "restaurant" recipe can be made at home when making ice cream to be stored in the freezer.

Ingredients

Home recipe:
1 L (1 qt) whole milk
8 egg yolks
300 g (10 oz) sugar
35 ml (1 fl oz) heavy cream
1 vanilla bean

Restaurant recipe
1 L (1 qt) whole milk
7 egg yolks
275 g (9 oz) sugar
120 ml (4 fl oz) heavy cream
50 g (1 2/3 oz) evaporated skim milk powder
2 vanilla beans

Procedure

Bring the milk to a boil with the cream and half of the sugar and the vanilla bean(s) split in half. Whisk together the egg yolks and remaining sugar until light and thick, stir in the milk powder.

Stir the hot milk into the eggs then return to the pot and cook over low heat, stirring constantly, until the custard thickens enough to coat the back of a spoon.

Cool the mixture quickly, straining it thorough a fine-meshed sieve into a bowl set in another bowl of ice or cold water. Stir occasionally as it cools to keep a film from forming on the top. This is an important step as it is recommended by health officials to bring the temperature down as quickly as possible to avoid bacterial growth.

As soon as the crème anglaise is no longer hot, freeze in an ice cream maker according to manufacturer's instructions.

(P. Paillon)

Traditional Mardi Gras "Bugnes"

Mardi Gras is not only celebrated in New Orleans and Nice. In the lyonnais region of France this "bugne", a deep fried yeast cake, is made to enjoy fat one last time before Lent.

At this time of year (the whole month of February), bugnes are found in all the pastry shops of Lyon.
The name is traced to the Celtic word "bigne" which means inflated.

Ingredients

500 g (1 lb) high gluten flour
25 g (scant 1 oz) dry yeast
10 g (2 tsps) salt
100 g (3 1/2 oz) sugar
8 large eggs
1 tbl rum
Vanilla extract
100 g (3 1/2 oz) unsalted butter, softened

Procedure

The dough for the bugnes is essentially like a brioche and is mixed in the same way. Dissolve the yeast in a little warm water or milk. Mix the yeast, eggs, sugar salt, vanilla and rum into the flour and mix well. Work in the butter until the dough is smooth. Cover and leave to rise at room temperature for 2-3 hours.

Punch the dough down, roll out to about 3/4 in and cut out oval pieces of dough. To make the distinctive bugne shape, cut a slit in the center and pull the edges through the hole to form a little top knot. Place the bugnes on a floured surface to rise again for 15-20 minutes.

Cooking and Presentation

Deep fry the bugnes in a large, deep pot filled with peanut oil heated to 365 F.

Drop five bugnes at a time into the hot fat. As soon as they come to the surface, turn them to brown on both sides. When puffed and golden, transfer to a rack to drain excess fat. Sprinkle with powdered sugar on both sides and serve warm.

(P. Paillon)

Information about the Chefs and their Restaurants

AIGLE (L') - 61300
Hôtel du Dauphin - Place de la Halle
Tf : 33 84 18 00 - Fax : 33 34 09 28
Michel BERNARD
Jean-Pierre FULEP

Scallop Salad with Endive and Clementines	*(P. 23)*
Veal Kidneys with Mustard Butter	*(P. 59)*
Foie Gras Cooked in Salmon	*(P. 63)*
Apple Mille Feuille with Frozen Calvados Soufflé	*(P. 160)*

"Le Dauphin" has been a restaurant and hotel in the heart of Pays d'Ouche since 1618.
Jean-Pierre Fulep has been the chef here since 1979. He is assisted in the kitchen by Yvon Brageul (Hotel School in Dinard, worked with Guérard and Vergé) and together they make a creative and dynamic team.

AUBIGNEY - 70140
Auberge du Vieux Moulin - Route de Sauvigney
Tf : 84 31 61 61 - Fax : 84 31 21 75
Elisabeth MIRBEY

Sweetbreads with Morels	*(P. 60)*
French Andouillette with White Wine	*(P. 64)*
Braised Trout	*(P. 68)*
Chicken with Crayfish	*(P. 112)*
Caramelized Apples	*(P. 147)*

Situated in the Saône valley at the gates of Burgundy, is the 18th century mill that Louise Mirbey transformed into a restaurant 30 years ago. The mill, abandoned after the industrial revolution has found a new life as a country auberge set on the edge of a forest with ponds, streams and parks all around.

Elisabeth Mirbey, chef de cuisine, is passionate about her chosen career and is dedicated to the special foods and traditions of her region. She works hard to preserve "the memory of how good things taste."

"To learn about and rediscover the wonderful flavors of our traditional cuisine using the new technology and products of today...that's the secret of good cooking.

The future of our profession depends on the next generation to have the desire to learn and follow the rigorous apprenticeship with a respect for the past and eye to the future.

These young chefs must remember that our profession takes dedication to every facet of the business--from the warm welcome at the door and courteous service to top quality products prepared quickly, efficiently, hygienically.... these are the secrets of succeeding!"

Elisabeth Mirbey is a founding member of "Les Dames Cuisinières de France"s, which promotes the role of women chefs and their place in the kitchen equal with men.

Les Dames Cuisinières de France
Siège Social: Auberge du Vieux Moulin
70140 Aubigney
January 7, 1985

Following in the footsteps of our ancestors, the "Mères Cuisinières", we would like to introduce the "Dames Cuisinières" of the present.
This association, "Les Dames Cuisinières de France" has been formed to make female chefs better known.
Recognition of their work will begin when they are apprentices and follow them throughout their training so they know they are not alone in a profession dominated by men.
But our goals are more far reaching!
We are the guardians of the culinary traditions passed from mother to daughter. It is now our turn to continue the indipensible harmony between cuisine, wines and cheeses that makes each of our regions unique.
French women everywhere, above all, be proud of your regional traditions!
Each of us in our own region should work to preserve the "cuisine"
du terroir". Our fellow chefs working in Paris can bring a taste of their native region to their cooking.
Finally, the "Dames Cuisinières de France" extends their support and wishes to work with women chefs in other countries as well.

Madame Elisabeth Mirbey
(President and Founder)

AUVILLERS LES FORGES - 08260
Hostellerie Lenoir
Tf : 24 54 30 11 - Fax : 24 53 75 64
Jean LENOIR

Sweetbreads and Crayfish Salad	*(P. 18)*
Sea Bass Soufflé with Asparagus and Sorrel Sabayon	*(P. 87)*
Lamb Medallions with Morels	*(P. 104)*
Chicken Breast with Leeks	*(P. 110)*
Rock Cornish Hens with Green Peppercorn Sauce	*(P. 115)*
Venison Medallion «à la Normande»	*(P. 127)*
«Delice» of Pineapple with Cointreau	*(P. 132)*
French Toast «Ardennais»	*(P. 140)*
Bouzy Granité	*(P. 156)*
Ratafia Sorbet	*(P. 158)*

Few chefs have enjoyed a career as successful as Jean Lenoir who has attained many prestigious titles; "Maître Cuisinier de France", Cuisinier d'Honneur de l'Europe", "Medaille d'Or de l'Academie Nationale de Cuisine 1995". Known worldwide, Jean Lenoir has participated in many culinary competitions, 70 culinary festivals and served on several jurys as well during his 40 year career. His name is now on a trophy presented annually by the Académie de Reims, "Have Faith, Young Cuisiniers and Maîtres d'Hotel". Chef Lenoir works with his wife Maryse, who is in charge of the dining room.

Salad of Sweetbreads with Crayfish (p. 18)
Here is a lovely salad with a variety of colors. The bright red garnish of crayfish heads contrast beautifully with the greens and golden sweetbreads. Easy to assemble, this salad can serve as an inspiration for variations using chicken, fish or charcuterie.

Lamb Medallions with Morels (p. 104)
For cooks who love fresh morels, it is important to point out that there is a similar mushroom found in the woods that is in fact toxic. "Gyromites" have the same tall pitted cap and hollow stem but are more rounded. The true morel (morchelloc conico) has a pointed cap.

Venison Medallions à la Normande (p. 127)
This is a classic dish that has been improved by Chef Lenoir. He has flambéed the cooking juices with Champagne liqueur and added aged Port before the final addition of cream--the indispensible ingredient for all dishes "à la Normande".
Lamb medallions could be used in a variation of this dish.

Granité of Red Wine (p. 156)
Granité is a lightly sweetened sorbet with an icy texture. It is more a frozen drink than a frozen dessert and it is often served between courses to refresh the palate and "rest the stomach". This granité made with the only still red wine produced in the Champagne region is very good for the digestion.

BEAURECUEIL - 13100
Relais Sainte-Victoire
Tf : 42 66 94 98 - Fax : 42 66 85 96
René BERGÈS

Monkfish and Tomato Terrine	*(P. 10)*
Filet Mignon «Paul Cézanne»	*(P. 97)*
Pine Nut Tart	*(P. 135)*

Founded in 1952 by Mr. Jugy, the team of the Relais de Sainte-Victoire continues to serve refined and inventive dishes while perpetuating traditional cuisine.
The passion for cooking of the Jugy and Bergès families over three generations has established their restaurant as one of the best in the Pays d'Aix.
Chefs Jugy and Bergès welcome their guests to share in this family tradition.
Chef René Bergès has developed a menu of dishes inspired by the products and traditional cuisine of Provence. His creativity and experience guarantees wonderful dining.
The "Relais de Sainte-Victoire" also has a wonderful wine list to choose from.

Filet of Beef "Paul Cézanne" (p.97)
Grande Dame of cooking Gabrielle Jugy has created a wonderful dish using the local red wine and herbs of Provence. The black olive tampenade and anchovies bring to mind the countryside around Aix-en-Provence that Cézanne loved so much.
This is an easy dish to prepare and assemble and is a nice variation for serving beef with a Provence accent.

BELLEGARDE-sur-VALSERINE - 01200
La Belle Epoque - 10, Place Gambetta
Tf : 50 48 14 46 - Fax : 50 56 01 71
Michel SEVIN

Lamb Brains with Avocado and Walnut Oil	*(P. 62)*
«Pot au Feu» of Chicken with Tarragon Sabayon	*(P. 111)*
Duck «Gigot» with Wholegrain Mustard	*(P. 114)*
Frozen Nougat Swans with Blue Curaçao	*(P. 159)*

"La Belle Epoque" is well situated at the crossroads of Bresse, Jura, Savoie and Switzerland on the way to the Alps. Chef Michel Sevin's menu reflects the traditions of "bressane" cuisine.

Lamb's Brains wirth Avocado and Walnut Oil (p.62)
Chef Sevin has created a delicious combination of flavors with brains served on a bed of greens with a lemony dressing accented with walnut oil. The fanned out slices of avocado and bit of tomato make this a lovely dish as well.

Chicken with Tarragon Sabayon (p.111)
Sabayon is a sweet sauce made with Marsala that is a delicious accompaniment to fruits. The delicate tarragon sabayon in this chicken dish is a clever variation of the sweet Sicilian dessert.
Here, the savory tarragon sabayon made with chicken stock and Champagne is the ideal sauce to serve with poached or steamed chicken.

BERGERAC - 24100
Le Cyrano - 2, Bd Montaigne
Tf : 53 57 02 76 - Fax : 53 57 78 15
Jean-Paul TURON

Mussel Gratin with Saffran Sauce	*(P. 33)*
Strawberry Gratin with Monbazillac	*(P. 138)*

Mussel Gratin (p.33)
This dish could also be made with crayfish.
Clean the crayfish and sauté over high heat with oil and butter. Flame with Cognac.
Add a little more wine to the dish made with crayfish since they do not add juice to the sauce like the mussel do. If Monbazillac is not available, choose another good quality sweet white wine.

Strawberry Gratin with Sabayon (p.38)
This sabayon is made with the Monbazillac of the region.
For best results, whisk the sabayon until very thick over low heat. The smoother and thicker it is, the better the sabayon will coat the berries and it will brown more evenly under the broiler.

BOUC BEL AIR - 13320
L'Etape Lani - Route de Marseille - CD. 6
Tf : 42 22 61 90 - Fax : 42 22 68 67
Lucien et Joël LANI

Vegetable Pyramid with Balsamic Vinegar	*(P. 17)*
Duck Foie Gras with Watermelon Preserves and Sweet and Sour Sauce	*(P. 57)*
Turbot with Green Olive Purée	*(P. 77)*
Red Mullet with Artichoke «Barigoule»	*(P. 84)*
Saddle of Rabbit with Celery Root and Poivrade Sauce	*(P. 122)*
Chocolate Millefeuille with Fresh Cheese	*(P. 131)*

The restaurant "L'Etape" was created by Lino and Marguerite Lani in 1967 (and actually built by the chef himself). It is a wonderful Provençale restaurant with a warm ambiance, featuring products purchased at the local market.

Their three children have all completed their culinary studies (Lycée Bonneville in Marseilles) and apprenticed in great restaurants around France (Relais Sainte-Victoire in Beaurecueil, Clos de la Violette in Aix, Petit Nice in Marseille and Troisgros in Roanne).

Message to young chefs:
"The restaurant business is a satisfying profession for those who cook with passion. This begins with studying in the top schools and apprenticing with accomplished chefs.

Message to our customers:
In order to bring the joy of eating to our customers, we must give a lot of ourselves, work professionally and always use the best products.

CASTILLON DU GARD - 30210
Le Vieux Castillon - Vieux Village
Tf : 66 37 00 77 - Fax : 66 37 28 17
Gilles DAUTEUIL

(Scallops Sautéed in Olive Oil with Eggplant Roulade	*(P. 34)*
Snails in Filo Pastry	*(P. 39)*
Fresh Cod Fougasse with Brandad	*(P. 86)*
Lamb Medallions	*(P. 107)*
Thyme Cookies with Lavender Honey Ice Cream and Chocolate	*(P. 152)*

This "Relais et Châteaux" establishment is in the picturesque village of Vieux Castillon near the famous Pont du Gard. Chef Gilles Dauteuil offers an inventive menu of delicate dishes inspired by the products and traditions of Provence.

How to prepare fresh snails
(for the Snail "Pannequet""p.39)
Buy 10 dozen snails. Purge them for 4-5 days with fresh thyme and wild fennel.
Degorge them in coarse salt for 4 hours before boiling. Pull the cooked snails from their shells and rinse them well 6 times in a basin of cold water, drain.
Cook them in olive oil with a chopped onion, 2 finely diced carotts, 4 crushed garlic cloves, bouquet garni with extra thyme, 1 L (1 qt white wine, 2 cups water, and season lightly with salt and pepper).
Simmer gently 4-5 hours.

CHAMPAGNAC de BELAIR - 24530
Le Moulin du Roc
Tf : 53 54 80 36 - Fax : 53 54 21 31
Solange et Alain GARDILLOU

Salmon Trout with Cepes	*(P. 70)*
Caramelized Apple «Gâteau»	*(P. 141)*
Walnut «Fondant»	*(P. 146)*

Hidden away in the heart of Dordogne near Brantôme is the "Moulin du Roc" an old mill that is decorated with beautiful antiques.
Chef Solange Gardillou has passed the baton to her son Alan who has earned a national reputation for his cuisine.

Salmon Trout with Cepes (p.70)
Solange Gardillou has created an innovative variation of carp stuffed with sausage by using salmon trout stuffed with goose rillettes. The fat in the rillettes melts slowly during cooking, adding flavor and moisture to the fish. This marriage of flavors goes very well with the cepe garnish.
Rillettes could be used as a ready made and delicious stuffing in several types of dishes.

Apple Gâteau (p.141)
This apple cake is similar in taste to Tarte Tatin. Many steps are the same as the famous upside down carmelized tart but with different results.
The addition of vanilla ice cream and crème anglaise is delicious and is best when the apples are warm.

Chocolate Sauce to go with "Walnut Fondant" (p.146)

Walnut fondant is always served with this chocolate sauce.

250 g (8 oz) bittersweet chocolate
400 ml (14 fl oz) strong coffee
2 tbls heavy cream
6 tsp sugar
75 g (2 1/2 oz) unsalted butter

Chop the chocolate and melt in a double boiler. Add the coffee and sugar and stir over very low heat. When the sugar has dissolved, remove from the heat, add the cream and butter then stir until melted and the sauce is perfectly smooth.

CORDES - 81170
Le Grand Ecuyer - Rue Voltaire
Tf : 63 56 01 03 - Fax : 63 56 18 83
Yves THURIÈS

Pike Perch with Pitty Pan Squash	*(P. 91)*
Banana Délice with Créole Sauce	*(P. 136)*
Strawberries and Kiwis in Flaky Pastry	*(P. 137)*

"Le Grand Ecuyer" in the medieval town of Cordes needs no introduction.
Chef Yves Thuriès who has earned every honor and trophy in the culinary arts and authored a prestigous collection of books and magazines has shared three of his recipes with Pierre Paillon.

Pike Perch with Spinach and Pittypan Squash (p.91)
The pittypan squash, which is grown in Provence, is an ideal compliment to the fish in this recipe. Steamed with butter, the flesh of the squash is slightly sweet and the color adds interest to the dish.
There are several varieties of pittypan sqaush ranging from white, light green to orange)

CUERS - 83390
Le Lingousto - Route de Pierrefeu
Tf : 94 28 69 10 - Fax : 94 48 63 79
Alain RYON

Vegetable Tart with Anchovy Vinaigrette	*(P. 27)*

"Le Lingousto" in Cuers is home to a young chef who expresses his personal ideas in the kitchen and knows how to take risks. Situated in the middle of the Pierrefeu vineyards, far from any big city, "Le Lingosto" offers a diversified menu of original dishes inspired by provençale traditions.

EPINE (L') - 51460
Aux Armes de Champagne
Tf : 26 69 30 30 - Fax : 26 66 92 31
Patrick MICHELON

Warm Bouquet of Seafood with Field Greens	*(P. 38)*
John Dory with Potatoes	*(P. 80)*
Suckling Pig with Sage, Polenta, Cepes and Foie Gras	*(P. 102)*
Galette of Pig's Feet and Potatoes	*(P. 103)*
Fruit Minestrone with Almond Raviolis and Cheese Ice Cream	*(P. 149)*

In the heart of eastern France, conveniently located at the juncture of several autoroutes, the hotel-restaurant "Aux Armes de Champagne" faces the beautiful gothic cathedral of l'Epine.
Young chef Patrick Michelon was trained in the kitchens of "Haeberlin" in Illhaeusern, "Hostellerie Reeb" in Marlenheim, "Hotel de la Poste" and "Lion d'Or" in Vezelay, and the "Hostellerie du Château" in Fère-en-Tardenois.
The chef proposes a menu rich in regional specialties featuring local products.

FONTVIEILLE - 13990
La Regalido - Rue Frédéric Mistral
Tf : 90 54 60 22 - Fax : 90 54 64 29
Jean-Pierre MICHEL

Tomato Omelette	*(P. 55)*
Bouillabaisse «Régalido»	*(P. 89)*
Leg of Lamb Braised with Garlic	*(P. 106)*

Near the "Moulin de Daudet" near Carmargue in Provence, "La Régalido" (Relais et Châteaux) offers a warm and restful haven.
The original and creative cuisine of chef Jean-Pierre Michel is inspired by provençale tradition.

GERARDMER - 88400
Hostellerie Les Bas Rupts
Tf : 29 63 09 25 - Fax : 29 63 00 40
Michel et Sylvie PHILIPPE
François LACHAUD

Tripe in Riesling	*(P. 65)*
Rabbit with Basil	*(P. 120)*
Blueberry Tart	*(P. 133)*

"Les Bas Rupts" offers a beautiful setting to its guests in the heart of a pine forest in the Vosges mountains.
Michel Philippe is one of the best known chefs in eastern France having earned the titles "Maître Cuisinier de France", "Chevalier des Palmes Académiques". He advises young chefs, "work hard and persevere, strive for work well done, be disciplined and honest."

"Tripes with Riesling" (p.65)
Tripes (chitterlings) can be prepared in many ways.
In addition to the famous "Tripes à la Mode de Caen" made with cider, other flavorings include tomato concentrate (specialty of the charcutiers from Yssingeaux) or cream as in this recipe.
This dish is so well loved in France that prizes are givien for excellence at the "Confrérie de la Triperie d'Or".

Rabbit with Basil (p.120)
The legs of rabbit tend to be dry and tasteless if simply roasted. Boning and stuffing with basil makes the meat very flavorful and moist.
The sauce adds flavor as well and the garnish of apples with cranberries makes this an excellent dish.

ILLHAEUSERN - 68150
L'Auberge de l'Ill - Rue Collonges
Tf : 89 71 89 00 - Fax : 89 71 82 83
Marc HAEBERLIN

Tagle with Sesame Seeds, Sweet Peppers and Pumpkin Sabayon	*(P. 73)*

"L'Auberge de l'Ill" has been one of the top restaurants in France for many years. The accomplishments and the remarkable cuisine of chef Marc Haeberlin is too extensive to describe here.
His recipe for this volume features the local freshwater fish tagle.

Information on tagle
Tagle is a white-fleshed fish with just one central bone like monkfish which is rare for a freshwater fish.
The flavor is delicate and the texture is supple and firm. Tagle can be cooked whole, in steaks or fillets using any cooking method. For example it is great on the grill or smoked which makes the skin delicious.
This fish can be combined with a wide range or ingredients and be served hot or cold.
Unlike many fish, tagle must be stored for 48 hours in ice before being prepared.

ISSOUDUN - 36100
La Cognette - Bd Stalingrad - Rue des Minimes
Tf : 54 21 21 85 - Fax : 54 03 13 03
Alain NONNET

Sweetbreads and Foie Gras Terrine with Jerusalem Artichokes	*(P. 14)*
Lentil Soup with Truffles	*(P. 42)*
Lentil and Chestnut Gâteau	*(P. 143)*

"La Cognette" was described in one of Balzac's great works, "La Rabouilleuse". It is in this historic place that Alain Nonnet prepares his high quality dishes. Message to young cooks:

"Work, work, work are the three rules of success. It is important to be yourself and live up to your own high standards and not worry about being better than someone else."

LOURMARIN - 84160
La Fenière - 9, rue du Grand Pré
Tf : 90 68 11 79 - Fax : 90 68 18 60
Reine SAMMUT

Whiting in Filo Papillotte with Puréed Garlic	*(P. 74)*
Civet of Hare	*(P. 123)*

Near Lubéron in the quaint village of Lourmarin, Reine Sammut cooks original dishes inspired by Mediterranean culture based on the freshest ingredients possible from local producers.

Since 1975 when she founded "La Fenière", her reputation has grown and spread beyond her region of Provence.

MAGNY COURS - 58470
La Renaissance - Au Village
Tf : 86 58 10 40 - Fax : 86 21 22 60
Jean-Claude DRAY

Lobster Salad	*(P. 20)*
Foie Gras with Pineapple Compote	*(P. 56)*
Salmon with Sherry Vinegar	*(P. 71)*
Filet of Beef with Morels	*(P. 96)*

A stone's throw from the famous racetrack at Magny Cours is the quiet retreat where Chef Jean-Claude Fray welcomes his guests and makes their dining experience a memorable one.

He grew up in Charolais and apprenticed in kitchens in his region before going to Paris to work at the Crillon, Louvre and Palais d'Orsay.

Mr. Dray worked under Raymond Oliver at the Grand Vefour then returned to La Nièvre to become chef of "La Renaissance". He earned the title "Maître Cuisinier de France" and joined the "Académie Culinaire" and "Toques Blanches Internationales".
"My cuisine is made with the freshest, most natural and best quality products available. Each season brings something new to discover. I enjoy cooking traditional rabbit "civet" as well as a modern seafood "navarin" with seaweed butter sauce. I like arranging all my dishes directly on plates and try to add a little "fun" to each presentation. After all, the appearance is the first impression before enjoying the taste. We make all our own bread and I love to make pastries. We have 25 desserts to choose from. Breakfast at our inn is given the same attention to detail, we make our own croissants, brioches and jams.

This is a small business and we maintain an intimate and refined atmosphere and make sure our guests enjoy themselves to the fullest.

Foie Gras with Pineapple Compote (p.56)
Foie gras is prepared in a myriad of ways.
Here, Chef Jean-Claude Dray combines the rich liver with an exotic compote of pineapple with a tang of spicy ginger and tart lime. It's a wonderful marriage of flavors that is a pleasure to eat.

MANOSQUE - 04210
Hostellerie de La Fuste
Tf : 92 72 05 95 - Fax : 92 72 92 93
BUCAILLE

Oysters Remoulade	*(P. 16)*
Pumpkin Soup with Polenta and Truffles	*(P. 43)*
Monkfish Simmered with Seasonal Vegetables	*(P. 81)*

In the heart of Provence near the town of Manosque you will find the "Hostellerie de la Fuste", a lovely restaurant set among the trees in the Grande Bastide.

The Jourdan and Bucaille families welcome you to enjoy the natural setting and dine on tradition and innovative cuisine.
Although Chef Bucaille has modernized many dishes, the menu is filled with classic provençal specialties.

Remoulade with Oysters (P.16)
This dish is prepared with "poutarque" (also "boutarque") which is made with eggs from mullet or bonito that have been salted, dried in the sun then pressed into a large oval shape.
For a typical Mediterranean hors d'oeuvre, the poutarque is thinly sliced or it can be broken apart and sprinkled on a green salad.
Poutarque is also found in the Middle East where the Tunisians enjoy it sprinkled with olive oil.

NIEUIL - 16270
Château-Hôtel de Nieuil
Tf : 45 71 36 38 - Fax : 45 71 46 45
Luce BODINAUD

Salad with Scrambled Eggs and Fricassé of Snails	*(P. 26)*
Stuffed Cabbage «Grand Mère»	*(P. 49)*
Monkfish with Smoked Pork and Potatoes	*(P. 83)*
Beef Braised in Red Wine	*(P. 100)*
Veal Shank Braised in White Wine	*(P. 101)*
French Cheesecake with Candied Angelica	*(P. 130)*

Luce Bodinaud is unique among French chefs. After teaching the art of drawing for 5 years, she married and together with husband jean-Michel they renovated an old hotel that became a "Relais-Châteaux" in 1968. Five years later, she decided to take charge of the kitchen and followed the traditional appenticeship alongside students half her age. She earned the CAP at age 35 and went on to gain experience in the kitchen of many great chefs. Within a year her efforts were rewarded with a star in the Michelin restaurant guide.

Chef Bodinaud is assisted in the kitchen by a dynamic team led by Pascal Pressac.

All the products come from nearby--the vegetables from a local farm and the herbs from the church garden. The menu is inspired by the local products of the Charentes-Poitou with attention given to lighter sauces and beautiful presentations.

Chef Bodinaud and her staff welcome student cooks at certain times of the year.

Chef Bodinaud's messages to customers, young cooks and colleagues:
"I derive great pleasure from cooking and try to share that joy with my customers and my staff."
"Our customers will discover the wonderful flavors of our region and we are here to share what we know of the region with our guests."
To young cooks, "remember that this profession demands a lot but is always greatly rewarding."
"We must adapt to change and embrace the evolution of cuisine and stay fresh in our approach."

Stuffed Cabbage Grand Mère (p.49)
The "Farci Charentais Grand-Mère" is a traditional dish that has been loved by the people of the Charentes region for generations.
Chef Bodinaud and her team have updated the dish with precise directions so it can be duplicated in any kitchen.
To maintain the shape during cooking, the cabbage can be placed in a large pot of simmering rice which prevents the cabbage from bursting.

PORT-SUR-SAONE - 70170
Château de Vauchoux
Tf : 84 91 53 55 - Fax : 84 91 65 38
Jean-Michel TURIN
Snail Raviolis with Morels	(P. 40)
Turbot with Caviar	(P. 76)
Lamb and Spinach «Millefeuille»	(P. 108)
Saddle of Wild Rabbit Stuffed with Kidneys	(P. 121)
Chocolate Marquise	(P. 145)

Jean-Michel Turin warmly welcomes his guests to his beautiful restaurant situated in the elegant château de Vauchoux. The refined cuisine is in perfect harmony with the surroundings

Turbot (p.76)
Turbot is a very delicate fish and the cooking process needs to be closely monitored. If the poaching liquid should boil the fish may break apart and be hard to handle. The sauce for this dish is also fragile. The reduction of the stock must be done carefully and the butter whisked in just before serving.

Lamb and Spinach "Millefeuille" (p. 108)
This "millefeuille" (napoleon) is a wonderful way to present the lamb and is very attractive with the sauce around the meat. I personally advise that the meat be larded before roasting which will make the meat more tender and improve the presentation. (Note: The French title of this dish refers to a "grenadin", which is a small veal roast threaded with long strips of barding fat.)

RUEIL-MALMAISON - 92500
El Chiquito - 126, av. Paul Doumer
Tf : (1) 47 51 00 53 - Fax : (1) 47 49 19 61
PICHOIS
Marinated Scallops with Truffles and Cabbage Salad	(P. 22)
Red Mullet with Sherry Vinegar	(P. 85)
Bream with Lemon	(P. 88)

"El Chiquito" originated in the Basque region then opened in Puteaux in 1953. It moved to Courbevoie before settling in Rueil-Malmaison in 1967.
The present chef, Jean-Pierre Pichois specializes in fish and seafood dishes and goes personally to the market at Rungis to choose his ingredients. He buys the freshest fish available from small boats that have fished in the waters off Brittany and the Vendée. The service attains the same high standards as the cuisine.
In summer the beautiful garden around the restaurant is in full bloom, which offers a calm get away from nearby Paris.

ST BONNET LE FROID - 43290
Auberge des Cimes
Tf : 71 59 93 72 - Fax : 71 59 93 40
Régis MARCON
Bass «St-Joseph»	(P. 90)
Rack of Veal «Margaridou»	(P. 99)

In the Rhône Valley where beautiful vineyards and fields of sunflowers dot the landscape, the "Auberge des Cimes" is fast becoming a mecca for gourmets. Chef Régis Marcon is constantly creating new dishes based on a solid foundation of traditional regional cuisine. He was awarded for his talents with the coveted "Bocuse d'Or" in 1995.

Bass "St Joseph"
We are inspired by this wonderful dish that won the "Bocuse d'Or" in 1995 in a contest that included creations from 25 top chefs from the around the world. We thank its creator, Régis Marcon who is an ambassador "par excellence» of French cuisine.

Veal "Margaridou" (p.99)
Régis Marcon first prepared this intricate dish at the Bocuse d'Or competition.
The presentation of this dish is spectacular. The number of beautiful garnishes makes it complicated for most occasions, but each element is useful on its own.

ST JULIEN CHAPTEUIL - 43260
Restaurant Vidal - Place du Marché
Tf : 71 08 70 50 - Fax : 71 08 40 14
Jean-Pierre VIDAL

Snails in a Crispy Crust with Garlic Cream and Field Greens	(P. 24)
Blood Sausage Lasagna with Prawns	(P. 45)
Cabbage Stuffed with Salmon Mousseline	(P. 47)
Open-Faced Grilled Blue Cheese Sandwich	(P. 50)
Cured Ham Galettes with Fresh Goat Cheese Sauce	(P. 51)
Lentil Tarts with Cured Ham	(P. 53)
Trout Stuffed Lentils Served with Mussels in Verveine	(P. 69)
Warm Chocolate Madeleines	(P. 134)

At the age of 35, Pierre Vidal has already been chef of his own restaurant in St-Julien-Chapteuil for 10 years.
"I strive to discover all there is to know of the local country cuisine. I use the best ingredients of the region--the green lentils from Puy, lamb and milk-fed veal from Velay and locally grown red and black currants. I am against the standardized cooking we are finding in many restaurants. We must be proud of our own region and search out its culinary treasures."
"I am proud to be living in this province and cooking with the local products."

Salad with Snails and Garlic Cream (p.24)
The garlic cream served with this dish should not be too strong. Follow the advise of Chef Vidal: remove the green sprout from each clove of garlic, blanch them until soft and rinse well under cold running water. Gently simmer the blanched garlic in cream and stock (for 300 g (10 oz) garlic, use 2 cups cream and 2 cups stock). The sauce is then blended until smooth and creamy in the food processor.

Open Face Blue Cheese (p.50)
This is an easy dish to make which features the special blue cheese of chef Vidal's region "Fourme d'Yssingeaux". (Outside France, use a creamy, not too salty blue cheese.) This open faced sandwich is garnished simply with a colorful bunch of currants.

Trout Stuffed with Lentils (p.69)
Vervain is infused to flavor this dish. It is recommended to use fresh leaves if possible, infused quickly for a light taste. Vervain is often used to flavor steamed mussels.

Warm Chocolate Madeleines (p.134)
For these cakes, Chef Vidal uses trimoline, a syrupy inverted sugar.

Honey, a naturally inverted sugar can be substituted for a richer flavor.
Inverted sugar is more concentrated (120%) than granulated sugar (saccarose) (100%) and will keep baked products moist for a longer time.

SALON DE PROVENCE - 13300
Le Mas du Soleil - 38, chemin Saint-Côme
Tf : 90 56 06 53 - Fax : 90 56 21 52
Francis ROBIN
Garlic Terrine with Parsely and Pink Peppercorns	(P. 11)

In the heat of the provençale summer, the "Mas du Soleil" is a place to unwind and relax. It is ideally located near the Camargue, Lubéron and the Alpilles for those visiting historical central Provence.

Chef Francis Robin's cuisine is subtle and spontaneous, inspired by the flavors of the wonderful products he finds in the region.

SARTROUVILLE - 78500
Le Jardin Gourmand - 109, route de Pontoise
Tf : (1) 39 13 18 88
Régis LIGOT
Lobster Blanquette with Basil	(P. 25)
Veal Kidneys with Sweetbreads and Sauternes	(P. 61)
Pears Poached in Cassis	(P. 148)

Régis Ligot has succeeded in establishing his lovely "Jardin Gourmand" in the northern suburbs of Paris. His classical and diversified training is evident in his menu of high quality dishes.

Veal Kidneys and Sweetbreads with Sauterne (p. 61)
Chef Ligot chooses the ideal Sauternes for this dish. The "Château Les Justices""has honey and floral flavor with a light roasted taste that combines very well with the meats.
A "Barsac" could be used as well.

SAUMUR - 49400
Les Délices du Château - Les Feuquières - Château de Saumur
Tf : 41 67 65 60 - Fax : 41 67 74 60
Pierre MILLON

Duck Foie Gras Marinated with Four
   Peppercorns   *(P. 13)*
Zucchini Blossoms with Prawns   *(P. 44)*
Pike Perch with Potato «Scales»   *(P. 93)*
Beef Tenderloin «Pot au Feu» with Foie Gras *(P. 98)*
Roasted Figs with Sabayon   *(P. 154)*

After training in Brussels, Pierre Millon returned to France to be chef of his own restaurant.

In 1988, he opened the "Les Délices du Château" in the beautiful château of Saumur.

This site was destined to become a great restaurant. This lovers' hide away was often visited by Roi René who appreciated good cuisine and had many fabulous parties there.

The cuisine of the present owner is refined and "fit for a king". Here one finds the local ingredients made into traditional dishes with a modern flair.

The chef rises at dawn several times a week to buy fresh, high quality produce at the local markets.

With "savoir faire", he combines these ingredients in surprising, harmonious ways.
The wine selection matches the quality of the cuisine.

SUCÈ-sur-ERDRE - 44240
La Châtaigneraie -
156, route de Carquefou
Tf : 40 77 90 95 - Fax : 40 77 90 08
Jean-Louis DELPHIN

Oysters with Hazelnut Butter   *(P. 30)*
John Dory with Wild Mushrooms   *(P. 78)*
Turbot Cooked with Muscadet   *(P. 79)*
Muscadet Sorbet with Mint   *(P. 157)*

Father and son cook side by side in the kitchen of "La Châtaignerie".

Chef Delphin, Sr. is Maître-Cuisinier de France, member of the Académie Culinaire and laureat of "Vase de Sèvres du Présidnet de la République Française".

His young son Jean-Louis has already distinguished himself with many awards and together they offer some of the best fish dishes in western France.

Their restaurant is located in a park along the banks of the Erdre, one of the most beautiful rivers in France.

TALLOIRES - 74290
L'Auberge du Père Bise -
Route du Port
Tf : 50 60 72 01 - Fax : 50 60 73 05
Sophie BISE

Lobster with Two Vinaigrettes   *(P. 19)*
Crayfish Gratin   *(P. 32)*
Prawn Brochettes with Pesto Noodles   *(P. 35)*
Braised Chicken with Tarrgon   *(P. 113)*
Squab with Figs and French Toast   *(P. 118)*
Salad of Venison Medallions with Caramelized
   Apples   *(P. 124)*
Chestnut Dome with Frozen Coffee Parfait *(P. 153)*

Marie and Francois Bise opened their restaurant in 1901 on the banks of the breathtaking Lac d'Annecy on the bay of Talloires.

The auberge became well known for its luxurious cuisine and fanciful decor. Over the years the secluded location has attrracted an illustrious clientel including artists and royalty.

Sophie Bise is following in the grand tradition of the family and is the fourth generation to cook at the auberge. She apprenticed in the great kitchens of her father's colleagues and succeeded him in the kitchen in 1986.

She now works with her mother to run the restaurant with the care and attention that is a family tradition. Her seasonal, refined cuisine combines classic dishes and new creations.

Crayfish Gratin (p.32)
Sophie Bise chooses not to cover her gratin with grated cheese. This is wise as the strong taste of cheese, that covers classic gratins, would mask the delicate flavor of the crayfish.
She has discovered that a thin skin formed on the surface of the sauce after it sits for 30 minutes browns evenly.

TOURTOUR - 83690
Les Chênes Verts
Tf : 94 70 55 06 - Fax : 94 70 59 35
Paul BAJADE

Venison with Juniper Berrie   *(P. 125)*
Golden Delicious Apples in Truffle Cream   *(P. 144)*

Here in the Haut-Var, land of truffles, Chef-owner Paul Bajade founded his restaurant "Les Chênes Verts".

Although his training was very classical, he brings a personal touch to his cuisine making it original and fresh.

"My friend Fredy Girardet, with whom I worked, wrote a book, "La Cuisine Spontanée" (Spontaneous Cooking) that influenced my own cuisine. With him I learned to make the most of each ingredient and not hide the flavors with complicated combinations. I believe that good cooking is founded in precision and simplicity."

VALENCAY - 36600
Hôtel d'Espagne -
9, rue du Château
Tf : 54 00 00 02 - Fax : 54 00 12 63
Maurice FOURRÉ

Shrimp in Red Wine   *(P. 36)*
Pumpkin Galette   *(P. 54)*
Chicken in Chive Sauce   *(P. 109)*
Quail Confit with Lentils   *(P. 119)*
Caramel Meringues with Rich Chocolate Sauce *(P. 142)*

"Hôtel d'Espagne" is found near the château de Valençay which Georges Sand described as "the most beautiful on earth". The hotel itself was a "relais de poste" (stop on the postal route) and was once the residence of Talleyrand and housed the general to the Prince of Spain when he was exiled at the château. Pierre Fourré transformed the builing into a hotel in 1875 and it later became a "relais-château".
Maurice Fourré and his family are now carrying on the family tradition. Chef Fourré is "Maître Cuisinier de France", member of the "Académie Culinaire" and "Cercle Prosper Montagné" delegate of "Régional Euro-Toques France".
His traditional cuisine uses the products of Sologne, du Berry and Touraine.

(Chicken with Chive Cream (p. 109)
The success of this dish depends on the perfect cooking of the chicken. After browning the chicken, the pan is deglazed (simmer the white wine to eliminate all flavor of alcohol) and the cream that is added takes on an ivory color and wonderful flavor.
Reduce the sauce so that it coats the chicken well.

VERDUN - 55100
Le Coq Hardi - 8, av. de la Victoire
Tf : 29 86 36 36 - Fax : 29 86 09 21
Roger HYEULLE

Duck with Raspberry Vinegar   *(P. 117)*

Duck in Raspberry Vinegar (p.117)
For a flavorful sauce, use fresh raspberries whenever they are in season. Frozen, unsweetened berries can be used when fresh ones are not available.
The sautéed apples are delicious and go well with the sauce. Choose tart, firm apples that will hold their shape when cooked.

VERVINS-en-THIERACHE - 02140
La Tour du Roy
TF : 23 98 00 11 - FAX : 23 98 00 72
Annie et Claude DESVIGNES

Warm Oysters with Paprika   *(P. 31)*
Truffle Soufflé with Foie Gras Mousse   *(P. 46)*
Medallions of Game with Two Sauces   *(P. 126)*
Frozen Nougat Bûche with Raspberries   *(P. 155)*

In the location of this restaurant, halfway between Paris and Brussels, Henri IV was recognized as the King of France.

"La Tour du Roy" would be a perfect stop for those visiting Belgium, the Ardennes, the Marne and the champagne cellars of Reims.

In this historic spot, Annie Desvignes follows in the footsteps of her mother who was also an accomplished chef. After working with many illustrious chefs (Raymond Oliver, Lenôtre, Claude Peyrot of the "Vivarois" Parra of "Petit Ruinais") and spending three years at the "Auberge de 'Abbaye à Bec Hellouin", she returned to Vervins to open her own restaurant in 1972.

Chef Desvignes is a member of "Entente Nationale des Cuisinières de Métiers" and the "Académie Prosper Montagné".

Oysters with Papkrika (p.31)
This recipe combines the wonderful flavors of braised lettuce and spicy paprika. The presentation of the oysers on the half shell with the bright tint of paprika is stunning. In addition this lovely dish is not difficult to prepare.

VILLENEUVE-Lès-AVIGNON - 30400
Le Prieuré - 7, Place du Chapître
Tf : 90 25 18 20 - Fac : 90 25 45 39
Serge CHENET
Marie-France MILLE

Asparagus with Marinated Salmon (P. 15)
Foie Gras Raviolis with spring Vegetables (P. 52)
Monkfish with Caviar and Egg Vinaigrette (P. 82)
Panaché of Lamb Provençale (P. 105)
Beggars'Purses with Pears Cooked
 in Spiced Wine (P. 150)

In this beautiful "Relais-Château" establishment, the young talented Chef Serge Chenet proposes a provençale menu that is refined and creative.

Beggars' Purse with Caramelized Pear (p. 150)

The pear in this dessert is lovely with its coating of caramel.
The "hypocras" (spiced wine) that Chef Chenet suggests for this dish has an interesting history.
The hypocras one finds today is not the richly flavored wine enjoyed by the royal court. The best quality white or red wine was infused for 7-8 hours with cinnamon, ginger, star anise, honey, a few peppercorns and iris root from Florence. The merchants of the city would offer this drink to the king each New Year's day, a tradition that continued into the 18th century.

VILLENEUVE-sur-LOT - 47300
La Toque Blanche - Pujols
Tf : 53 49 00 30 - Fax : 53 70 49 79
Bernard LEBRUN

Terrine of Duck Foie Gras (P. 12)
Salad with Foie Gras, Prawns, and Duck
 Gizzards (P. 21)
Turbot with Red Wine (P. 75)
«Demoiselles» of Duck Served Fruit (P. 116)
Prune Bavarian Cream (P. 139)

"La Toque Blanche" has a stunning view of the medieval village of Pujols which is perched on the hill facing the restaurant.

Chef Bernard Lebrun built and opened "La Toque Blanche" in 1981 after gaining experience in 14 different restaurants throughout France. He has earned several titles including "Maître Cuisinier de France".

"I am lucky to be in a region of France that provides such wonderful products--the fruits, vegetables, poultry and the wines of the Aquitaine. I am blessed to know dedicated and small-scale producers who bring their products directly to me. Our chickens are farm-raised in the old-fashioned way and the ducks are force fed by hand!

To know these people and have the chance to visit them is a rich experience. It is a privilege to work with

such wondeful products and share them with my customers."

Turbot with Red Wine (p.75)
There are two secrets to the success of this recipe.
The sugar in the sauce balances the acidity of the wine. The turbot is cooked perfectly--it is quickly seared and cooked in the court bouillon just long enough to firm the flesh.

YSSINGEAUX - 43200
Le Bourbon - 5, Place de la Victoire
Tf : 71 59 06 54 - Fax : 71 59 00 70
André PERRIER

Gambas with Wild Mushrooms in Red Wine (P. 37)
Snails with Smoked Trout in Honey Sauce (P. 41)
Cabbage «Beggars'Purses» with Scallops (P. 48)
Foie Gras with Sausage and Ham Brochettes (P. 58)
Salmon with Chinese Artichokes (P. 72)
Pike Perch with Crispy Skin (P. 92)
Frozen Soufflé with Batavia (P. 151)

Yssingeaux is a region with rich volcanic soil that produces many flavorful ingredients.
André Perrier uses all these wonderful foods in his cuisine. The titles of the four menus proposed at the restaurant show his enthusiasm for the good earth; "Grand Plaisir", "Parfum" (original dishes), "Purs Sucs" (regional dishes), "Alliance et Passion" ("symphony of flavors").

Salmon with Chinese Artichokes (p.72)

Chinese artichokes ("crosnes") are cultivated in Yssingeaux so it is natural that chef Perrier would use them as a garnish.
The texture is similar to Jerusalem artichokes. (Note that both of these vegetables are tubers and not related to globe artichokes.) "Crosnes" are fragile and cook very quickly. They should be cooked "al dente" so that they are easier to handle. They can be sautéed in butter or cooked in meat juices.

Pike Perch with Almond Oil (p.92)

Pike perch is a delicious fresh water fish that is available in the summer in France.
Recipes calling for pike perch can also be made with perch or bass.

Additional Recipes

P. BEEKES (P. 170)
30250 - SOMMIERES (L'Enclos Montgranier)
C. BEX (P. 166)
46210 - LATRONQUIERE (Hôtel du Tourisme)
M. CASALIS (P. 175, 175)
28000 - CHARTRES (Restaurant Henri IV)
R. DANGUY (P. 162)
89450 - VEZELAY (Hôtel de la Poste et du Lion d'Or)
E. DEMORNEX (P. 163)
01830 - ST-JEAN-de-GONVILLE
M. DERBANE (P. 169, 175, 181)
75018 - PARIS (Les Chants du Piano)
F. DESROYS DU ROURE (P. 168)
77000 - MELUN (Auberge Vaugrain)
D. DUCROUX (P. 162, 174, 176, 178)
75002 - PARIS (Les Pavés de Tiquetonne)
Mme GOUTTES (P. 174)
31290 - PONT-LAURAGAIS (Restaurant «La Dînée»)
HÔTEL DE LA POSTE (P. 165, 168)
61700 - DOMFRONT
J. HOUBRON (P. 164, 180)
21130 - AUXONNE (Hôtel du Corbeau)
P. LARIPIDIE (P. 162, 173)
75008 - PARIS (Restaurant «Le Clovis»)
T. LARIQUE (P. 171, 172, 183)
88000 - EPINAL (Le Mouton Blanc)
F. LAUSTRIAT (P. 165, 167, 167, 177, 179, 182, 183)
03000 - MOULINS
D. LECADRE (P. 165, 172)
83980 - LE LAVANDOU (Au Vieux Port)
S. LETRONE (P. 164, 171, 176)
28210 NOGENT-Le-ROI (Mélodie)
J.L. MARTIN (P. 164)
54460 - LIVERDUN (Restaurant «Les Vannes»)
R. MOSER (P. 170, 170, 173, 178, 182)
57130 ARS-sur-MOSELLE (Hôtel de la Gare)
P. PAILLON (P. 165, 168, 169, 173, 174, 177, 178, 184, 184)
43200 YSSINGEAUX (MOF)
C. PARRAIN (P. 175, 180)
63600 - AMBERT (Restaurant «Le Livradois»)
A. PARVEAUX (P. 173, 176, 177, 182)
19240 - VARETZ (Domaine de Castel-Novel)
P. PAUMEL (P. 163, 167, 181)
77960 - CHAILLY-en-BIERE (Le Châlet du Moulin)
H. PAUTARD (P. 172, 176, 177)
11000 - CARCASSONNE (Auberge du Pont-Levis)
L. PIGUET (P. 164, 165, 166)
25310 - ROCHES-Lès-BLAMONT (Auberge de la Charrue d'Or)
P. POMARÈDE (P. 166, 182)
12100 - MILLAU (International Hôtel)
M. PRADES (P. 165, 178)
43300 - LANGEAC (Le Châlet de la Source)
F. ROBADEY (P. 171, 183)
21000 - DIJON (Lou Pescadou)
J. ROGLIARDO (P. 166, 179, 179)
69003 - LYON (La Bonne Auberge)
O. RUELLAN (P. 163, 170, 172)
22750 - ST-JACUT-de-la-MER (Restaurant «Le Terrier»)
J. C. SCHNEIDER (P. 162, 168)
57200 - SARREGUEMINES (Auberge St-Walfried)
C. SEYSALLES (P. 169)
24620 - LES EYZIES (Hôtel Cro-Magnon)
D. SIMUNIC (P. 180)
M. VESSAT (P. 169, 182)
24420 - SAVIGNAC-les-EGLISES (Hôtel du Parc)

Arrange (dresser)
The final stage of preparing a dish is to carefully arrange or "dress" all the elements harmoniously on a platter or plates. This final presentation of the dish is an important part of any recipe.
(See also "pipe out".)

Barding fat (bardes)
Thin sheets of fatback used to wrap around meats and line molds for making terrines and pâtés.

"Bouquet garni"
An aromatic 'bouquet' of thyme sprigs, bay leaves, parsley stems (sometimes one small rib of celery). The bundle is tied and added to stocks and marinades to add flavor and removed at the end of cooking.

Baste (bouillir)
To moisten poultry as it roasts with water, wine, stock or a combination.
The French term "mouiller" (to moisten) also means to add liquid to a braised dish or to sautéed vegetables. The French term can also mean to add liquid to a sauce to make it smoother and more fluid (see "thin out").

Blanch (blanchir)
To plunge vegetables or other foods into boiling water a few minutes to cook completely or partially and to set the color and flavor. They are then "refreshed ("rafraîchir") in cold water.

Blend (travailler)
The French term means literally to "work". In cooking it means to blend vigorously to combine elements of a mixture.
"Travailler" is also used to describe the whipping or beating egg whites to stiff peaks.

Bind/thicken (liaison)
To give body and texture to a sauce by adding a thickening agent of some kind. Beurre manié (flour and butter paste), potato or corn starch will thicken a liquid, egg yolks give rich body to a sauce.

Blind bake (cuire à blanc)
To bake a tart shell without a filling. Line the mold with pastry, prick the entire surface with a fork, line with aluminum foil or parchment paper. Fill to the top with pie weights, (or beans, rice) to maintain the shape of the pastry. When the pastry is half baked remove the weights and foil and either add a filling and bake or finish baking until light brown then fill with fresh fruit or other filling.

Glossary of Professional Terms

Each profession has its own terminology that describes equipment and procedures. In France, cooking has many specific terms that help to make cuisine a very precise art. French terms, for which there is no English equivalent (and are used often in professional American kitchens) are in "parenthesis".

Braise (braiser)
To cook meat (or vegetables) over medium low heat in a heavy pot with a tight fitting lid so that all the moisture is contained.

Brown (revenir)
To brown vegetables or small pieces of meat briefly in oil or butter (or both) to seal in juices and flavor before liquid is added or the heat is turned down to finish cooking. (See "sear/saisir".)

"Brunoise"
Very small dice (3-4 mm (1/8 in)) of vegetables added to a sauce or soup for color and flavor.

Butter/spread a thin layer (masquer)
A thin layer of butter, mayonnaise or other spread is "buttered" in a thin layer on bread slices to make canapés.
Foie gras purée can be "buttered" on a slice of toasted French bread for an hors d'oeuvre. (The bread is then "masquée" with foie gras.)

"Chaudfroiter"
Meaning "hot/cold"; to cover foods with a hot sauce (or one that requires cooking) that is then chilled, coated with aspic and served cold.

China cap/conical sieve (chinois)
A hand-held, cone-shaped metal sieve, (either mesh or perforated), used to strain sauces to make them smooth and eliminate aromatics (cloves, bay leaves, etc.)

Clarify (clarifier)
To remove the impurities from an aspic so that it is perfectly clear. Egg whites, which absorb the fat, can be added to a very cloudy stock to clarify it. The aspic is then ladled through a fine cheesecloth or muslin (see "filter/chausse") to eliminate all particles that may cloud the aspic.

Clean crayfish (châtrer)
Although the French word means literally to castrate, the culinary term refers specifically to wild crayfish that must have the intestine removed while they are alive. This is done by twisting the middle tail fin, twisting and pulling the intestine out.

Coat with sauce (napper/marquer)
To cover a food (or the bottom of a plate or platter) with a thin coat of sauce. The sauce needs to be fluid and of coating consistency and just enough is used to coat evenly.

"Corser"
This French term has two meanings:
1) to work a dough to give it body and elasticity.
2) to give more flavor to a sauce by either concentrating by reducing or adding additional seasonings.

"Court bouillon"
A quickly, prepared flavorful liquid used to poach fish ("court bouillon" means "short-boil"). Made of water, wine, vinegar and a bouquet garni, the liquid is brought to a boil to infuse the aromatics and used right away.

Croutons
French "croutons" are delicate, tiny cubes of close-textured bread ("pain de mie"/Pullman loaf) that are toasted in the oven or fried in butter to add to soups. For traditional fish soups, "croutons" are made with thin slices of toasted French "baguette" and rubbed with garlic.
Crouton also refers to a baked puff pastry decoration (see "fleuron").

Decant (decanter)
A wine is decanted when it is carefully poured from the bottle into a carafe leaving the mineral deposits in the bottom of the bottle.
A stock is decanted when the fat that rises to the top is separated from the meat juices that settle to the bottom.

Deglaze (deglacer)
To dissolve the "sucs" or browned meat juice exuded during cooking that adhere to the pan (or a stock that has been reduced to a thick "glaze"). Various liquids are used to deglaze depending on the dish: water, white or red wine, clarified stock (meat, fish), cream or vinegar.

"Duxelle"
A flavorful combination of finely chopped mushrooms and shallots (or onions) cooked in butter. Can be added to sauces or soups, forcemeats or used on its own as a filling.

Filter (chausse)
A muslin cone-shaped filter used for straining and degreasing stocks and aspics. A paper coffee filter will also absorb fat from a stock and could be used for the same purpose.

"Fleuron"
From the French "fleur" (flower), a crescent-shaped decoration of puff pastry. Other shapes can be made with small cutters to "identify" the main ingredient of the dish--fish, ducks, etc.
They are brushed with egg glaze before baking to make them golden and one or two are placed on each plate. Sometimes called "croutons".

Glaze (glacer)
To make a food shine by coating with melted aspic (on cold foods) or melted butter (on hot foods).

Grease/butter (enduire)
To coat the inside of a mold with melted or softened butter, so that the filling will not stick to the mold.

"Julienne"
Delicate matchstick-shapes of vegetables or cooked meats (3-4 mm (1/8 in) wide X 4-6 cm (1 1/2-2 in) long).
Julienned vegetables can be cooked and served as an attractive side dish or decoration or used to add color to terrines and stuffings.

Line a mold (chemiser)
The first step in assembling some fancy terrines is to line the mold with a thin layer of mousseline or forcemeat, then fill the center with other mixtures that compliment the color and flavor.
Each slice of the cooked terrine shows the attractive "frame" made by lining the mold.

"Ciseler"
This French term, which means to cut, has two culinary meanings. When fish fillets are "ciselés", the surface is slit across the grain so that the fish will not curl up during cooking.
It is also refers to cutting leafy vegetables into strips known as "chiffonade".

Macerate (macerer)
To immerse meat, vegetables or fuits into a liquid to augment the flavor. The food absorbs some of the liquid and some flavor from the food is infused into the liquid.
Technically, any brined or marinated meat has been macerated.

Usually the term refers to fruits macerated in wine or alcohol of some kind.

"Mignonette"
Refers specifically to black pepper that is not ground in a mill but rather crushed very coarsely (often with the bottom of a heavy pot). It is usually placed in cheesecloth with other spices to add flavor to a liquid then removed at the end of cooking.

"Mirepoix"
The classic aromatic blend of carrots, onions and celery cut into small or medium dice and cooked in butter. For stews, the mirepoix becomes part of the dish while in a marinade it is discarded at the end. Mirepoix and bouquet garni are often used together to give a foundation of flavor to many dishes.

Mixture ("appareil")
The result of mixing several ingredients together. The general term "appareil" in French usually refers to fluid or creamy "mixtures" such as batters and custards as opposed to "pâtes" or doughs. The mixture is then cooked or frozen.

Pastry bag (poche a douille)
Conical pouch made of cloth or plastic with a hole at the point. Thick mixtures are placed in the bag, the large open end is gathered and kept closed and the mixture is pushed out in the desired shape.
An indispensible tool for the pastry chef for making cream puffs and to decorate cakes, the pastry bag is also used by the "cuisinier" to add fillings and decorate (see "pipe out/dresser").

Pastry cutter (emporte pièce)
Pastry cutters come in a variety of shapes and sizes for cutting pastry, aspic, truffle decorations. Professional chefs invest in a few well-made stainless steel cutters in classical shapes.

Pipe out (dresser)
To pipe out forms on a baking sheet with a pastry bag (with cream puff pastry, for example). The pastry bag is also used to pipe out decorations on a plate or platter (potatoes Duchesse or whipped cream).

Plastic scraper (corne)
A flexible hand held scraper used to scrape down the sides of a bowl and remove mixtures from a bowl.

Poach (pocher)
To cook in gently simmering liquid. Fragile foods like brains and quenelles are poached so that they do not fall apart during cooking.

191

Reduce (*réduire*)

To concentrate the flavor and texture of a stock or sauce by simmering gently and slowly evaporating the liquid.

Reduce to a glaze (*réduire à glace*)

To concentrate a stock to a thick, syrupy consistency. This flavorful essence can be the base for a sauce (add cream) or added to sauces to intensify the taste (see "corser"). Reducing also deepens the color and the resulting gaze is often brushed on cooked meats to give a flavorful, golden shine.

Refresh (*rafraîchir*)

To stop the cooking and set the color of blanched or boiled vegetables by plunging into ice water.
The French term "rafraîchir" also means to "freshen" a sauce made in advance by adding fresh ingredients.

Ribbon (*ruban*)

Eggs and sugar that have been whipped until thick, light and lemon-colored will form a "ribbon" when the whisk is lifted. The mixture will fall in a thick ribbon from the whisk and the trail of the ribbon will hold its shape for a second when it lands on the surface.

Sabayon

Sabayon is a dessert of egg yolks, sugar and wine that is whisked over a water bath until thick and warm.
In French cooking, "sabayon" also refers to all egg preparations that involve the same technique as the dessert. For example, the first stage of a hollandaise before the butter is added, the first stage of genoise before the flour (and butter) is added are "sabayons". Modern cooking has also developed savory sabayons

that are egg yolks whisked until thick and warm with stocks of various flavors to make delicate sauces for fish, chicken or vegetables (a hollandaise without the butter).

Salamander (*salamandre*)

Cast iron disk attached to a long handle. The puck-shaped disk is heated directly in the flame of the stovetop then is passed over the top of dishes like "crème brûlée" to caramelize the sugar on top without cooking the custard underneath. The broiler is sometimes referred to as the salamander as it is used for the same purpose.

"Salpicon"

Diced or coarsely chopped vegetables and/or meats that are usually combined with a sauce to make a kind of stew.

Sear (*saisir*)

Large cuts of meat are seared over high heat (with a little oil) to coagulate the protein on the surface and hold juices in during the remainder of the cooking process. (See "brown/revenir".)

Simmer (*frémir/mitonner*)

Just below boiling, a liquid has tiny bubbles and is the right temperature for poaching delicate foods. A court bouillon, for example is brought to a simmer to poach fish.
When a slow cooking stew or soup is simmered a long time, the term "mitonner" is used.

Sprinkle with flour (*singer*)

Adding a light dusting of flour to browned pieces of meat. The flour is them cooked in the fats and juices

of the meat, a liquid is added which is thickened by the cooked flour to make a stew.

Spatula (*spatule*)

The flat wooden spatula is an important tool in the French kitchen for checking the coating properties of a sauce. By running a finger across the spatula one can see how well the sauce will coat the food.
The spatula is also an efficient shape for stirring.

Steam (*étuver*)

To cook a food in its own juices. This French version of steaming requires just a little fat of some kind and a little salt. The pan is covered and the vegetables, meats or fish steam with the moisture contained in them.

Stock (*fumet*)

A flavorful liquid obtained by simmering vegetables, aromatics, bones and meat trimmings in water (with or without wine) to infuse their flavors.
Once strained, the stock is used as a base for soups and sauces and can be reduced to a glaze and used as a flavor enhancer.

Sweat/steam (*suer*)

To cook vegetables or meats in a covered pot to draw moisture out. This method cooks and concentrates the flavor of foods like onions without browning.

Thin out (*détendre*)

When a sauce, dough, or other mixture is too thick it is thinned out with liquid.
This is sometimes necessary after a batter has "rested" and the flour has expanded in the liquid element.

Small amounts of water, milk, wine or eggs (depending on the recipe) are added to rectify the consistency.

Trim (*parer*)

To trim a cooked product just before the final presentation to give it a beautiful form.

Turn (*tourner*)

In English and in French "turn" has two meanings:
When a sauce separates due to spoilage or overheating it has "turned" (or curdled).
"Turning" is also a French method for trimming vegetables (by turning with one hand and trimming with the other) so that they are all the same size. The classic "turned" vegetable is a football shape with 7 sides which rolls easily in the pan for even cooking.

Truffle essence (*essence de truffe*)

The liquid in which truffles have cooked and as a result smells and tastes of truffles can accurately be labeled "essence de truffe". A synthetic product is now available in France that is called "truffle flavoring".

Water bath (*bain-marie*)

A water bath is used to cook fragile mixtures, usually with eggs, that should not come in direct contact with the heat of the stove and for keeping delicate sauces warm. For the stovetop, a larger pot is filled with simmering water and a smaller pot is place inside (double boiler).
For cooking many items or larger preparations in the oven, fill a roasting pan with hot water so that it comes about 1/2-2/3 up the side of the mold(s).

WATERCOLORS

Olivier TAFFIN, born in Paris in 1946, is a self taught artist and writer who is passionate about his work. He is a painter, author-illustrator of comic strips and children's books and since 1992 has worked as a playwright.

He loves a challenge, which explains the wide variety of his creative activities in which his spirit of discovery shines through.

His most important work was the ORN Series, published between 1982-90 by Dargaud.

In 1983, his play, «L'incrust», was well received at the «Petit Odéon» theater in Paris.

Photography Credits

The photographs in this book were taken by Pierre MICHALET, except for :
. Le Prieuré (Villeneuve-Lès-Avignon) : Ph. Giraud
. Le Grand Ecuyer (Cordes) : Editar/Yves Thuriès
. Auberge de l'Ill (Illhauesern) : TAG (Fenétrange)
. Auberge des Cimes (St-Bonnet-Le-Froid)
. Le Coq Hardi (Verdun) : Eliophot

Translation

Translator Anne Sterling is a graduate and the former director of La Varenne École de Cuisine with over two decades of culinary experience. She is a food columnist, recipe consultant and teaches cooking to adults and children.

WILEY

ISBN 0-471-16062-8

John Wiley & Sons, Inc.
Professional, Reference and Trade Group
605 Thrid Avenue, New York, N. Y. 10158-00012
New York • Chichester • Brisbane • Toronto • Singapour

CICEM S.A.
36, rue St-Louis-en-l'Ile
75004 PARIS

ISBN 2-86871-000-X

Dépôt Légal 2e Tr. 96
Photogravure : FOTIMPRIM (Paris)
Photocomposition : BOA (Paris)
Impression : QUEBECOR (La Loupe 28)
Reliure : SIRC (Marigny-Le-Châtel 10)